ENCYCLOPAEDIA OF INDIAN GOVERNMENT: PROGRAMMES AND POLICIES

ENCYCLOPAEDIA
OF
INDIAN GOVERNMENT:
PROGRAMMES AND POLICIES

Vol. 25

Planning and Development

Edited by

Satish Tiwari

ANMOL PUBLICATIONS PVT. LTD.

NEW DELHI - 110 002 (INDIA)

ANMOL PUBLICATIONS PVT. LTD.
4374/4B, Ansari Road, Daryaganj
New Delhi - 110 002

Encyclopaedia of Indian Government: Programmes and Policies

First Edition, 2000
ISBN 81-261-0515-1 (Set)

[Responsibility for the facts stated, opinions expressed, conclusions reached and plagiarism, if any, in these volumes is entirely that of the Editor. The Publisher bears no responsibility for them whatsoever.]

PRINTED IN INDIA

Published by J.L. Kumar for Anmol Publications Pvt. Ltd., New Delhi - 110 002 and Printed at Mehra Offset Press, Delhi.

Contents

Preface vii

1. Role and Performance 1

2. Planning and Development Plans 5

3. Member of Parliament Local Area Development Scheme 92

4. Decentralisation and Planning 100

5. Common Minimum Programme 160

6. Monitoring of Twenty Point Programme 162

7. Monitoring of Performance of Infrastructure Sectors 166

8. Management of Projects Implementation 175

9. Nineth Plan: Objective, Strategy and Approach 242

Preface

Encyclopaedia of Indian Government: Programmes and Policies contains authoritative information on about fifty departmental policies and their future developmental programmes.

Organised to be completed in 40 volumes, this gigantic work covers Agriculture; Atomic Energy; Chemicals and Fertilizers; Coal; Commerce; Communication; Culture; Defence; Education; Environment and Forests; External Affairs; Finance; Food & Consumer Affairs; Food Processing Industries; Health and Family Welfare; Home Affairs and Internal Security; Human Resources; Industry; Information and Broadcasting; Labour; Law, Justice and Company Affairs; Non-conventional Energy Sources; Ocean Development; Parliamentary Affairs; Personnel, Public Grievances and Pensions; Petroleum and Natural Gas; Planning and Programme Implementation; Planning and Statistics; Posts and Telegraphs; Power; Rural Development; Science and Technology; Social Justice and Empowerment; Space; States Affairs; Steel; Steel and Mines; Sugar and Edible Oils; Surface Transport; Textiles; Tourism; Urban Development; Water Resources; Women and Child development etc.

Based on the information derived from authoritative sources, this work contains authentic facts and figures. I am deeply beholden to all the scholars whose writings are cited or substantially made use of in the present work. I am also thankful to Anmol Publications Pvt. Ltd. for undertaking publication of this encyclopaedia. I am solely responsible for shortcomings in presentation of matter.

Encyclopaedic in nature, this will prove a dependable reference work for scholars and academics besides those appearing for different competitive examinations.

—**Satish Tiwari**

Preface

1

Role & Performance

The Department of Programme Implementation, formerly known as Ministry of Programme Implementation was set up in 1985 with the sole purpose of independently monitoring Central Sector Projects and key infrastructure sectors including the social sectors. During past few years this Department has built up a rich data bank, acquired professional expertise and developed capability for carrying out objective monitoring and evaluation.

This department has five divisions, namely,

- Twenty Point Programme & Common Minimum Programme Division
- Member of Parliament Local Area Development Scheme Division
- Infrastructure Monitoring Division
- Project Monitoring Division
- Administration Division

Twenty Point Programme (TPP) & Common Minimum Programme (CMP) division:

The Twenty Point programme (TPP) Division monitors the implementation of Twenty Point Programme. Package of programmes consisting of schemes relating to poverty alleviation, employment generation, education and health etc. The TPP has been in operation since 1975.

This package was restructured twice in 1982, and, 1986. The present programme TPP-1986 has been in operation since 1st April, 1987 in its present form. With the globalisation of Indian Economy and adoption of modern liberalisation process, the TPP86 provides much needed safety net to the deprived and adversely affected population. The TPP plays a vital role to ensure growth with equity and social justice. It plays an important role in removing rural poverty by providing sustainable employment and creation of assets for raising the income level of the targeted poor people in the rural areas.

Common Minimum Programme (CMP) division:

The Department of Programme Implementation was a nodal Department to monitor the CMP which was being implemented by the concerned Ministries/Departments. This programme include taking important steps in the field of economy and financial administration, social justice in the interest of SC & STs, backward classes, minorities and improving international relations particularly with the neighbouring countries.

Members of parliament local area development (MPLAD) scheme division:

Monitors the implementation of various works/activities under the MPLAD Scheme. The scheme has made a very good impact on the development of various areas throughout the country. The works of different varieties have come up for the benefit of general public at large. These works consist of construction of libraries, school buildings, approach roads small bridges, community centres, installation of computers in the schools etc.

Infrastructure monitoring division (IMD):

The IMD monitors the performance of infrastructure sectors with the special focus on removing the bottlenecks standing in the way of accelerated growth.

For this purpose, this Division is monitoring on monthly basis the performance of 11 infrastructure sectors viz., Power, Coal, Steel, Railways, Cement, Telecommunication, Ports, Fertilizers, Petroleum & Natural Gas. Roads and Civil Aviation with focus on the production targets which are included in the MOU of the various infrastructure sectors.

Project Monitoring Division (PMD)

The Project Monitoring Division (PMD) is monitoring all Central projects of the Government costing Rs.20 crores and Above and review the impact of Accelerated Irrigation Benefit Programme Since 1996-97. This division has also been charged with the responsibility of monitoring major infrastructure projects in private/joint sector. This Division makes appraisal of the Projects from the point of view of the state of preparedness, examining causes of time and cost overrun of the projects and identifies the bottlenecks in the implementation thereby playing an important role as coordinator and facilitator. Evaluation of compilation report and carrying out system study also fall within its purview. Sometimes this Division is called upon to examine the causes of time and cost overrun in specific projects for fixing the responsibility. Through its studies and evaluation reports the Division has contributed in identifying strengths and weaknesses in the entire system of projects formulation, appraisal, implementation, monitoring and evaluation. Besides, the constraints of the resources, the other serious weaknesses identified by the Division, are incomplete feasibility study, delays in land acquisition, delays in the tieup of technology, delays in preparation of engineering design and drawing etc. It has been observed that pace of implementation of many projects could be improved by better management as is shown by some projects in PSUs which have been implemented within the gestation period. In the light of experience gained in different sectors of economy, this Division has been suggesting various remedial measures to be adopted by the administrative Ministries and Project Authorities. The importance of project management has been analysed by the Department from time to time. One of the important contributions of the Division has been to bring about improvement in the system of project management.

2

Planning and Development Plans

India's per capita consumption of power is estimated at a low 380 KWH against a global average of approximately 2,250 KWH. Financial constraints have been the chief impediment in tapping the abundant energy resources in the country. Initially, a need-based capacity addition of 48,000 MW was estimated during the Eighth Plan (1992-97) which was scaled down to 30,538 MW taking into account the availability of resources. The actual capacity addition, however, is anticipated to be substantially less. As of now, the country faces an energy shortage of about seven per cent and peaking shortage of 16 per cent. The situation is likely to get worse due to the anticipated slippage in the planned capacity addition.

The average plant capacity factor is around 60-61 per cent and, out of the 40 per cent is on account of forced outages. It is worth appreciating that an improvement of one per cent in plant load factor means the availability of 800 MW additional capacity, equivalent to a new plant which would cost Rs. 3,000 crore. Greater stress, therefore should be given to increased capacity utilisation, renovation and modernisation and re-powering of aged plants. These options require only a fraction of the investment needed for capacity addition with quick and rich results. The sound economics of such improvements can be read in the fact that a 10 per cent improvement in thermal plant load factor in the existing capacity will be equal to 8,300 MW of new installed capacity at a lesser cost.

Though India has a long way to go in meeting the enormous demand, the vast Indian electricity market offers the highest growth opportunities. The soaring demand for power for the Indian power sector to grow at a rapid pace. It is expected that in the post-liberalisation period, the power sector would see an average annual growth rate of nine per cent and the capacity addition during the periods 1997-2002 and 2002-2007 is projected at 57,000 MW and 67,000 MW respectively. The country also offers great potential for hydropower generation which is largely untapped at present. Its total hydropower resources are estimated to be 84,044 MW. It is estimated that an uncovered gap of about 80,000 MW of the projected requirements by year 2007) will need to be bridged by private sector investment. A capacity addition of such magnitude will require investments of $90 billion.

Small power projects with a short gestation period could be a viable alternative to the current impose. Small power plants offer several advantages over their bigger counterparts. While the mega plants could take anywhere between three to four years to be set up, the smaller ones can be set up within a period of 18 to 24 months. The time saved allows the smaller plants to be completed at a lower cost owing to savings in pre-operative expenses. The cost per MW of a small power plant would be around Rs. 3 crore as compared to Rs. 4 crore for the larger plants. Moreover, these plants can be set up close to the load centres, thus minimising transmission losses.

Some SEBs have shown an interest in setting up smaller plants. Rajasthan issued letters of intent to six private firms for setting up 19 naptha-based power projects of 50 MW capacity each. When these six power developers start production within the next one-and-half years, they will generate around 850 MW.

Captive power plants are largely used as a back-up supply of power to supplement the power supply from an SEB. A regular supply of power is critical in the case of various industries where a break in production can prove to be very costly. Besides ensuring a reliable alternative source of supply, captive power plants also make commercial sense given the high costs of energy from the SEBs.

Recognizing the urgent need to augment the power supply to industry, the government announced substantial tax concessions for setting up captive power plants. The import duty on capital power plant equipment has been cut from 25 per cent to 20 per cent. Also the power ministry has done away with the stipulation requiring clearance from the CEA for power plants with an investment of less than Rs. 1,000 crore. This will speed up the process of obtaining clearance for small projects.

The market for captive power plants in the next then years is estimated to be around 3,000 MW (Rs. 12,000 crore at current cost). Though the capital cost per MW for setting up a captive plant may be slightly more than that of amega plant, it is cheaper to operate because the steam generated from the plant can be recovered and used in production.

The government's perspective plan for the power sector implies the creation of nearly 12,000 MW per year over the next ten years. The increasing gap between the supply and demand of power and the huge investment required to meet this made the government change its policy on the power sector in 1991-92. The sector was opened up for private investment with a lot of incentives. The government's policy offers virtually all areas of power production and supply to private entrepreneurs for investment, be it power generation, distribution, renovation and modernisation or cogeneration. Driven by the large demand for power in the country, the policy offers enormous opportunities for the investors.

Private sector companies can set up enterprises to operate either as licensees for distributing electricity in a specified area or as generating companies. The debt equity ratio should be 4:1 and the promoter's contribution should be at least 11 per cent of the total outlay. To ensure that private entrepreneurs bring in additional resources to the sector, not less than 60 per cent of the total outlay must come from sources other than Indian public financial institutions. Up to a 10 per cent foreign equity participation can be permitted for projects set up by foreign private investors: The rates for depreciation in respect of assets have been liberalized and customs duty for the import of power equipment and excise duty has been reduced.

A 16 per cent guaranteed rate of return on equity has been provided. For the portion of foreign equity, returns up to 16 per cent can be designated in the currency of the subscribed capital to protect it from foreign exchange fluctuations. If these measures are implemented effectively the power situation could well brighten.

Mandi (Kutch), May 24. Gujarat is poised to become Asia's largest wind energy producing state by this year-end with an estimated investment of Rs. 600 crore to generate 150 MW by setting up wind farms on the Kutch and Saurashtra coastline.

These turnkey projects have been undertaken by two companies, city-based Sun Source (India) Limited, which has entered into collaboration with the Cannon Energy Corporation, California and Madras-based Natural Energy Processing Company-Micon Ltd., which had pioneered the setting up of wind farms in the country.

Both companies have entered into this low-technological area following the incentive scheme announced by the state government to tap wind farm energy by private entrepreneurs and also to encourage them to go in for non-conventional methods of generating power.

The survey undertaken jointly by the department of non-conventional energy sources, New Delhi, Gujarat Energy Development Agency, and Indian Institute of Meteorology, has revealed that Gujarat has the longest coastline in the country. The potential for wind energy has been estimated at around 5,000 MW on the coastline of Kutch and Saurashtra. The total installed electric power capacity in the state is 8,100 MW. The state's coastline is considered to be a potential "energy gold-mine."

The survey has also indicated that the long coastline has good winds throughout the year, averaging around 20 km. Per hour or more. The relatively cyclone-free coast between Mandvi, Mundra and Tuna in the Kutch district and between Lamba and Okha in Jamnagar district also have a wind power potential of about 2,000 MW.

In addition, a promising terrain site for wind power generation has bee identified near Dhank in Rajkot district, where an annual average wind speed of more than 25 kmph has been recorded. These areas have large tracts of wasteland which can be made available for setting up wind farms.

With 17,000 industrial units, the state ranks second in the country in terms of industrial production. The demand for power supply is increasing at the rate of 12 per cent per annum. The industry's energy needs are likely to treble in the coming 10 years.

To meet the demand for power, the state government has announced several concessions to tap non-conventional sources. Due the efforts of the GEDA, the nodal agency for promotion of renewable sources of energy, the state has become one of the leaders in wind energy exploitation. To prove the viability of wind electric power generations systems, six wind farms with 120 wind turbines and a total installed capacity of about 17 MW have been set up along Saurashtra and Kutch. The all-India wind power capacity is 41.5 MW, of which about 17 MW is in the state. Most wind turbine generators in the state are imported from Denmark.

The NEPC-Micon Ltd. has taken over the Gujarat Wind Farm Limited at the coastal town of Mandvi in Kutch district Asia's first commercial wind farm was set up by the gujarat Wind farm Ltd. at Mandvi way back in 1986. This wind farm, with 23 wind turbine generators channelises 2.4 million KV per annum into the Gujarat Electricity Board grid for supply to various GEB consumers.

A spokesman of the NEPC-Micon said that the Mandvi wind farm would be expanded by adding 10 more turbine generators. Its capacity would be increased from 1.5 MW to 2.5 MW. A model wind farm at an estimated cost of Rs. 8 crore would be set up by the company at Dhank near Rajkot district. The company has already identified 25 potential entrepreneurs, who have agreed for setting up the wind farms.

At least 12 places have been identified by the NEPC-Micon Ltd. on Kutch and Saurashtra coast for setting up wind farms at a cost of around Rs. 250 crore. For setting up on MW capacity wind farm, four turbine generators were needed and the total estimated cost involved in it was Rs. 5 crore. The company has a target of setting 50 MW capacity wind farms on the Gujarat coastline.

When the Mandvi wind farm was set up, the technological assistance of a Danish company, Micon Ltd. was taken by the GIIC and GEDA for installation of the turbine generators. But now NEPC-Micon would go for indigenous technology.

NEPC-Micon Ltd. has also set up a national-level research foundation with an investment of Rs. 200 crore for carrying out extensive research on non-conventional resources and energy production.

The Sun Source (India) Ltd. has decided to set up 100 MW capacity wind farms on places earmarked on the Saurashtra and Kutch costline. It has planned to set up one of the largest wind farms in Asia at Dhank in Rajkot district.

Two Gujarat entrepreneurs, Mr. Rajni Patel and Mr Ashok Gajjar, chairman and the vice-chairman of Sun Source (India) Ltd. have with the help of an NRI, Mr Bhal Pandya, entered into technological colloboration with Cannon Energy Corporation of California, USA. The latter is the third largest wind power producer in the world. Financial arrangements of $140 million have already been made by the company with the help of private sources in USA.

The five-year incentive scheme, launched by the state government, includes several concessions to entrepreneurs. GEB would permit the industrial undertaking to utilise the electricity generated by their wind farms for a maximum period of six months and the GEB will purchase electricity at a fixed rate of Rs. 1.75 per unit.

Duty Exemption: The electricity generated by the wind farms will be exempted from the electricity duty. The beneficiary unit will be given an exemption from demand cut to the extent of 30 per cent of the installed capacity of the wind farm, and the import duty on goods for wind farms will be waived.

Moreover, Central excise duty exemption will be given to renewable energy devices and systems including wind turbine generators. The state government will also give sales tax exemption to boost the movement.

The situation regarding electrical power is worsening and indeed the new year started rather disastrously for the residents of Delhi and north India. In some areas of Delhi there was hardly any power for a number of days.

Apart from the environmental concerns as a result of pollution created by burning of fossil fuels to generate electrical power are causing concern particularly in areas such as Ladakh with fragile and sensitive ecology.

It is matter of regret that in a poor country like ours with enormous resource crunch, little attention is being paid to demand side management i.e. using our available electrical generating capacity efficiently and economically.

In rest of the world there has been a rapid shift from the inefficient short life incandescent GLS lamps to Compact Fluorescent Lamps (CFLs). Indeed in Japan, a country which is most conscious on energy consumption, there is virtual absence of incandescent GLS lamps and the country is using the latest energy efficient lamps for lighting. The same is true to a lesser extent for Canada, Switzerland, Scandinavia, South Korea, Taiwan and Singapore.

Emphasis in these countries is not only to use energy efficient lamps, but also to use longer life lamps, so that the total consumption is minimized because the production of lamps and its components also use a great deal of energy and scarce raw materials.

Likewise the 40 w fluorescent tubes which are generally used in India became obsolete in rest of the world more than a decade ago. In most of the countries the shift has been to 36 W Triphosphor tubes which are–

— 55 per cent more energy efficient than the 40 W tubes.

— Use 183 gms of hours against only 3000 to 4000 burning hours of 40 W tubes.

The shift from 40 W fluorescent tubes to 36 W Triphosphor tubes would mean that the total requirement of the country will be only 30 million pieces per annum against the current consumption of over 110 million pieces.

Another item which guzzles too much of electrical energy are Electro Magnetic Ballasts (chockes for fluorescent tubes). A choke for a 40 W tube consumes approximately 18 W electrical power. In many developed countries the use of Electro Magnetic Ballasts are no longer permitted because these are grossly energy inefficient and also pose a fire hazards. In several countries the shift has been towards Electronic Ballasts which use less than 2.5 W and have a high power factor of over 0.95. It means it saves power and does not pose any fire hazards.

The use of Compact Fluorescent lamps is place of GLS must be promoted vigorously as has been dome in the USA, Japan, Canada, Europe, Australia and most recently in the Third World countries South America, Malaysia and Sri Lanka. Serious consideration must be given to allow the import of components for Compact Fluorescent Lamps (CFL) without import duty to reduce the cost of the lamps to the consumers.

Both for the purpose of public safety as well as saving of energy, the use of Electro Magnetic Ballasts should be prohibited in high rise buildings, hotels, schools, hospitals, cinemas and places where large number of people gather.

In remote places like Ladakh which have a fragile ecology and where the electricity has to be generated by diesel oil which is to be transported over long distance from Mathura to Ladakh at great expense, the switch over from incandescent GLS lamps to CFL, from 40 W tube to 36 W Triphosphor tubes and from Electro Magnetic Ballasts (choke) to Electronic Ballasts must be done without delay.

Electrical power should not be subsidized because it is a disincentive to save energy and it effects the viability of the Electricity Boards. Instead one-time subsidy may be allowed to switch over to energy efficient solutions as been done in several other countries.

Considering the extremely poor quality of our coal and the inevitable compulsions to use clean-coal technologies in the future, the cost of thermal power, the mainstay of electricity production in India, will invariably rise. In this context, we have to take a serious look at nuclear power, since it could become a potentially viable option in the future. In fact, comparative studies of the long-term cost-effectiveness of different modes of electricity generation show that it would be profitable to increase nuclear-based electric supply to a level of about 15-20 per cent of the total demand by 2015 AD, if the country is to maintain an adequate pace of industrialization and overall economic growth.

Over the past our decades, India has invested considerable public funds in the nuclear sector. The expectation was that the department of atomic energy

(DAE), which has been responsible for this sector all along, will produce returns commensurate with these investments in the long run, especially through the delivery of safe and economic nuclear power in good measure. But, it is now evident that the DAE has so far failed in this task.

Following the Pokhran explosion in 1974, the developed countries isolated India and blocked it from deriving the benefits of global technological developments in the nuclear field. But, this also gave the necessary impetus to indigenous development. In this backdrop, the DAE has indeed made some valuable contributions in different segments of activity. For example, the R&D institutions of DAE have been developed into some of the best of their kind, even though much is yet to be learnt about effective management of their functions and personnel. DAE institutions have also indigenously developed or successfully adopted the technologies for crucial aspects of the pressurized heavy water reactor (PHWR) based nuclear fuel cycle. They have also gloomed a large number of talented scientists and engineers at the working level.

Thus, with the mixed performance of distinct success in patches along with the concurrent failure in meeting their primary mission on nuclear power, the DAE today stands out as an enigma among the scientific departments of the government. What then are the reasons for DAE's current predicament with the management of its nuclear power programme?

Unfortunately, there is no comprehensive analysis of the performance of the nuclear power sector which is openly available from the DAE and Nuclear Power Corporation (NPC). No detailed data or information on the performance and safety status of this sector are available, with which others can carry out an independent evaluation. An assessment done by one of the past members of the Atomic Energy Commission (AEC), at the request of DAE, has been kept confidential even within the department. Such unwarranted secrecy about civilian nuclear activities has prevented the DAE institutions from receiving any technological inputs or management advice from elsewhere.

In the area of safety, the DAE is yet to learn that the functioning of a truly independent Atomic Energy Regulatory Board (AERB) to oversee the safety of their nuclear installations will not only ensure a standard of safety comparable to international levels, but also help enhance its own credibility and public confidence. Instead, DAE is insistent on keeping the AERB a subordinate organisation, so that it can continue to influence and control the regulatory decisions in its favor.

Interaction between DAE's R&D managers and NPC engineers is another area which needs substantial improvement. It has to be realized that the nuclear power sector is the primary customer for DAE's R&D output and, therefore, the relevance and priority for such work should be mainly determined by the NPC. But, today NPC finds itself at the mercy of organizations like the Bhabha Atomic Research Centre (BARC), which set their own priorities and agenda with little concern for the pressing needs of the power sector. While not meeting NPC's targets for development inputs, BARC also wields the veto power to block NPC's proposals to acquire technological assistance from any non-DAE sources.

The time has definitely come to clearly delineate and separate our civilian nuclear activities from those which relate to the perpetuation of our nuclear weapons' option. Today, the DAE appears to be responsible for both these areas, which gives it an added excuse for keeping the nuclear power sector under a cover of secrecy.

The country has waited long enough for the DAE and the AEC to take the necessary corrective steps to salvage the nuclear power sector. It is now imperative that the highest levels of the government directly intervene and carry out an in-depth evaluation and policies, plans, organizational structures and management practjices of the nuclear sector, in order to set matters right without further delay. They Prime Minister's Office, the Planning Commission, and the ministry of power must be fully involved in this exercise. DAE and NPC should be asked furnish their detailed suggestions, plans and milestones in this connection.

With bold new policy initiatives, NPC should be able ·to succeed in attracting technical and financial participation from the private sector, both from within the country and abroad. Long-term planning for this sector has to be comprehensive and it will require an assured stability and continuity in essential elements of our nuclear policy.

Activities in the nuclear power sector have to be sequenced and dovetailed appropriately, taking into account realistic time schedules and the resources position for key nuclear materials. The current uranium reserves in the country may not be able to sustain a programme is excess of 6000 MW of PHWR-based power generation. Also approximately 45,000 MW years of PHWR operation has to take place before enough plutonium can be produced to fuel one 500 MW fast breeder reactor. Obviously, accelerating the uranium exploration programme and seeking substantial policy changes which will permit acquisition of fuel from abroad should, therefore, take precedence over many other matters.

Today, we have about 1100 MW of nuclear power available to the grid on an annual average. The four 220

MW reactors at Rajasthan and Madras will have to be shut down at least for three years i the near future for changing their deficient pressure tubes. DAE's 40 MW fast breeder test reactor which should have gone to full power a decade ago as per plants, is still to go beyond the 10.5 MW power level. Under these circumstances, DAE must relent from making misleading promises and grandiose projections without undertaking a detailed planning exercise.

Revamping the organisational structures and management approaches in the nuclear sector will involve substantial changes, going beyond mere tinkering with the prevailing outmoded practices in DAE.

It would also be wise to consider the induction of experienced personnel with proven techno-managerial capabilities from the department of space, DRDO and the major power sector companies into DAE and NPC. The infusion of fresh talent and thinking from outside will indeed help the nuclear sector at this juncture. These changes must be aimed at bringing in the required dynamism, accountability and vision, without which NPC cannot survive much longer as a power sector business enterprise.

Planning

Planning in India derives its objectives and social promises from Directive principles of State Policy enshrined in the Constitution. Public and private sectors are viewed as complementary. Private sector covers not only organised industry but also small scale industries, agriculture, trade and a great deal of activity in housing, construction and other fields. Individual effort and private initiative are considered necessary and desirable in national endeavour on development with optimkum of voluntary cooperation. Although in the past, economic planning did envisage a growing public sector with massive investments in basic and heavy industries, now the emphasis on the public sector is less pronounced and the current thnking on planning in the country, in general, is that it should increasingly be of an indicative nature.

Planning Commission was set up in 1950 to prepare the blue-print of development, taking an overall view of the needs and resources of the country.

First plan

The First Plan (1951-56) had a two fold objective to correct the disequilibrium in economy caused by the Second World War and partition of the country and also to initiate simultaneously a process of all-round balanced development. This was ensure increase in the national income and steady improvement in living standards. Keeping in view large-scale imports of foodgrains in 1951 and inflationary pressure on economy, the Plan accorded the highest priority to agriculture including irrigation and power projects. About 44.6 per cent of the total outlay of Rs. 2,069 crore in the public sector (later raised to Rs. 2,378 crore) was allotted for its development. The Plan also aimed at increasing the rate of investment from five to about seven per cent national income.

Second plan

In 1954, Parliament decleared that the broad objectives of economic policy should be to achieve a 'socialistic pattern of society' under which the basic criteria for determining the lines of advance would be social gain and greater equality in income and wealth and not private profit. The Second Five Year Plan (1956-57 to 1960-61), therefore, sought to promote a pattern of development which sould ultimatley lead to the establishment of a socialistic pattern of society in India. In particular, it stressed that the benefits of economic development should accrue more to the relatively less privileged sections of society and there should be a progressive reduction in the concentration of incomes, wealth and economic power.

The main aims of the Second Plan were: (i) an increase of 25 per cent in the national income; (ii) rapid industrialisation with particular emphasis on the development of basic and heavy industries; (iii) large expansion of employment opportunities; and (iv) reduction of inequalities in income and wealth and more even distribution of economic power. The Plan also aimed at increasing the rate of investment from about seven per cent of the national income to 11 per cent 1960-61. The Plan laid special stress on industrialisation, increased production of iron and steel, heavy chemicals including nitrogenous fertilizers and development of heavy engineering and machine-building industry.

Third plan

The Third Plan (1961-62 to 1965-66) aimed at securing a marked advance towards self-sustaining growth. Its immediate objectives were to: (i) secure an increase in the national income of over five per cent annum and at the same time ensure a pattern of investment which could sustain this rate of growth during subsequent Plan periods; (ii) achieve self-sufficiency in foodgrains and increase agricultural production to meet the requirements of industry and exports; (iii) expand basic industries like steel, chemicals, fuel and power and to establish machine-building capacity, so that the requirements of further industrialisation could be met within a period of 10 years or so mainly from the country's own resources; (iv) utilise fully the manpower resources of the country and ensure substantial expansion in employment opportunities; and (v) establish progresively greater equality of opportunity and bring about reduction in disparities of income and wealth and a more even distribution of economic power. The Plan aimed at increasing the national income by about 30 per cent from Rs. 14,500 crore in 1960-61 to about Rs. 19,000 crore by 1965-66 (at 1960-61 prices) and per capita income by about 17 per cent from Rs. 330 to Rs. 385 during the same period.

Annual plans

The situation created by the Indo-Pakistan conflict in 1965, two successive years of severe drought, devaluation of the currency, general rise in prices and erosion of resources available for Plan purposes delayed finalisation of the Fourth Five Year Plan. Instead, between 1966 and 1969, three Annual Plans were formulated within the framework of the draft outline of the Fourth Plan. They took into account the conditions prevailing at that time. The state of the economy and the non-availablity of financial resources for Plan purposes kept down the size of development outlay during this period.

Fourth plan

The Fourth Plan (1969-74) aimed at accelerating the tempo of development and reducing fluctuations in agricultural production as well as a the impact of uncertainties of foreign aid. It sought to raise the standard of living through programmes designed to promote equality andsocial justice. The Plan laid particular emphasis on improving condition of less privileged and weaker sections especially through provision of employment and education. Efforts were also directed towards reduction of concentration and wider diffusion of wealth, income and economic power.

The Plan aimed at inincreasing net domestic production at 1968-69 factor cost from Rs. 29,071 crore in 1969-70 to Rs. 38,306 crore in 1973-74. In terms of 1960-61 prices, this implied an increase from Rs. 17,351 crore in 1968-69 to Rs. 22,862 crore in 1973-74. Average annual compound rate of growth envisaged was 5.7 per cent.

Fifth plan

The Fifth Plan (1974-79) was formulated against the backdrop of severe inflationary pressures. Major objectives of the Plan were to achieve self-reliance and adopt measures for raising consumption standards of people living below the poverty line. This Plan also gave high priority to bring inflation under control and to achieve stability in the economic situation. It targeted an annual growth rate of 5.5 per cent in national income. Four Annual Plans pertaining to the Fifth Plan period were completed. It was subsequently decided to end the Fifth Plan with the close of Annual Plan 1978-79 and initiate work for a new Plan for next five years with new priorities and programmes.

Sixth plan

The Sixth Plan (1980-85) was conceptualised keeping in view achievements and shortcomings of the past three decades of planning. Removal of poverty was foremost objective of the Plan even though it was recognised that task of this magnitude could not be accomplished in a short period of five years. The strategy adopted for the Plan consisted essentially in moving simultaneously towards strengthening infrastructure for both agriculture and industry so as to create conditions for an accelerated growth in investments, output and exports and provide through special programmes designed for the purpose, increased opportunities for employment especially in rural areas and unorganised sector and as well meeting minimum basic needs of people. Stress was laid on dealing with inter-related problems through a system-approach rather than in separate cmpartments, greater management efficiency and intensive monitoring in all sectors and active involvement of people in formulating specific schemes of development at local level and securing their speedy and effective implementation.

Sixth Plan s actual expenditure stood at Rs. 1,09,291.7 crore (current prices) as against the envisaged total public sector outlay of Rs. 97,500 crore (1970-80 prices) accounting for a 12 per cent increase in nominal terms. Average annual growth rate for the Plan was 5.2 per cent, targeted growth rate for this period.

Seventh plan

The Seventh Plan (1985-90) emphasised on Policies and programmes, the aim of which had been rapid growth in foodgrains production production, employment opportunities and productivity within the framework of basic tenets of planning, namely, growth, modernisation, self-relience and social justice. Due to overall fovourable weather conditions, implementation of various thrust programmes and with concerted efforts of the government and the farmers, foodgrains production during the Seventh Plan grew by 3.23 per cent as compared to along term growth rate of 2.68 per cent during 1967-68 to 1988-89 and a growth rate of 2.255 per cent in eighties. To reduce unemployment and, consequently, the incidence of poverty, special programmes like Jawahar Rozgar Yojana were initiated in addition to the already existing programmes. Due recognition was also accorded to the role small scale and food-processing industries can play in this regard. Various policy instruments were used to improve the productivity and the international competitiveness of the Indian economy. Instead of creating new facilities, the thrust was on improvement of existing facilities, and fuller capacity utilisation.

The total expenditure during the entire Seventh Plan stood at Rs. 2,18,729.62 crore (current price) as against the envisaged total public sec tor outlay of Rs. 1,80,000 crore, resulting in a 21.52 per cent increase in nominal terms. During this Plan period, Gross Domestic product (GDP) grew at an average rate of 5.6 per cent per year exceeding the targeted growth rate by 0.6 per cent

Annual plans

The Eight Five Year Plan (1990-95) could not take off due to the fast changing political situation at the Centre. The new government which assumed power at the Centre by June 1991 decided that the Eighth Five Year Plan would commence on 1 April 1992 and that 1990-91 and 1991-92 should be treated as separate Annual Plans. Formulated within the framework of the earlier Approach to the Eighth Five Year Plan (1990-95), the basic thrust of these Annual Plans were on maximisation of employment and social transformation.

Eighth plan

The Plan proposes a growth rate of 5.6 per cent per annum on an average during the Plan period. The level of national investment is proposed at Rs. 7,98,000 crore and the public sector outlay of Rs. 4,34,100 crore. Consistent with the expected resource position, the size of the plans of the states and union territories is projected at Rs. 1,86,235 crore and of the Central Plan at Rs. 2,47,865 crore.

Annual plan 1992-93

The Annual Plan 1992-93 envisaged a total public sector outlay of Rs. 80,771.96 crore, actual expenditure came down to Rs. 72,853 crore which is lower by one per cent than the Budget Estimates for the Plan. The actual size of the Plans for states and union territories was lower by nearly 10 per cent i.e. from Rs. 32,364.88 crore (BE) to Rs. 29,159 crore. The main reasons for the shortfall in State Plans were deterioration in the balance from current revenues, erosion in the contribution of state electricity boards and in some cases of state road transport corporations, negative opening balances,mounting non-plan expenditure, shortfalls in the collection of small savings, etc.

Annual plan 1993-94

The envisaged total public sector outlay of Rs. 1,00,120.16 crore for the Annual Plan 1993-94 on revision came down to Rs. 92,623.64 crore which is lower by 7.48 per cent that the budget estimates for the Plan. In the Central Sector, the approved outlay was Rs. 61,453.53 crore. The total outlay of the plans for states and union territories on revision was lower by 13.84 per cent i.e. from Rs. 36,184 crore in the budget estimates to Rs. 31,175.11 crore in revised estimates. The main reasons for the shortfall in states plans were deteriorating in the balance from current revenues, erosion in the contribution of state electricity boards and in some cases of state road transport corporations, negative opening balances, mounting non-plan expenditure, shortfall in the collection of small savings, etc.

Annual plan 1994-95

The Annual Plan 1994-95 provides for a public sector outlay of Rs. 1,12,197 crore at current prices. At 1991-92 prices it would be about 20 per cent of the envisaged Eighth Plan public sector outlay. The state plans outlay is Rs. 39,992 crore at current prices, which works out to 35.64 per cent of public sector outlay and 17.17 per cent of the Eighth Plan provision for the states at 1991-92 prices. In the first three years, assuming that the actual outlays will be the same as the revised estimates of 1993-94 and the budget estimates of 1994-95 will be reallised, the public sector outlays in the Central Plan and the State Plans will work out to 59 per cent and 44 per cent of the respective Eighth Plan provisions, at constant prices.

An overview:

An era of planning thus started in 1951, when the First Five Year Plan was launched. This was followed by the Second Five Year Plan (1955-56) and the Third Five Year Plan (1960-61). All these developments, from the Grow More Food Campaign in 1942 to the planned economy, are discussed separately. On the whole, the country lacked any well-defined policy of agriculture up to the end of Second Five Year Plan. Many improvements have taken place since then.

Cooperative farming, declared at one stage as the ultimate form of organisation for agricultural production, did not receive wide acceptance and that accounts for lack of any serious effort or enthusiastic response to its implementation. To achieve social justice, ceiling on the size of holdings is being imposed but there is considerable confusion in matters of detail and execution. Adequate investigations are lacking to justify the measure economically. There is good cultivable land which is lying waste in some states not because the ownership rights are vested in persons who are not able to farm it themselves but also because they do not lease it out for fear of losing their title to it. To the extent such land is brought under cultivation, the measure may prove beneficial. But where the holdings are pushed down below a certain minimum size, it is not easy to predict the effect on agricultural efficiency and production.

Quite often the emphasis on increasing the production of foodgrains has led to a fall in the production of commercial crops, leading to shortage of such products. In turn a cry is raised to increase the production of cash crops. Such an action can hardly be called a policy. Not much thought was given to preparing the estimates of cost-benefit ratio in undertaking programmes of large-scale irrigation and land reclamation. Therefore, emhasis has been changing from major to minor irrigation projects and vice versa; similarly from land reclamation to raising the standard and intensity of cultivation on land already under the plough.

These instances make it clear that hardly any well-defined policy existed and much less was pursued. A sound policy calls for precise and detailed information on cost-benefit relationships of various developmental projects, efficiency standards, and farms in various size groups in different farming type regions. First, it is necessary to have a census of agricultural resources, surveys on land use, investigations on factors inhibiting agricultural efficiency regionwise and the demand projections for the current and future needs in respect of food, cash crops, and export. Then taking the country and regions as units, sound plans need to be drawn up for land use, agricultural production, and needed supplies. To support the fulfilment of these targets, ancillary measures need be taken, namely, land reclamation, assistance in raising the intensity of cultivation, credit support, educational programmes, irrigation, etc. All such measures, for successful implementation, need a watchdog in the form of adequate farm management and agricultural economics research to guide and evaluate simultaneously the execution of the programmes in order to make them efficient and effective and to stop those measures which, on experience, have a retrograde effect.

No doubt, steps have been taken towards the direction suggested above, the major lacunae in them may be listed as follows:

(1) The carrying out of developmental activities on a piecemeal basis with the result that full benefits expected from such programmes have not been

obtained. In UP, tube-wells, for example, were dug but could not be commissioned for lack of energisation.

(2) The budgetary provision for efforts in various directions were made on the basis of administrative divisions and not on a properly estimated requirement of expenditure with the consequence that the efforts were too thinly spread and proved almost futile. The early Grow More Food Campaign is an appropriate example of this.

(3) The approach where an investment could be most effective from the point of view of natural factors like land, climate or economic factors like demand, particularly in the case of livestock products, has been conspicuous by its absence.

(4) Duplication and overlapping has often led to futility of efforts which cold never be enough according to needs and urgency.

If we examine any one of the policy measures on prices of foodgrains, production, distribution, land tenure, irrigation, land reclamation and settlement, we will see that each one has some woeful tale to tell. In the functions of the Ministry of Community Development and Cooperation and the Ministry of Agriculture, there was a considerable overlapping till they were recently merged. Between them and even within the same ministry there is duplication of positions. This leads not only to wastage of scarce funds but also to confusion in working.

A number of committees have from time to time gone into the problem of agricultural administration and machinery. All of them have helped to expand agricultural organisation. Mention may be made of the Patel Committee (1945-46) as a result of whose recommendations the Directorate of Economics and Statistics became a separate unit of the Ministry; the enquiry by N. Gopalsawami Ayyanger (1949), which recommended the creation of the Bureau of Natural Resources and Agriculture with a coordinating minister for the Ministries of Agriculture, Food and works; the W.R. Natu Enquiry 1951; and more recently the enquiry Mr. Keifer (1965). Full-scale general enquiries have also been made of the machinery of the Government of India leading to proposals for its reorganisation by Richard Tottenham in 1945, by Shri R.A. Gopalsawami in 1952 and Dr. Appleby in 1954. It may also be mentioned here that the Food Grains Policy Committee, 1947, the Grow More Food Committee 1952 and the Balwantrai Mehta Committee, 1957 also have made recommendations for the reorganisation of the machinery of agricultural administration at different levels. The desire for administrative improvement has been continuous, the suggestions for reform numerous, but the practical results of the enquiries have been rather disappointing. Piecemeal changes and adjustments have been made from time to time. There has been some bureau shuffling off and on but no thorough reorganisation that could assure the efficient functioning of the machinery for accelerating development.

In order to streamline agricultural production in the country, an Agricultural Board was constituted in 1963. The main function of the Board was to bring about expenditious implementation of the programme for the development of agriculture including animal husbandry, forestry and fisheries. The working of the board was recently reviewed and the Minister of Food, Agriculture, Community Development and Cooperation is its Chairman and the Minister of State in the Ministry of Finance, and the Member Agriculture, Planning

Commission, are its members. The function and powers of the board are: (i) to secure effective and continuous coordination between the *Centre and the states, in matters relating to the formulation and execution of development programmes; (ii) to review the progress of development programmes, ensure efficient arrangements for supplies and services, locate difficulties, if any, and endeavour to remove them; and (iii) to take such other measures as would ensure speedy and effective implementation of the development programmes at the Centre and in the states. The decisions of the Board will be treated as the decisions of the Government of India as long as they are within the plan provisions and within the framework of the approved budget provisions of the ministries concerned.

The Ministry of Agriculture was reorganised in 1964 on the initiative of the then Minister of Food and Agriculture who had found it a poor instrument for carrying out a dynamic and forward-looking policy aimed at making the country self-sufficient and even surplus n the foodgrains and assuring the prosperity of the farming population. The reorganisation was aimed at making the Ministry "function more effectively and to enable it more actively to associate itself with the implementation of development schemes by the states." It attempted (i) a redistribution of subjects and responsibilities among the various units of the Ministry so as to make the assignments of the units compact and specific; (ii) to assign to scientific and technical officers of the Ministry executive functions and operational responsibilities for planning, implementation and supervision of programmes, in addition to their advisory functions, to secure through "better administrative machinery"; and (iii) closer and more continuous contact between the Central and State Governments in the implementation of agricultural plan schemes and to improve Centre-State relations.

The apex of the structure of administration consists of the Minister of Food and Agriculture, who is a senior member of the Cabinet, and Ministers of State and Deputy Ministers who constitute the political executive. The Secretary of the Ministry is the official head of the Ministry and the principal adviser to the Minister. The Department of Agriculture which is one of the three departments included in the Ministry is organised in eight wings, and has besides five specialised offices, a number of supervisory and operational agencies and some cells and units for certain specific purposes.

The eight wings of the department are: (1) Production; (2) Forestry; (3) Fisheries; (4) Inputs (F) (Fertilisers); (5) Inputs (M) (Machinery); (6) Land problems; (7) Special development programmes; and (8) Coordination. The specialised of offices are: (1) The Indian Council of Agricultural Research; (2) The Directorate General of State Farms; (3) Agricultural Prices Commission; (4) The Directorate of Extension; and (5) The Directorate of Economics and Statistics.

Lastly, reference may be made to the numerous subordinate and attached offices ot the Department which operate various programmes of the Ministry, expert committees and other agencies. The more important attached offices are the Directorate of Plant Protection, the Office of the Agricultural Marketing Advisor, the National Seeds Corporation, the Warehousing Corporation, etc.

Committees, both official and unofficial, expert or representative of interests, have been established to advise the Ministry on many important matters. Fifteen of these have been listed as functioning at present. These are Panel of Economists, Panel of Experts on Agricultural *Demonstration and finally Panel of Farmers to advise the Agricultural Prices Commission.

The other agencies falling in this category are: Committee for the Improvement of Agricultural Statistics; National Committee on the Preparation of Farm Management; Manual for the use of Extension Workers; Study Group on Wild Life and Wild Life Products; Indian Board for Wild Life; Central Forestry Commission; Board for Agricultural Machinery and Implements; Standing Committe of Experts on Manures and Fertilisers; National F.A.O. Liaison Committee; Central Council of Gosamvardhana; Central Variety Release Committee; Central Board of Fisheries; and Central Fisheries Research Committee.

The areas covered by these boards and committees are of vital importance to the development of agriculture and it is necessary, therefore, that they should be active bodies manned by competent personnel.

The Planning Commission's role in agricultural administration needs to be examined. It is directly and intimately connected with agricultural development at all stages from policy formulation and planning to plan implementation and evaluation. The Planning Commission's concurrence is required for the ministry's policies and programmes in detail. In fixing the targets of production, in making financial allocations in the five year plan and in the annual plans, in negotiations with the states, the Planning Commission plays a leading, if not dominant role. The working relations between the Planning Commission and the Ministry have not been always smooth and are not infrequently marked by friction.

Role of planning

The role of planning, therefore, continued to be highly relevant. The nature of instruments available to implement the Plan, however, has undergone a significant change in the wake of liberalization and economic reforms. Fixing specific targets for various sectors and deciding who should produce what, when and how is no more the responsibility of the Plnning Commission. Market signals will decide these. To ensure that market signals are consistent with the society's requirements, however, will continue to be a planning function. The planning process will have to focus on planning for policy so that the signals that are sent out to the economic system induce the various economiic agents to behave in a manner which is consistent with the national objectives.

Recognizing the federal character of our system and to encourage meaningful fiscal federalism involving the Centre, the States and local bodies, the planning process has to develop a common policy stance which would be adopted both by the Centre and the States. The role of planning in the coming years would, therefore, involve a considerable degree of policy co-ordination between the Centre and the States, among the States and between the States and the Sub-state level tiers of government.

People's participation and PRI: The role of the government, in general, has to shift from being the provider to the facilitator for people's participation in the development process by creating right types of institutional infrastructure and environment conducive to broad based economic development of people's initiatives cannot be achieved without the active support and involvement of the political system at all levels. In the IX Plan, the Panchayati Raj bodies in rural areas and municipalities in urban areas will be directly involved in the development process. People's involvement via their elected representatives is expected representatives is expected to be realized through genuine democratic decentralization.

The approach to the IX Plan recognezes the need to restore the fiscal health of the government at all levels. The fiscal deficit, especially the revenue component of the deficit, will remain a central concern of macro-economic management. Every effort will have to be made to contain the non-plan, non-development revenue expenditure will be minimized. The borrowings of the government will be regulated so as to maximize the productive potential of the economy.

Subsidies, both direct and indirect, constitute a heabvy burden on the public exchequer. Most of them are untargeted or open-ended. While the costs of indirec6subsidies are hard to measure. Fixation of administered prices of goods and services produced in the public sector on extra-economic considerations is an important element of non-transparent subsidies. Such subsidies are openended and often accrue to those who are not envisaged to benefit from them. Further, th;ey lead to misallocation of resources in l;the economy resulting from wrong price signals apart from placing heavy burden on the exchequer.The Ninth Plan is expected to move away from untargeted hidden subsidies to a system of transparent subsidies directed towards specific target groups in a selective manner.

Adequate quantity, quality and reliability of infrastructure are essential preconditions not only for economic growth and development but also to make the country internationally conpetitive and attractive for investment. The investment needs in this sector are of magnitudes that are beyond the resources available to the government. There is an imperative need, therefore, to motivate the private sector to participate in the development proces, if the infrastructure gap has to be bridged. The public sector which has carried the burden of infrastructure development so far will also benefit by the competition and partnership with the private sector. Successful development of this crucial sector will require bold policy initiatives, framing of schemes and seting up of an institutional environment which would provide a level playing field to all competitors whilst simultaneously safeguarding the rights of consumers.

The overview of the approach to the Ninth Five Year Plan outlined in the preceding paragraphs clearly indicates that it Plan'. The true test, of course, is in the implimentation. The deprived sections of our society certainly deserve a better deal than what they have got so far. Let us hope that their time has come.

Coming to specifics of the Ninth Plan, it may be noticed that as compared to the earlier approach plan documents which used to give prominence to growth of aggregate GDP, the Ninth Plan gives prominence to growth of agriculture. This is based on the logic that it is agricultural prosperity which brings down povety and generates more employment and, therefore, higher rate of growth of GDP should be achieved through achieving higher rate of growth of agricultural output. In the earliear plans, industrial development was given prominence and the public sector usually occupied commanding heights. But during th Ninth Plan, it is agriculture which is going to occupy commanding heights and the public sector outlay constitutes only about 35 per cent of the total estimated plan investment of Rs. 8,75,000 crore. So this is a shift of emphasis in terms of priority from public sector industrial development to agricultural development which is mostly in the private sector. This was necessary because the public sector investment in agriculture had stagnated in the name of providing inputs subsidies like fertilizers subsidy. Correspondingly, public sector investment in agriculture infrastructure like irrigation had come down. This was rectified even during 1996-97 by allocating Rs. 900 crore for accelarated irrigation development. But that amount was diverted from other sectors and the overall public sector investment in agriculture remained around 12.8 per cent. Therefore, the Ninth Five Year Plan has decided to increase budgetary support and public sector investment in irrigation, rural roads, rural markets and a host of other infrastructures. What is more, while the overall growth of GDP envisaged during the Ninth Plan is seven per cent, which was made mandatory by the Common Minimum Programme, the rate of growth of agriculture envisaged during the Ninth Plan is as high as 4.5 per cent. This can be achieved only by promoting commercial agriculture through modernization and bringing in vast amount of private invesment. This pattern of development is envisaged for agriculture during the Ninth Five Year Plan.

Industrial development will continue to receive priority as it received during the Eighth Five Year Plan but there will not be much public sector investment in new industrial units. Most of whatever investment that will be undertaken will go for providing industrial infrastructure for small-scale industries paricularly in food processing activities. Recently, the Government of India enhanced the investment limit of small-scale industries to Rs. 3 crore. This will help technological upgradation of small-scale industries. Foreign direct investment is assumed to play a very prominent role in the development of industry. In this context, several measures have been taken. all of them are aimed at mobilizing private investment for industrial development.

Other than agriculture, the second most important priority of the Ninth Plan is infrastructure development like power generation, ports, railways, national highways, etc. Most of these except railways are left to the private sector. But wherever necessary, such as in the case of power generation and distribution and development of railways, public sector investment will continue. But the magnitude of the problelm is so much that these infrastructure facilities cannot be provided without massive investment from the private sector both domestic and foreign.

Finally, the Ninth Plan recongnizes the failure of the past efforts to provide basic minimum services to the rural areas. Accordingly, this task was taken up during 1996-97 itself. It is going to be a prominent programme during the Ninth Plan. it is hoped that by the end of the Ninth Plan, the people in rural areas will have access to basic minimum services like safe drinking water, roads, primary health and primary education.

The Planning Commission has also decided to pay more attention to protection of biodiversity in Himalayan region and cleaning the rivers polluted by industrial and urban effluents.

Besides, the State governments are asked to formulate appropriate development strategies and programmes to reduce intra-State economic disparities.

No doubt, creation of employment opportunities, reduction of poverty, empowerment of women and other weaker sections of the society, fostering environmentally sustained development and promoting self-reliance are all continued in the Ninth Plan. but most of these programmes are ongoing which are carried forward from the previous plans. Relative emphasis may differ. But the top priority is given to agriculture, infrastructure and basic minimum needs during the Ninth Plan. They are the priorities of the Ninth Plan and they are intended to make the country a reasonably decent plane to live in.

Planned growth

The Central as well as state governments have taken some measures to ensure planned growth of towns and check speculation in land. Many states and Union Territories have formulated Master Plans for many of their towns under the Town Planning Acts and have also set up development authorities. The Central Government has enacted the Urban Land (Ceiling and Regulation) Act, 1976. In addition to these, there are Acts like Periphery Acts, Agricultural Tenancy and Lands Act, and Vacant Lands Act enacted by different States and U.Ts In many states/U.Ts there is taxation on vacant land or conversion of agricultural land to urban uses. In almost all the States/U.Ts, Housing boards/development authorities have been set up which are directly participating in the urban fringe land market either as developer of land or at times, even as builder of houses mainly for the lower income groups. Recognising the sensitive nature of fringe areas, the 73rd and 74th constitutional Amendments have been enacted, to give more powers to Gram Panchayats and Nagar Panchayats for transitional areas.

No doubt, many of the measures taken by the government have gone a long way in checking speculation in land and ensuring regulated development. However, the problem has not been completely eliminated or brought to a satisfactory level. Legislative enactments have not been fully effective either in containing speculation or making land available for the poor. These enactments have succeeded in encouraging the phenomenon of speculation and sprawl beyond the jurisdiction of the Acy. In quite a few cases, these have been by-passed by the speculators through benami deals or various other measures. Even the fiscal measures have not deterred speculation. The rate of tax has normally been low. The expected price of land is high enough to pay for all the extra charges. In order to tackle the problem effectively especially the problem of the fringe, the following recommendations are made:

Firstly, administrative control should be tightened and no unauthorised development should be allowed under any cirumstances. The political interference in enforcing rules and regulations relating to urban development should be discouraged by a Central legislation. At the same time a set of development control and building regulations should be framed and enforced by the designated agencies for development of urban fringe.

Secondly, speculation in land cannot be checked by imposition of greater penalty or bigger taxes, etc. A Central legislation should empower state governments to acquire plots which are vacant for more than two years. Coloniser/developers who may purchase lands from farmers should be asked to make development within a period of three years. If not, the state government should have the power to acquire the land at the price at which the developer originally purchased the land from the farmer or impose heavy tax and compounding tax rate on vacant land.

Thirdly, as regards infrastructural facilities, the local bodies should be made responsible for providing basic facilities in the colonies falling in the fringe. In order to enable these local bodies to provide these facilities, their financial position needs to be improved. It is, therefore, desirable to create a separate scheme for developing colonies in the fringe. The scheme can be formulated based on people's participation or matching grants.

Fourthly, no individual should be allowed to own more than two or three plots in the country as whole. One could be in his home town, another in his home state and third one in any part of the country.

Fifthly, the public housing schemes should be pursued more vigorously. Housing boards/development authorities should not only construct flats but also allot plots at reasonable prices. Considering the shortage of urban land within the various cities, the housing boards/ development authorities should develop land lying in fringe areas, especially those lands which are unproductive.

Sixthly, in authorised colonies, there still exist certain residential pockets which should be regularised alongwith development charges immediately to obtain additional revenues. Longer and delay for approval, greater the financial loss for the local bodies. All the colonies, whether authorised or unauthorised, enjoying certain civic facility should be made to pay taxes to increase local revenue. There should be periodical review of property tax based on land values.

Finally, the Master Plan that is made for any metropolitan city is normally for 15-20 years and for a specified boundary. In TCPO's study it has been seen that in certain cases like Chennai, fringe area grows faster than the corporation area in terms of population. Hence, provision should be made in the Master Plan that the areas closer to the corporation boundary are included in the corporation limit periodically and development measures are taken simultaneously by the government. This would ensure speedy disposal of applications for the approval of the layouts, construction, plans. etc.

By adding fringe areas to the main city every year or once in two years or three years the burden of expenditure on the infrastructural facilities for the newly added areas is reduced considerably higher than that has been collocted by the local bodies. This could be well utilised for the development of the respective areas.

Some drastic steps ought to be taken to tide over the existing situation in the urban fringe. To check the haphazard growth of the fringe areas, it is imperative that the administrative control is tightend, if need be, a Central legislation may be enacted in this regard. The developers should be asked to make development within three years of the purchase of land, failing which allotment of land made to the developers should be cancelled by the Government by paying the same price at which developers bought it. Moreover, no individual should be allowed to own more than two or three plots in country. To check speculation in land prices, a Central legislation empowerning the State Government to acquire plots which are vacant for more than two years should be framed and enacted. Moreover, the local bodies under whose jurisdiction the fringe areas fall, should be provided adequate financial support to enable them to provide the essential infrastructural facilities like municipal water supply, sewerage and drainage in the colonies falling in the fringe areas.

At the time of Independence, understandably, there were a few industrial concentrations: the steel complexes at Jamshedpur and Burnpur supporting a good number of steel and heavy engineering units in Bihar and West Bengal. The coal industry, again largely confined to these eastern states, supporting a wide range of allied industries, the railways and roadways. The jute mills of eastern India, plantation industry in Assam and the Nilgiris, textile units around Ahmedabad, Bombay, Coimbatore, Madras, Madurai and Pondicherry, in turn, support allied engineering industries around Bombay and a few chemical units were handsome but entrepreneurship was scarce.

The launch of the First Five year Plan in 1951 was the first step in deciding priorities and channelling resources towards these. There was understandably the stress on agriculture. The seeds were sown for expanding agricultural production through handsome investments on massive irrigation-cum-hydroelectric projects. The construction of massive irrigation dams like the Bhakra Nangal, Hirakud, Koyna, Nagarjuna Sagar... was envisaged during these years. The foresight of the planners could be appreciated much later when several lakhs of acres were brought under irrigation and cheap hydroelectric power flowed from these.

In the early fifties, capacity for steel production was less than 1.5 million tonnes, through the two steel works of Tata Steel and Indian Iron and Steel Company. Jawaharlal Nehru T.T. Krishnamachari and visionary bureaucrats like S. Boothalingam believed in steel triggering a lot of activity in downstream capital goods and consumer industries. When the Russians, the Germans and the British offered handsome credit and technology for building a million tonne integrated steel plant each, these visionaries boldly opted to accept all the three offers! It was thus that in just five years, the three integrated steel plants at Bhilai, Durgapur and Rourkela, built on green field sites, started delivering a rich mix of basic steel. Mother factories like the Heavy Electricals india (which later merged with BHEL) and the Heavy Engineering Corporation took shape during this period.

Several of these were long gestation projects that involved large investments. Unlike in most countries of the West, the public sector was not the result of nationalisation: S. Swayambu, Chairman of Heavy Electricals in the late Sixties, graphically pointed to the compulsions of the government to enter industruy: "the private sector at that time could not think beyond producing fraction horse power motors or electric bulbs. They neither had the resources nor the holding power to invest in large, long gestation projects," he pointed out.

Unfortunately, several of these investments like those in HEC, did not yield the returns envisaged; the inability to make sustained investments in the user industries, of steel making and mining also led to poor levels of capacity utilisation. In contrast, with the full complement of staff recruited, there was heavy over-manning related to output; thus the twin evils of a very high incremental capital output ratio (ICOR) and low productivity plagued the Indian industry.Three decades later, these continued to affect competitiveness despite the tremendous advantage of building capacity at modest costs.

In the mid-Sixties, India suffered two successive droughts that led to a preciptious fall in foodgrains production. The shortfall zoomed to around 10 million tonnes per year. The impact was so severe that the very concept of planning over five year span had to be given a holiday. But, this adversity had its beneficial fallout: in triggering the green revolution. Within five years, the coordinated work of policymakers, scientists and farmers ensured self-sufficiency in foodgrains.

The technology spread to a range of commercial crops, notably cotton and sugarcane, that triggered spectacular expansion of the textile and sugar industries.

Coming of age of public sector

The decade also witnessed the coming of age of the public sector. Several large industrial units came out of gestation and started earning handsome profits. The Bharat Heavy Electricals showed remarkable enterprise and growth during this period. BHEL undertook manufacture of the entire gamut of power equipment that supported the massive additions to capacity witnessed over the last three decades.

Equally spectacular was the success of the Oil and Natural gas Commission in exploring and producing oil and gas wells at Bombay offshore and in Gujarat onshore. The western region, through mostly offshore wells, accounted for production rising to a level of 20 million tonnes in just about a decade. ONGC became one of the large, globally renowned enterprises in just around two decades.

The public sector thus was reacing commanding heights in several areas, notably oil, power, steel, coal, state trading.... With the nationalisation of 14 major banks and with industrial development catalysed and funded massively by the public financial institutions of IDBI, ICICI, IFCI and dozens of state financial and industrial development corporations, almost the entire financial sector was under the public sector.

Yet, the third decade of independence was one marked by serious industrial strife. While the beginning of this decade was marked by the precipitous fall in food production, the country's involvement in the liberation struggle of Bangladesh in 1971 proved costly. The economy went through two years of massive inflation (1973-75).

For the first time since independence, a non-Congress party, the Janata Party, came to power at the Centre in 1977. There was so much comfort on the agricultural front that efforts were made even to export some wheat. The government attempted large transfer of resources to rural India. But the insistence that MNCs should offer equity in their Indian ventures, led to IBM and Coca opting to quit India. The spree of nationalisation of the foreign oil companies, the coal companies andthe 103 textile mills further accentuated by the tightening of FERA, led to a slowdown of direct foreign investment.

The corrections that came in the early eighties proved beneficial and set the pattern for opening up later. The advent of Maruti Udyog and four other Japanese manufacturers to produce light commercial vehicles, and financial collaborations for two-wheelers helped Indian industry catch up with technology. In just three years 1984-87, Maruti Udyog zoomed to a production level of 100,000 vehicles and set new standards for productivity and work ehtics. Foreign trade was given a lot of importance during these ten years. The Minerals and Metals Trading Corporation too scaled new heights. The seeds for building Indian multinationals were truly sown during these eventful years.

The Asiad '82, the Non-Aligned Meet 1983, the Commonwealth Heads of Government Meet 1984 and, more importantly, the expansion of the television network, contributed a lot to expanding awareness on the severe shortcomings of Indian economy. Comparison of notes became more frequent. Apart from Japan, the emergence of the Asian Tigers and the first attempts of China to open up shook off the complacency and smug satisfaction over modest achievements. The emergence of a middle class whose numbers expanded rapidly, also triggered demand for a vast range of consumer goods and new products like time share resorts.

This decade marked a major break with the past in regard to trade, industry and nvestment policies. And this was largely due to the near collapse of the economy during 1990-91 when foreign exchange reserves nose-dived to just two weeks' import requirements and with no one willing to bail us out. The debt burden was increasing beyond prudential levels of servicing; inflation was soaring; budget deficits were at unconscionably high levels, further stoking inflation and interest rates. The near impossible situation required drastic remedies. Sweeping changes were made.

Over four decades of licensing, controls and permits were abolished for all but a handful of strategic industries. The MRTP Act was almost totall scrapped excepting retaining control over restrictive practices. tariffs were being comprehensively reduced. Subsidies were sought to be contained. A beginning was made in broad-basing the ownership of public sector undertakings. Financial sector reforms were initiated. Foreign direct investment and investment by foreign financial institutions were sught as never before. The results were encouraging. There was considerable success in containing inflaton, which was brought down to around 5 per cent last year; in stepping up growth rate to over 6.6 per cent; in building foreign reserves of around $ 20 billion; in stepping up export growth to over 20 per cent per annum over the last two years; and in attracting investments over vast areas.

However, unlike in China, there is no clarity and unanimity with regard to industrial policy, especially in attracting foreign investments and privatisation. In an employment scare economy, understandably, there is the concern to protect employment in the organised sector. Unfortunately, ths has been carried toa bizarre extent: of keeping alive dozens of public sector undertakings with little or no productive activity but only for the purpose of protecting employment of a few. In the Ministry of Heavy Industry alone, some 34 of the 48 undertakings have been kept running on this basis. The National Textile Corporation provides an even more depressing example: with no prospects of viability, the mills are run largely for keeping a few thousands in employment despite pumping in massive resources that also became unproductive. Productivity levels at the public sector banks are low.

Encouraged by the results of the new techniques and recovery on the economic front, "Approach to the Fourth Five Year Plan" described "growth with stability" as its main aim. During the previous few years, instability on the economic front had primarily been associated with wide fluctuations in the agricultural production and consequent rapid rise in prices. The "Approach Document," therefore, recommneded the building of buffer stocks of main agricultural commodities to meet such fluctuations besides evening out physical supplies between years. Such stocks were also to be utilised for stabilising the levels of agricultural prices. All this could, however, be possible only in the context of a steady rise in agricultural production. The other major object of the Fourth Plan was to move towards self-reliance as speedily as possible because it was felt that the process of development sustained by continuous foreign aid (inclusive of food aid) was not healthy. This could be possible both by reducing imports and increasing exports. Here again agriculture was required to play a major role in both these objectives.

If the country could achieve self-sufficiency in foodgrains and remove constraints on supplies of most of the traditional export commodities based on agricultural raw materials, this objective could be fulfilled. The general approach for stabilisation of agricultural prices and supplies from buffer stocks and open sale arrangements could in part look after this. There was also need to investigate new types or varieties of agricultural products when international demands and inducements come to increase their supply. Where domestic consumption of these products was to be restrained in order to make physical availability for export possible, the means used would have to be the imposition of excise or direct purchase by a state agency for export.

Programmes for research and market surveys in order to find new uses and new markets for traditional export commodities and adequate measures for augmenting their production and availability for export were also recommended.

In the agricultural sector, the Fourth Plan had two main objectives. The first objective was to provide conditions necessary for a sustained increase of about five per cent per annum over the next decade. The second was to enable as large a section of the rural population as possible, including the small cultivator and the farmer in dry areas, to participate in development and share its benefits. Accordingly, the priority programmes of development in agriculture fell broadly in two categories, namely, those which aim at maximising production and those which aim at remedying imbalances.

The creation of conditions necessary for a five per cent agricultural growth was basic to the approach of the Fourth Plan. The crucial position of agriculture and the extreme urgency of achieving rapid growth in production were brought home, more than ever before, by the experience of previous years. The pace of development in the agricultural sector sets a limit to the growth of industry, of exports, and of the economy as a whole and constitutes a major condition for achieving economic and social stability and improving the standard of living for the mass of the people.

Role of central government

The activities of the Central Government in relation to agriculture at present may be summed up as follows ;

— The planning of agricultural development jointly with the Planning Commission;

— Coordinating state agricultural plans, watching their implementation and evaluating performance;

— Providing financial assistance to states for their agricultural schemes by way of grantsin-aid and loans;

— Ensuring the supply of agricultural inputs such as improved seeds, implements, fertilisers, etc., in sufficient quantities and in time;

— Providing credits and facilities for marketing, storage, and transport of produce;

— Providing economic incentives to farmers in the form of remunerative prices and enforcing the minimum and maximum prices;

— Extension work among farmers including extension education to make farmers receptive to scientific farming practices;

— Providing technical advice and assistance to states in implementing programmes;

— Development of livestock, dairying and fisheries;

— Development of forests;

— Land reclamation, soil conservation, utilisation of water resources;

— Fundamental and applied research in agriculture, veterinary science, forestry, agricultural economics, fisheries, etc.; maintaining the standards of higher education;

— Home science and nutritional needs of the population; and

— The administration of external assistance.

The National Commission on Agriculture was constituted during 1970. The Commission was expected to look into almost all the problems that were gone into 48 years ago by the Linlithgow Commission. Though much has been done to develop agriculture since then, and especially after independence, the basic problems remain almost the same.

For instance, the Linlithgow Commission (1925) was to examine and report on the "present conditions of agriculture and rural economy in India and to make recommendations for the improvement of agriculture and promotion of the welfare and prosperity of the rural population." Another important term of reference of the 1925 Commission was to investigate "the existing methods of transport and marketing of agricultural produce and stock."

The new Commission too will "examine and report on the present conditions of agriculture and rural economy and make recommendations for the improvement of agriculture and the promotion of the welfare and prosperity of people." It will also report on the "development of infrastructures including facilities for transport, marketing together with the lines of future development."

In view of the vital changes that have occurred since the last Commission reported, the terms of reference of the new Commission have been widened in their scope and made as broad-based as possible.

One of the important terms of reference is to investigate the structure and organisation of the agricultural services, spelling out the relative responsibilities of the Centre and the states. An equally important term of reference is to establish in clear terms the inter-relationship between industry and agriculture.

The Commission was also to investigate and report on:

— The pattern of land utilisation and the nature of the cropping thereon and the methods of land improvement.

— The principles of development of water resources.

— Utilisation of the science of soil conservation and land shaping.

— So far it has submitted 23 interim reports on different subjects, including fertiliser distribution, seed multiplication, some aspects of agricultural research, extension and training, credit services for small and marginal farmers and agricultural labourers, reorientation of programmes for Small and Marginal Farmers and Agricultural Labourers Development Agencies, modernising irrigation system and integrated development of command areas, desert development and certain important aspects of selected export-oriented agricultural commodities, agricultural price policy and certain important aspects of marketing and prices of selected commercial crops.

— Implementation of the land reforms policy and the changes that may be necessary in the pattern of crop sharing.

— The new strategy of agricultural development based on the package of practices, and modifications required for better results.

— Forecast for the decade 1970-71 to 1980-81 on the magnitude of the requirements of fertilisers, good seeds, pesticides and agricultural implements and machinery; the organisation necessary for their production and distribution.

— Forecast for the decade 1970-71 to 1980-81, the requirements of credit for the agricultural programme.

— The strategy of agricultural research, education and extension, and

— Integrated development of agriculture, animal husbandry, farm forestry and inland fisheries, to avail of the economic of mixed farming.

The Commission submitted its final report on 31 January, 1976. The main emphasis in the report is on the modernisation of agriculture through application of science and technology, keeping growth with social justice as the guiding principle. The Commission has spelt out the implications of establishing a prosperous egalitarian agricultural economy in another 25 years. It has estimated in quantitative terms, the potential growth in various sectors of agriculture—crop production, animal husbandry, fisheries and forestry—and also indicated in detail the technologies, inputs, infrastructural and institutional development required for achieving this.

With good agricultural season during 1967-68 and the adoption of the new strategy over the years, agricultural development a great success and the country reaped the richest crop of 108.4 million tonnes of foodgrains during 1970-71. The subsequent two years have, however, again proved that nature can play havoc and reduce the effect of the 'new strategy' as well. Agriculture in rainfed areas presents a more formidable problem. There it is not only low yielding, but also precarious, and poverty is acute and widespread.

In the past the focus of the overall agricultural development effort was, to a large extent, on areas with the maximum promise of agricultural growth. In the Fifth Plan, when intensive agricultural programmes such as multiple cropping and high yielding varieties programme generally based on irrigation will continue to receive attention, it will be necessary simultaneously to place stress on agricultural programmes in rainfed and other less promising areas. The Fourth Plan provided for (i) intensification of research into improved dry-farming technology, and (ii) pilot projects for testing the efficacy of the new technology and for providing demonstration-cum-training in this technology. The progress so far has been rather slow on account of, among other things, a late start, personnel problems and absence of effective tie-up between the pilot projects and the research centres. It is proposed to intensify efforts towards evolution and propagation of appropriate dry farming technologies. Many of these areas are suitable for the development of animal husbandry which will receive added emphasis. Intensive efforts to develop animal husbandry in the rainfed areas could make an appreciable addition to the incomes of the rural poor. Finally, public rural works will have to form an important component of the employment generating activities in dry-farming and other rural areas where normal programmes of agricultural development are not likely to make a significant impact.

In recognition of the considerations mentioned above, certain special programmes such as the Small Farmers' Development Agency (SFDA) and Marginal Farmers projects, Crash Scheme for Rural Employment and Drought-Prone Areas programme were initiated in the Fourth Plan. By and large, these programmes were conceived in isolation and their operations were locationally dispersed. In the Fifth Plan, it will be necessary not only to accelerate the pace of implementation of these programmes but also to make distinct operational improvements. The experience with these programmes has shown that, if an impact is to be made, the development programmes in general and the special programmes in particular will have to be integrated. In these areas, an effort towards integrated area development will be a necessary condition for improving the economy of small and marginal farmers and agricultural labourers. Such integrated rural development programmes will vary in terms of different land and water resource situations and will have to be tailored to suit local conditions.

Lead banks

One of the innovations introduced in the wake of bank nationalisation in 1969, from which a great deal was expected, was the lead bank scheme. The intention was to assign districts to the nationalised, and some non-nationalised banks in which they would perform the function of the catalyst in development. The lead bank was expected to be in close touch with other development agencies in the district, particularly the district authorities, to locate viable schemes that would then be financed by it alone or in collaboration with other banks in the district. It was to adopt a "consortium approach" as the leader of the banking institutions in the district and help diversify credit facilities even as it brought hoarded cash into the banking system. It was a challenging task in which the past was no guide. The original allotment of lead districts was made rather mechanically, more in the manner of an "equitable distribution" of a rather unprofitable and difficult assignment than on a proper assessment of banks. Some banks were assigned lead districts far from their traditional and historical areas of operation. This was unavoidable to an extent because there were large parts of the country which were "underbanked." To rectify this, it was difficult to avoid the hardships that go with any pioneering venture. Even in relatively developed districts, the lead bank required exceptional qualities of leadership from local managers. Very often they were working in a vacuum because they had no techno-economic plan, or properly evaluated projects, in the district for which they could provide the credit. Lack of coordination and cooperation among the several agencies engaged in rural development is a familiar complaint about Indian planning. The lead bank is yet another institution that has failed to mesh in the development process. The concept of integrated area development has been accepted in principle but the links betwen institutions have yet to be worked out. There have also been complaints that the consortium spirit was missing in the relationship between the lead and other banks (including those in the cooperative sector) in the district. An intensive programme of training and orientation of banking staff working in rural areas is overdue.

It is easy to be censorious about the rather poor record of the lead banks, but in fairness one should record that a lead bank manager's task require infinitely more complex skills than his counterpart needs in conventional urban banking. There are new additions to his tasks every day. None of them lends itself to easy definition or clear guidelines. A directive issued by the Union Government, for examble, seeks to dovetail the 20-point programme into the general pattern of duties of a lead bank. In a sense, this is merely a restatement of the functions of the lead bank in a different way. But unless detailed instructions are given to the field staff on how they should act in a specific situation they would rather play safe, particularly because they may be held accountable for avoidable financial losses.

The rapid and widespread development of small industries including cottage, household and small scale industries is one of the major objectives of the Plan as a part of the primary goals of reducing unemployment and underemployment in the country. The major components of the strategy proposed to be adopted in formulating and implementing the development programmes for these industries to be taken up in the new Plan are:

(i) to generate opportunities for fuller and full-time employment by

  (a) revitalising and developing the existing traditional and other small scale industries, and

  (b) promoting intensive development of new viable small industries;

(ii) to raise the level of earnings of rural artisans, handloom weavers, craftsmen and others employed in these industries;

(iii) to promote the growth of these industries in rural areas and small towns; and

(iv) to reduce progressively the role of subsidies by providing these selectively for credit and development of skills, designs and marketing.

According to the new Statement on Industrial Policy announced in December, 1977, the main thrust of the policy will be on effective promotion of cottage and small industries widely dispersed in rural areas and small towns. The statement contains several policy measures for accelerating the pace of growth of these industries which are outlined subsequently along with the contents of the development programmes for different cottage and small industries. It has already been decided that no more licences should be issued to new industrial units within certain limits of large metropolitan cities having a population of more than 1 million and urban areas with a population of more than 5 lakhs as per the 1971 Census.

While the number of industries reserved for exclusive development in the small scale sector has been significantly expanded, the Government will also consider introducing special legislation for protecting the interests of cottage and household industries with a view to ensuring that these activities which provide self-employment in large numbers get due recognition in industrial development.

Some assistance is already being provided for the development of selected small 'service' industries covering units engaged in repair and maintenance of machinery and equipment. The integrated rural-urban growth contemplated under the Integrated Rural Development Programme which will bring into its fold towns of the unemployed educated youth. Such opportunities like starting retail shops and various household services would be available to such youth who are enterprising. With a view to help them in avialing of a variety of employment opportunities, it is proposed to consider provision of margin money assistance for starting selected small business and enterprises.

The Industrial Development Bank of India has taken steps to set up a separate wing to deal exclusively with the credit requirement of the cottage and small industries sector. It will coordinate, guide and monitor the entire range of credit facilities offered by other financial institutions for the sector, for whom separate wings will be set up in these institutions particularly the nationalised banks. The banks will be expected to earmark a specified portion of their total advances for promotion of these industries. The policy of the government will be that no worthwhile scheme for these industries is given up for want of credit.

In the light of the experience gathered from the working of the scheme of margin money assistance referred to earlier, a new scheme has been taken up for promotion of tiny industrial units in the rural and semi-urban areas. Varying rates of interest are being charged by the financial institutions from artisans, craftsmen, handloom weavers and others within and outside the cooperative fold and those being assisted by development agencies for different small industries. It is proposed to review the rates of interest with a view to remove certain anomalies. Institutional credit facilities will be suitably supplemented by the States and Union Territories particularly for the poorer sections of the society in backward areas, without involving overlapping.

As pointed out earlier, there has been a tendency to proliferate agencies and organisations for the development of different cottage and small industries. This has tended more to confuse the average rural and small entrepreneurs. To over-come this, it is envisaged under the new industrial policy statement that there will be one agency in each district called the District Industries Centre, mainly to provide and arrange a package of assistance and facilities for credit guidance, raw materials, training, marketing, etc., including the necessary help to unemployed educated young entrepreneurs in general and custom services. These centres will establish close linkages with the Development Blocks on the one hand and with specialised institutions concerned with the development of small industries on the other. It is the intention of the government to extend this improved organisational pattern to all the districts over the next two to three years.

Initially, it is proposed to establish the District Industries Centres in most of the districts already covered under the scheme of Rural Industries Projects. For establishing these centres, the staff of the Rural Industries

Projects and the State Boards for Khadi and Village Industries will be suitably deployed, trained and, wherever necessary, strengthened to deal with the problems of the existing rural and such other industreis which have potential for development in each district. The staff of the new Centres will work in close consultation and collaboration with the concerned State-level Departments and institutions as well as the Central and other institutions functioning in the districts including the financial and voluntary insititutions and associations engaged in the development of cottage, household and other small industries.

To ensure coordination, it will be necessary to constitute high-level committees not only at the district and State levels, but also at the Centre. The main functions of these committees comprising the representative of all the concerned departments, agencies and institutions including the financial institutions, would be to simplify the procedures and undertake a periodical review of the problems and monitor the progress.

Besides the continued dependence of a significantly large number of different rural and other small industries for marketing on middlemen, an increasingly large number of these industries have also been experiencing difficulties in marketing their products. Therefore, marketing assistance including those for market intelligence and surveys, testing facilities, quality control and standardisation of products of selected industries will receive special attention. Since the reservation of certain items of textiles for production in the handloom sector has not been effective, the government will enforce the existing reservation and further extend it to other items. The items reserved for exclusive development in the small scale sector will be reviewed annually with a view to ensuring their effectiveness and also expanding the list of new products and processes capable of being manufactured in the sector. Measures such as purchase preference and reservation for exclusive purchase by the government departments and the public sector undertakings will be used to support the marketing of their products. Greater efforts will be made to provide closer marketing linkages between the products of small scale industries and the requirements of medium and large industries particularly the public sector undertakings.

With a view to providing more extensive marketing assistance within the country for reducing the role of middlemen and intermediaries, it is proposed to provide margin money assistance particularly to the unemployed educated young entrepreneurs for setting up retail shops for the products of traditional and modern small industries, subject to the condition that a specified percentage of their total turnover is accounted for by the products purchased directly from these industries. A scheme on these lines will have to be supported by setting up of testing-cum-after-sale service centres for selected industries. Both these schemes will be taken up by the State-level corporations and entrepreneurs. It is also proposed to examine the feasibility of utilising the network of marketing outlets established by the Khadi & Village Industries Commission and organised industries for marketing the products of different small industries.

The existing activities of the institutions already engaged in promotion of exports of the products of different small industries will be suitably enlarged and diversified. More important activities to be undertaken by them will include promotion of linkages between the small producers and foreign purchasers, collection and dissemination of information about the pattern and potential of exports including suggestions for product development and design, freight charges, etc.

Training facilitis are another important input for raising the level of earnings of those employed in these industries as well as for creation of new employment opportunities. It is proposed to review the ongoing Central and States training schemes with a view to re-orienting these suitably in the context of the new strategy outlined earlier, making these more effective and avoiding any duplication. Besides training of the Central and State personnel engaged in extension and promotional activities, training facilities for artisans, craftsmen, workers and unemployed educated youth will be suitably expanded wherever considered necessary. Greater attention will be given to training of small entrepreneurs in management and unemployed educated youth so as to assist them to set up small industries and service units. In the light of the experience gained in the implementation of the craftsmen and apprenticeship training schemes, it is proposed to tie up more effectively the training programmes with the requirements of industries by introducing sutiable diversification in the trades and also by upgrading * Training Institutes are mostly urban oriented, a scheme is under consideration for rural artisans' training and a feasibility study-cum-survey is to be taken up in 1978-79. Besides, further efforts would be directed towards setting up of facilities for technical training in specialised and advanced categories such as electronics and processing instrumentation, chemicals, farm machinery trades and vocations suitable for women.

Special measures are envisaged under the new industrial policy statement for ensuring an effective and coordinated approach for the development and widespread application of suitable small and simple machines and devices for improving the productivity and earning capacity of those engaged in different small industries. It will further be the endeavour of the government to fully integrated such appropriate techniques of production with the broader programme of all-round rural development. Efforts will be made by the staff of the District Industries Centres to identify technological and other problems of small industries and to arrange for research and investigation on them through local and other concerned educational and technical institutions. For this purpose, the facilities for research and common services will be expanded.

The measures envisaged under the new industrial policy statement and also the development programme outlined subsequently are intended to promote viable rural and small industries ona decentralised basis. It would be possible to achieve this pattern of development by progressively reducing the role of subsidies including sales rebate by providing these selectively for credit and development of skills, designs and marketing. It is, however, realised that some subsidies may be required for limited periods in respect of the poorer sections of the society engaged in some traditional industries. Therefore, it is proposed to review the schemes involving subsidies and rebates so as to adopt a selective approach in regard to coverage and period.

Outlay

In the context of the proposed strategy, the development programmes will be reoriented and expanded. The Plan outlays will be supplemented by institutional finance as well as private investment. A total outlay of Rs. 1410 crores in the public sector has been provided in the Plan. The break-up is shown below:

The outlay of Rs. 45 crores for industrial estates will be supplemented by the outlay made for the schemes of industrial areas under the programme for medium and large industries. In addition to the outlays made in the public sector about Rs. 2,000 crores are expected to be invested from private sources including banking and financial institutions. Thus, under the Plan, a total outlay of about Rs. 3,400 crores would be available for the development of household cottage and other small industries.

The levels of employment and production anticipated in 1982-83 are indicated below:

In the context of the enlarged programmes to be taken up under the new Plan, it will be necesssary for the all-India organisations concerned with the development of different industries to take suitable steps for periodical reviewof the policies, programmes and problems of these industries. Besides a closer liaison with the concerned State departments and institution for monitoring the programmes, quick studies will also be undertaken for assessing the impact of some of the major programmes especially on the level of employment, earnings and exports. A reference has already been made about the need for setting up a high-level coordination committee at the Centre to review from time to time the progress of the programmes of all these Boards and the State Governments and also to ensure coordination in respect of important policies and programmes for credit, training, marketing and exports.

The first four years of the VIII Plan witnessed reasonably good performance as reflected in macro-economic indicatore in terms of higher than expected growth rate of Gross Domestic Product (GDP) accompanied by a sustainable current account balance, comfortable foreign exchange reserves and a moderation in the level of fiscal deficit and the rate of inflation. But doubts are expresssed in certain quarters as to the contribution of the Plan itself to these achievements.

A review of the progress of the VIII Plan, however, indicates a number of areas of concern—stagnant agiculture, soaring food prices, increasing inter-regional disparities, deceleration in employment growth, significantly lower growth in basic infrastructure like power, transport, irrigation, communication, etc and shortage of funds for social sectors, especially the basic minimum services (BMSs).

Efforts of the government to contain fiscal deficit have fallen disproportionately on investment in key infrastructure and social sectors which depend on budget support. There has been a decline in total Plan outlay. The high levels of government borrowings in recint years has also led to a sharp increase in interest rates, which contributed significanly to the interest burden of the government. Further, the crowding out effect of government borrowings might have adversely affected the investment in the private sector.

Sustained growth of the economy depends on adequate availability of basic infrastructural facilities like power, transport, irrigation and communications. The VIII Plan has fallen significantly short not only of the targets but also of the VII Plan achievements in these vital areas. This was mainly because of non-realization of the expected private investment in those sectors. There was already a demand-supply gap of over 10 per cent in the power sector at the beginning of the VIII Plan. By the end of the Plan, this gap is likely to be widened further.

The performance of social sectors like education, health and family welfare, women and child development, housing, water supply and urban development which are key to achieving equity and social justice and which depend exclusively on budget support for finaancing their plan outlays, have suffered serious shortfalls during the VIII Plan. As a result, the quality of life of a vast majority of the poor might have suffered a set-back. On the whole, during the VIII Plan the economic growth, though significant, is unlikely to have benefited the poor and the underprivileged substantially.

Shortfalls in the VIII Plan targets were observed in almost all infrastructure sectors like irrigation, power, transport and communication. For the first three sectors, the VIII Plan review gives the following estimates:

The figures and statements appearing in newspapers indicate shortfall in the target for power and irrigation being even larger than given in the review paper. In respect of irrigation potevtial created during the VIII Plan, the Minister of state for Planning, Prof Alagh has said that the shortfall may be the highest for any Plan since 1951.

The danger is that if the present government keeps dilly-dallying in the hope of private foreign capital in the infrastructure sector finally falling prey to various temptations, as the previous government had done, we may end up doing no better than before.

Perhaps the entire set of problems connected with tempting foreign capital is being sought to be iroued out with the help of what apears to be divergent interpretations of the Common Minimum Programme of the United Front government. Such divergence does not make for clarity in the government' policy postures. Not that clarity could have made any substantial difference to the inflows in the face of the fact that out of $ 20 billion wouth FDI agreements signed, hardly about a tenth or so has actually come in.

An issue recently raised at the Planning commission suggesting that the Commission be the sole arbitrator in matters of economic policy appeared amongst other things to aim at avoidance of interpretative confusions. Thus far that has not has not happened and therefore while in respect of fixing of targets, the Commission may have the last word, policies for raising and distributing resources are still with the government as before.

Whatever may be the pros and cons of vesting the Commission with final powers on economic policy, one thing is clear. The one-step forward and two-steps backward approach confirms that we have become victims of an artificial euphoria on the possibilities of attracting foreign capital. Being an open economy with statutory protection of rights to private property and an established legal system and bureaucracy, we should not have got less FDI than China when actually our FDI catch is much less than theirs. Perhaps it is a combination of the foreign investor's ethnic and geographical proximity to China which is responsible for the difference. but if that is so, at least in the Asian region, the attempt to attract foreign capital in terms of purely economic incentives may be misplaced and may not end up in a big inflow of foreign capital in terms of purely economic incentives may be misplaced and may not end up in a big inflow of foreign capital after all.

It is well-known that so far as Western developed countries are concerned, some 80 per cent of their foreign investment are only amongst themselves—the big seven—and just about 20 per cent remains for the rest of the world. Even in this, their pressures and compulsions may allow them to be induced more in the financial and the consumer goods sector than in the area of the infrastructure, as came out in the figures produced by the present government in Parliament not much after assuming office in June 1996. The figures indicated that more than fifty per cent of FDI in India, following reforms, had moved into the consumer and other non-priority sectors.

While the suggestion for a greater role for the Planning Commission in laying down policies may have been legitimately prompted by defferences between the Commission and the Union Ministry for Finance, the resolution of the real cirsi in respect of nuances will have to wait for a better clarity in regard to the necessity of planning for prioritising investment in the country.

Until the current clamour focusing on infrastructure, it had begun to appear as if all that India needed was higher investment somehow and not prioritised investment, which is what the planning process had itself rigthly tried to emphasize. The question is whether the advocates of a greater role for the Planning Commission in policy formulation are wanting it because they think that the Finance Ministry is ignoring our compulsion to plan and therefore not coming up with consistent policies or because while both are lukewarm in respect of priorities, they differ only on how higher investment whatever it is, is to be funded.

In fact, investment prioritisation is necessary not merely for building up infrastructure but also expanding supplies of such other goods as food, clothing, shelter, quality health and education. As infrastructure is a precondition for a greater elasticity of output and growth resulting from rising monetary investments, higher supplies of various wage goods are a precondition for removal of poverty and improving the quality of life. How dangerous vested interest propaganda playing up the quantum of investments and playing down their prioritisation is can be confirmed by the recent developments on the food front when immediately after trying to export 3 million tonnes of wheat we had to desperately rush to try to import 2 million tonnes of wheat again to arrest a sharply rising price of that commodity thereafter. One hopes the smugness that we have enough food security will now be shaken off. And in any case, one hopes that there will be renewed realization, as in respect of the infrastructure sector, that a worthwhile attack on poverty and poor quality of life would necessitate a very careful investment planning in respect of the wage goods sector as well. That sector would not automatically come to life through a higher quantum of investment or through a mere pumping of populist public expenditure.

As long as we are hazy about planning being concerned with, not higher investment alone, but also with right plan priorities, the debate about who sets policy may somewhat unreal.

Multi-level planning

Apex-planning body at state level is generally state Planning board comprising chief minister as chairman and finance and planning ministers of the state and some technical experts as members. Department of planning in state government provides secretariat for the board. In many states, planning process has been decentralised to district level and in some states even to sub-division or block levels. In most of the states, there is district planning committee or district planning council comprising both official and non-official members. Some states also have a separate set-up consisting of functionaries like district planning officers, economist, credit planners, project appraiser, export training coordinator and an area planner in some of the districts for formulation of district plans, which are integrated with state plan.

The Seventy Third and Seventy Fourth Constitutional Amendment Acts are the culmination of the evolutionaly process as far as secentralisation of democratic power is concerned. With passing of appropriate legislations by the state governments and the conduct of elections to the panchayati raj institutions, Zilla parishads, Nagar Palika, etc. will be empowered to plan, fund and implement appropriate developmental works at the local level.

Programme implementation

The Ministry of Programme Implementation (now Department of Programme implementation in the MInistry of Planning and Programme Implementation) was set up in September 1985 to usher in a new system of goaloriented management to closely monitor implementation of anti-poverty programmes, performance of all industrial infrastructure sectors of economy and implementation of Central Sector industrial projects costing over Rs. 20 crore each. The Department through its efficient system, prompt facilitative action and computerised network provided by the National Informatics Centre, is ensuring effective implementation of projects and programmes.

Infrastructure Monitoring by the Department of Programme Implementation aims at reviewing the physical performance with reference to the targets for the financial year of nine industrial infrastructure sectors namely, power, coal, steel, railways, telecommunications, shipping and ports, fertilizers, cement and petroleum and natural gas, which have a pivotal role in the economic development of the nation. This involves identifying problem areas requiring action on a priority basis and coordinating the efforts of administrative ministries with a view to overcoming critical bottlenecks, determining intersectoral linkages for achieving optimal results with emphasis on better capacity utilisation.

Physical targets (for each area in respect of each infrastructure sector) are examined at the beginning of the year. Overall growth in infrastructure performance from 1985-86 to 1994-95 is given in table 18.

The present author conducted an awareness survey with the morning and evening walkers of Vaishali and district parks of Pitampura in Delhi. Most respondents were retired teachers, government officers, businessmen and youth.

The teachers who taught economics had a fairly good idea about plans but with the exception of three or four, none had cared to read even in the newspapers about the import of the Ninth Plan approach paper. Teachers belonging to the disciplines of literature such as Hindi, Sanskrit and English had very little idea of even the concept of 'plan'.

The businessmen were more concerned with their "self-interests" and profits rather than plan/s. "The plans were the concern of Tatas and Birlas. " They were primarily concerned with the yearly budget to adjust their business accordingly.

The government officers, who retired as section officers, were hardly aware of the plan. Of course, they were concerned with their pensions and closely followed the annual budget.

The youth had hardly any time to read newspapers except about vacancies. They seemed to be a frustrated lot!

In rural India, the condition is worse. Hardly anybody knows about the plans except some of the various schemes which were advantageous to them. The common man has no knowledge or information about the plans and programmes.

In the absence of consciousness and awareness, it is extremely difficult to expect people to co-operate and participate in the schemes and programmes of plans. There appears to be a very big communication gap. In earlier times, "Planning Forums" in universities and colleges had made teachers and students aware of the plan/s. These should be revived. The teachers and students may take the message of plans to the people.

The funcftions of communication are, today, much wider. Besides, information and motivation, they include socialization which implies stimulation of people's active involvement in public issues. Communication has to be linked to people"s needs, both material and non-material, The mass-media, particularly the electronic media such as radio and television tend to claim a much higher degree of attention than the verbal media. This needs to be exploited fully.

Gandhi offers us a theory of non-violent communication which consists of four theoretical units. The first and foremost of theoretical units is non-violent speech and action; the second unit is the maintenance of relationships and enrichment of personality; and the third is openness; and the fourth is flexibility. Gandhi's theory of communication may be thought as instrumental in bringing about communal harmony and generating interest in the plan.

Kurukshetra, journal of Ministry of Rural Areas and Employment can become an effective instrument of communication. Other journals such as Yojana can also play an active role in this respect.

As per the 1991 census, the literacy rete in India was 52.11 per cent. The rate of literacy in urban male and female was 81 per cent and 63.9 per cent respectively, while in rural areas among males and females it was 57.8 per cent and 30.3 per cent respectively. The role of literacy among the Scheduled Castes and Scheduled

Tribes women was pretty low i.e. 23.76 per cent and 18.19 per cent respectively.

In villages, the girl's education is far behind. If 100 girls take admision in the first grade, by the time they reach fifth standard only 40 girls remain; in the eighth standard only 18, in the 10th, 9 and only one in the twelfth standard. The picture changes radically in urban areas. There are 82 in the fifth, 62 in the eighth, 32 in the tenth and 14 in the twelfth standard.

There are 27 per cent villages and 21 per cent cities, where safe driking water is available. In 1,62,000 villages, no potable water is available as per the data obtained from government sources by 1993. In fact, there are 60 per cent villages which have no safe drinking water, while liquor shops are there in 90 per cent villaves.

There is a shortage of 13.7 million houses in villages according to 1991 census. The living conditions in 36 per cent in cities and 73 per cent in villages are extremely poor.

As per oficial estimates, out of 1,29,852 villages with a population of 1,000 or more, 1,12,190 villages have links roads (1995-96). The late US President, John F. Kennedy once said : "It is not wealth that builds our roads but roads that build our wealth".

In 1991, per capita availability of food was 510 grams which has come down to 474.2 grams by 1994. Health: There are primary health centres in almost all the blocks of the country. Arrangement for a 30-bed hospital is made for a population of one lakh. Access to sanitation is available only to 16 per cent of the people of India.

The general difficulty recognized by all studies is that government schemes and programmes do not reach people for whom they are meant. The late Prime Minister Rajiv Gandhi had said that only 15 paise reach people out of the 100 earmarked. Thus the "citizen" is lost between leaders and bureaucrats.

Prof B.M. Bhatia says that vaious poplist programmes although thought of as poverty alleviating and job creation programmes, are in reality nothing more than vote catching devices used by politicians to keep themselves in power. And all this at the cost of the public exchequer. They are nothing but bribes to the voters for casting the vote in favour of ruling political party or parties which initiated the programes. It is time people understood that the public distribution system (PDS), dual pricing system, consumption articles, and running multitude of welfare schemes are all part of the game politicians play in a democracy. By coing so, they are promoting their own selfish interests, and by no means serving a public cause. The UF government, though in a minority in the Lok Sabha, has started giving the impression the it will act boldly in the matter. A Cabinet Minister said the other day: "We can's seconomy". This comes as a whiff of fresh air. Besides, he went on to add, "the previous...government which sougth to be populist and held back a price hike for petrol for three years and introduced a subsidy of Rs. 1,288 crore for sugar in 1992 could not come back to power".

Micro-level planning

The Planning Commission has indicated, in the Ninth Five Year Plan that the priorities for the public sector outlays are the seven basic minimum services that were identified and adopted by the Chief Ministers' conference of July, 1996 for attainment by AD 2000. It is believed that social development and rural development cannot take place in a noon-growth environment. Employment and social security are vital to social development. Hence, the focus of micro-planning is made on:

— Cent per cent coverage provision of safe drinking water in rural and urban areas;

—Cent per cent coverage of primary health service facilities in rural and urban areas;

— Universalization of primary education;

— Provision of public housing assistance to all shelterless poor families;

— Extension of midday meal programme in primary schools to all rural blocks and urban slums disadvantaged sections;

— Provision of connectivity to all unconnected villages and habitations;

— Streamlining the public distribution system with the focus on the poor;

— Growth and growth-related infrastructure particularly power and irrigation;

— Employment; and

— Social security.

Thus the seven basic minimum services, growth and growth-related infrastructure, employment and social security form the focus of micro-level planning.

Planning for and by the people: Two teams comprising officials and non-officials, visit the habitations and encourage people to participate in Shramdan and also apprise them of the need for and scope of micro-level planning. The teams also help the people to draw up their own plans in all the sectors which would reflected the vision of the villagers on different key areas in their ward, the desired and achievable goals in five years, the next one year and the next quarter. It indicates the specific action by the people and identify the assistance required from the government to achieve the goals set by them. Under this exercise, the students' team led by a lecture who is a group leader would act in close co-operation with the Sarpanch and the ward members, teachers and other village functionaries, youth clubs, literacy campaign volunteers, non-government organizations, women's groups, watershed committee members, Vana Samrakshana Samithi members et al. The micro-level plan so prepared would be handed over to the nodal officer for eventual transfer to the Gram Panchayat. It is the villagers who would implement the plan for themselves and by themselves and they could do so effectively. The implementation of the programme would be reviewed periodically.

Since the launching of the Janmabhoomi programme is the first of its kind in the country, the success of the programme would le ad to further effective implementation of the micro-level planning in Andhra Pradesh as well as other States. Against this background, an effort is made in the present article to evaluate the Janmabhoomi programme in Cuddapah district of Andhra Pradesh.

The study was conducted in Cuddapah, a backward drought-prone district in the Rajyalaseema region of the State. Out of 50- Mandals, 20 were randomly selected for the present study. From each selected Mandal, a sample of 15 group leaders were drawn and the primary data was collected using a pre-structured scheduled besides discussions with the nodal officers, parents and political leaders.

The Janmabhoomi programme was launched in all 2,494 habitations in Cuddapah district. The programme also covered 22 slums in Cuddapah municipality and 29 slums in Proddatur municipality. As many as 2,682 Prajala Vaddaku Palana teams were formed in addition to 2,552 roup leaders comprising lecturers, headmasters and teachers. The notable feature was the voluntary involvement of 21,337 junior and degree college students including 2,680 girls in the programme. And, the youth, voluntary organizations, political parties and leaders also enthusiastically participated in the programme. The government officials and the school teachers functioned as 2,835 facilitators to provide the required facilities to the teams and to-co-ordinate the villagers and the teams.

The group leaders and students stayed in the habitations from January 1 to 8 to serve and motivate the villagers to participate in Shramdan and improve their surroundings. Emphasis was laid on providing clean drinking water, health and hygiene, environmental cleanliness, primary education and family planning and inculcating a sense of unity and self-reliance, and enlightened people on achieving development through a positive approach. Under the health package, vitamin A was administered to children under five years of age to prevent incidence of night blindness and iron and folic doses were given to check anaemia. All the eligible couples with two children were motivated to undergo sterilization and oral contraceptive were distributed to recently married couples. The Department of Agriculture and the District Rural Development Agency also prepared packages and propagated the rural development schemes.

In the Janmabhoomi programme, the institution of Gram Sabha played a prominent role. Gram Sabhas or village meetings were conducted in the evenings where various problems were discussed. Solutions were worked out besides preparation of micro-level planning of the habitation for the next three months, one year as well as the vision statement in respect of all the sectors for the next five-year period with the help of the Sarpanch and other leaders in the villages. The team not only prepared the actual planning on the basis of locally available resources but also helped the villagers in identifying the problem areas and in planning for remedial action or further progress in different key areas. Cleaning of school premises, clearance of thorny bushes, cleaning and upkeep of sanitation, maintenance of potable water, laying of roads, digging of soakpits near hand-pumps, repairing the bore wells, white washing of school and government buildings, plantation of trees, and repairs to irrigation canals were some of the important services renders by the teams in the villages with the active participation of the public.

They also sensitized the villagers on issues like health, hygiene literacy, savings, environment, etc. Besides, the students surveyed the habitations under the supervision of their group leaders and collected all the details relating to literacy, size of family, drinking water, sanitation, health care, family planning, primary education, public distribution, power, transport, roads, communication, etc. which are evolved into basic data for the future planning of the habitation with allocations coming in the next budget.

Issues and priorities

The update to the Economic Survey 1995—96, published about seven months ago, had emphasised three key challenges for economic policy: how to control the fiscal deficit; how to provide adequate and reliable economic infrastructure services at a reasonable cost and with sustainable financing and pricing policies; and how to ensure broad—based employment–generating growth of agriculture, industry and other sectors, together with strengthened programmes for basic social services and anti—poverty programmes to ensure a rapid alleviation of poverty.

These challenges remain central to our concerns. It is essential to keep reducing the Centre's fiscal deficit to below four per cent of GDP as soon as possible in order to: reduce interest rates and free up resources to finance the high levels of investment, both public and private, envisaged in the Approach Paper to the Ninth Plan; to contain Central Government borrowing from the RBI and thus check the growth of inflationary potential and pressures; to moderate the growth of rapidly rising interest payments which preempt the resources available for spending on priority, social and infrastructure needs; to facilitate orderly development of the market for long—term debt securities which is so essential for fostering the financing of infrastructure: and to reduce the risks associated with excessive government borrowing from external sources.

The path of fiscal deficit reduction is well known in teory as it is difficult to implement in practice. We must preserve with our programme of tax reforms which has helped to raise the ratio of revenues to GDP. We must seek higher non—tax revenues in the form of larger dividends from Government equity in public enterprises. We must reduce the growth of subsidies through better targeting and much more systematic application of user charges for Government services. The normally difficult task of expenditure management will be accentuated in the coming years by the challenge of accommodatingthe recommendations of the Fifth Central Pay Commission. Finally Government must act expeditiously on the recommendations of the Disinvestment Commission.

The responsibility for fiscal consolidation and prudence does not rest with the Central Government alone. The States have to do their part in reducing their borrowing requirements through better design and implementation of their tax systems and through steps to curb low priority expenditures.

The recurring power failures even in the capital city of Delhi this winter underline the critical nature of the power problem throughout the country. Because of unavailable, uncertain or erratic supplies from the public grid, the economy is paying a heavy price in the form of foregone production, lost exports of goods and services, frustrated investment intentions, recourse to high cost captive power generation, loss of international competitiveness, and barriers to the spread of information technology which is redefininf the terms of production, technical progress and international specialisation thhroughout the world. The key elements of the Commonm Minimum National Action Plan for Power, which need to be pursued vigorously, include the establishment of independent State Electricity Regulatory Commissions, the rationalisation of retail power tariffs, induction of private participation in electricity distribution and the restructuring and corporatisation of State Electricity Boards to run on commercial principles.

Power is only one, albeit critical, component of our energy economy. Today, the development of our petroleum sector is under a serious threat, with crude oil production having declined, oil imports rising sharply and the deficit on the Oil Pool Account rising each day and expected to exceed Rs. 15,000 crore before the end of this financial year. There is no economically viable alternative to adjusting petroleum prices to reflect the impact of international oil price increases. Furthermore, if we are to reap the benefits of increased investment and efficient production in all stages of the petroleum sector (ranging from exploration and development to refining and distribution), We must carry out a phased dismantling of the existing administered price mechanism in this sector. The time for initiating this reform is already overdue.

A pick—up in the growth momentum of the economy will intensify the need for gerneing increasing amounts of foreign savings to meet the investment requirements of economy and to sustain the growth momentum itself. Foreign direct investment flows provide such savings without adding to the country's external debt. As indicated in the Common Mnimum Programme, foreign direct investment should rise to US $ 10 billion per year from the current level of US $ 2 to 3 billion. We must learn from the pragmatic nationalism of China which received around US $ 40 billion of investment in 1996, and expects to attract more in 1997. We must also learn from the flexibility and speed of Indonesia, which modified its policies rapidly in response to perceived competition from China and India, to double foreign investment inflows between 1994 and 1995. We must ensure that the regulations governing the inflow of foreign investment are transparent and attractive in comparison with what other Asian economies offer. A review of FERA is underway in this context.

Fifty years after achieving independence, poverty, illiteracy, disease and lack of minimum social services continue to afflict hundreds of millions of our afflict hundreds of millions of our people. Experience from all over the world shows that rapid all over the world shows shows that rapid, employment—generating growth is the most effective way of reducing poverty. Our policies and programmes must accord the highest priority to encouraging growth of sustainable and productive job opportunities in all sectors. In agriculture, income earning opportunities for farmers should be expanded by removing existing impediments to domestic and international trade in agricultural products and removing controls on key agro-processing industries. At the same time, there have to be renewed efforts to strengthen rural infrastructure in the form of irrigation, rural roads, soil conservation, seed development, research and extension, and rural credit systems. In many cases this may call for a review and redirection of existing programmes. Besides, it is imperative to find incrmental resources for public investment in rural infrastructure. Such resources can be raised only partly through the budget. Without hurting the poor, the bulk of the resources would from the larger and better—off farmers.

There is a tremendous scope for expanding productive employment in the construction and other service sectors, especially in the cities and towns. But torealise this potential, the Government must be prepared to remove impediments imposed by various laws and regulations, such as the Urban Land Ceiling Act.

For the vast majority of our people to benefit from extension of job opportunities stemming from rapid labour—intensive grwoth, there has to be acommensurate expansion and quality improvement in the basic social services such as primary eduction and primary health care. The experience of countries as diverse as China and Indonesia has demosntrated the critical requirement for priority attention to these basic services.

For those at the margins of a market driven economy the effective provison of minimum social services and special programmes, for employment and poverty alleviation fulfill an essential need. Over time these special programmes have proliferated, not always rationally. The maximise the beneficial impact of anti—poverty programmes, it would be desirable to seek ways of consolidation and rationalisation, and some attrition. The basic goal should be to enhance sustainable benefits to the poorest segments of the society, while reducing administrative duplication and wastage and minimising well—known "leakages."

Over the last 5 to 6 years the Indian economy has demonstrated enviable resilience and buoyancy as a result of wide ranging economic reforms and closer integration with the world economy. On the whole, those dimension of the economy have performed best where reform efforts have been most thorough and far reaching. We must learn from this experience as we look ahead to meet the challenges of the future.

The response to the Janmabhoomi programme was fascinating. The villagers responded generously and participated actively in the programme and carried out more work than they had been entrusted with, out of sheer enthusiasm in spite of the harvesting season. Politicians and local leaders were so fascinated by the work under the programme that they made it clear the were not worried about who gave the call for the Janmabhoomi programme but were only concerned with the good results it was producing by evoking a generous response from the participants. The MLAs and various party workers enthusiastically participated in the programme irrespective of their political ideologies.

The advantages of the Janmabhoomi programme to the students are manifold. To mention a few:

— Janmabhoomi is a new experience to the students who are given an orientation through the programme. They have begun to understand the life of the common man in the village. This is a good learning and rewarding experience for the students.

— The programme provided an opportunity to learn more by talking to people belonging to different social levels in villages and understanding their problems.

— The programme also provided an opportunity to the students to learn first hand the suffering of the disadvantaged sections of the society.

— The programme taught the students to understand the very essence of unity, co-operation, co-ordination and dignity of labour in a practical way. It helped to build the right attitude towards work and life besides developing the motive of social service, team spirit and leadership qualities.

— The change of working environment diverted the students to some sort of recreation from the burden of continuous study and widened their mental horizon. The experience instilled self-motivation and positive attitude and developed self-confidence in the students. It shaped them into responsible citizens of tomorrow.

In some villages, the programme seemed to have started more with a whimper than a bang because of ill-timing. Some of the parents of college students resisted their wards from taking part in the programme. They felt that the steps taken by the State government to involve college students in the ambitious programme was imprudent with public examinations round the corner and the syllabus yet to be completed by the end of January. It was also felt that it was not wise to allow the Intermediate students to take part in the programme as the course was a turning point in their career which will determined their future.

It was commented that a good programme was badly organized. The programme had been drawn up hastily and the people had not even been informed, let alone motivated, to participate in Shramdan works.

The teachers and academicians, who were the corner-stones of the programme, observed that they were not given a proper say in designing the programme and were sent to the habitations before they had even prepared themselves mentally for the assignment.

In spite of reservations over the method of execution, teachers, academicians, students and people from all walks of life have been appreciative of the concept of self-help and service.

The following are a few suggestions which may contribute to further success of the Janmabhoomi programme.

— Involvement of lectures/teachers and students in the programme is a good beginning and it should be encouraged by including it in the curriculum so as to ensure further dynamic participation. The need for adoption of villages in their areas is to be so promoted that the teams of students guided by lecturers could frequently visit and interact with villagers and win their confidence. Incentives may be awarded for the students to ensure their motivation and involvement. The programme should be considered as a assignment free from the interference of the revenue machinery and political parties.

— The students should be used as catalysts in the ambitious programme and their services should be further utilized imparting necessary training.

— The services of the educated unemployed youth should be utilized for the purpose and be made compulsory for consideration or registration for employment as they have to learn a lot from this kind of programme.

— Gram Sabhas should be provided with all the relevant details like how much money would be forthcoming to each habitation under various schemes like Indira Awaas Yojana, Jawahar Rozgar Yojana, Prime Minister's Rozgar Yojana, Chief Minister's Empowerment of Youth, etc. Gram Sabhas should be further activated and village Panchayats should be made answerable to them.

— All members of the doctors' association in the district or the area should be convinced in the habitations besides helping volunteers and involving them in preparation of micro-level planning.

— There is need to motivate the villagers and take necessary steps to boost the morale of the people. Once the concept is translated into active public support, the programme will be a total success.

— The success of the programme will always depend on the manifestation of the leader's will power. Further involvement of the elected representatives as well as officials will be the source of inspiration for the people in the villages.

The response and achievements of the Janmabhoomi programme are encouraging. Hence, there is need to study the results of the programme and implement it in such a way that it leads to the overall development of the rural areas. Effective implementation of the Janmabhoomi programme with systematic planning, organisation, training, follow-up, vigorous monitoring, efficient administrative machinery with proper orientation, whole-hearted participation and co-operation of the administrative machinery for rural development, elected representatives, pollitical parties and all sections of the people would eradicate poverty disease and achieve accelerated development in rural areas.

Achievements and failures

The late Eric P.W. Da Costa, Editor, Eastern Economist writes that In Indian planning still contains serious defects in statistical method.

He, commenting on the second Five Year Plan, wrote that it was good so far as it was on paper. This may be true of subsequent plans as well (italics added).

Da Costa felt that there was no guarantee that its figures were not as full of mistakes and misjudgements as the First Five Year Plan. Consider for example, some of the co-ordinates of First Five Year Plan. National income in the Indian Union in the First Five Year Plan was to rise by 11 per cent. In point of fact, as the draft outline of the Second Five Year Plan had shown, it had risen by 18 per cent. In other words, there was an error of over 50 per cent in these estimates on practically every item, the growth of the economy as a whole, the international account and resilience of internal production and the capacity of the country had been greatly underestimated. Planning, if that was synonymous with prediction, had been a resounding failure. This flaw of calculus continues. In the following pages, a brief review of eighth plans is given.

The First Five Year Plan was launched in 1951. It laid the foundation of development in agriculture, irrigation, community development, transport and communication. It provided for rehabilitation of refugees, provided a base for growth by improving land and tenure system. It aimed to revive the village, cottage and small-scale industries and prepared the ground for industrialisation. It laid down physical targets of production, in agriculture, particularly food grains, cotton and jute and in industrial the committed resources of Rs. 2,374 crore, the actual outlay came to Rs. 1,968 crore only.

The Plan was too small to be effective, particularly in industry. According to the late T.T. Krishnamachari, it was a plan of preparation and it was successful to a large measure.

The II Paln aimed at substantially increasing industrialisation, employment and national income and at reducing inequality of income and wealth. It laid great emphasis on public investment and rapid industrialisation. The basic pattern of investment was shifted from agriculture to industry, while in the industrial sector emphasis was laid on capital-intensive heavy industries, particularly steel. It envisaged setting up of three steel plants in the public sector, extension of two private sector plants, 75 per cent rise in coal production, cement production and extensive development of railway infrastructure.

It envisaged an investment of Rs. 6,200 crore of which Rs, 3,800 crore was to be in the public sector and Rs. 2,400 crore in the private sector and Rs. 2,400 in the private sector along with a current development of Rs. 1,000 crore. The Second Plan sought to create employment for about 80 lakh persons and it sought to open up new frontiers to build up a sound edifice of infrastructure and to promote industrialization involving capital-intensive projects.

Its programmes may be judged by the fact that the net national income rose by 20 per cent against a target of 25 per cent and per capita income rose by 8 per cent against a target of 18 per cent. The shortfall was due to the annual population growth at the rate of 2.2 per cent against an estimate of 1.2 per cent. The per capita consumption of basic necessities like food, clothing and shelter remained much below the target. It therefore, failed to improve the standard of living.

Exports during the Plan were Rs. 2,965 crore. There was a rise of 3.3 per cent in exports. The target in imports was Rs. 4,350 crore, but imports rose to Rs. 5,402 crore, recording a rise of 24.5 per cent. The balance of payments was adverse by Rs. 2,339 crore. A more disquiting feature was the steep rise of 30 per cent in prices and it could not create adequate additional opportunities for employment.

The Plan shifted the basic emphasis from agriculture to industry rather too soon with consequent failures in food grains, commercial crops. Price stability and exchange surplus. But it promoted the public sector for industrialization and resource mobilisation. It promoted infrastructural development in energy, transport, etc. and provided a foundation for accelerated economic growth.

The Third Plan (1961-66) was framed when there were crises on the financial, foreign exchange, and food fronts. Experts were critical of India's overambitious plan which laid emphasis on welfare at the expense of efficiency and at reduction of inequalities at the cost of raped economic development. This plan aimed at an annual increase of over 5 per cent in national income, self-sufficiency in food grains, expansion of basic industries like steel, chemicals, fuel and power, promoting industrialization and increasing employment. It sought to achieve a 5.4 per cent annual increase in national income and 3.2 per cent annual increase in per capita income.

The Plan envisaged a public sector investment of Rs. 6,300 crore, while investment in the private sector was to be Rs. 4,100 crore. The total outlay was thus Rs. 10,400 crores. The actual expenditure in the public sector was, however, Rs. 8,576.5 crore. The strategy was to expand the infrastructure in the energy, transport and communication sectors.

During the Plan period, inflationary pressure increased in the economy. There was a big rise in non-plan expenditure and deficit financing. During that Plan period, there was floods and droughts, wars with China and Pakistan, increase in defence expenditure and delays and uncertainties in external aid. The Plan failed to generate employment and there was stagnation in the absorption of surplus labour. There was an increase in the concentration of wealth. In the five years, prices rose by 36 per cent. The balance of payments crisis became deep, leading to a partial devaluation of the rupee.

There were three annual plans for the years 1966-67, 1967-68 and 1968-69 respectively. The annual plans were to prepare ground for the fourth Plan. Our agricultural strategy producing new high yield seeds etc., was laid in the Annual Plans and there was exploitation of irrigation potential.

The Fourth Five Year Plan (1969-74) envisaged an aggregate outlay of Rs. 24,882 crore of which Rs. 15,902 crore was assigned to the public sector. Unfortunately, there were shortfalls in achievements of the various targets laid down. There were failures in the energy and transport sectors. Inflation increased very much and unemployment rose and there was poplation explosion.

The Fifth Plan (1974-79) envisaged an outlay of Rs. 39,303 crore for the public sector and Rs. 27,050 crore for the private sector. In view of the Fourth Plan experience and galloping inflation, the Fifth Plan lowered the target growth rate to 4.4 per cent even compared to the darft Plan which envisaged a growth rate of 5.5 per cent Even the reduced targets were not achieved. about 25 million people were without employment. There was no self-sufficiency in financial resources and foreign debt increased.

The sixth Plan (1980-85) tried to raise the national income, modernise technology, reduce poverty and unemployment, develop the energy sector, improve th standard of living of the masses and reduce inequalities in income and wealth. It was to promote balanced regional development and control population through Family Planning and ecological improvement. The development strategy was to make a material contribution to remove poverty and to achieve full employment over a period of fifteen years. An annual growth rate of 5.2 per cent in per capita income was also contemplated.

The total plan investment was estimated at Rs. 1,58,710 crore of which Rs. 84,000 crore (53 per cent) was to be in the public sector and Rs. 74,710 crore (47 per cent) in the private sector. A total outlay of Rs. 1,72,210 crore was envisaged for the Sixth Plan. The public sector outlay was estimated at Rs. 74,100 crore. The resource mobilizations was to be through public savings, private savings, domestic savings and inflow from abroad. Furing the Plan period the balance of trade deficit had increased from Rs. 2,370 crore in 1979-80 to Rs. 3,970 crore in 1984-85. The balance of payments deficit was Rs. 9,053 crore.

The Seventh Plan was to consolidate the gains of past investment spread over three and a half decades of Indian planning and to take the country on the path of further development leading to equality and a tangible rise in social consumption and welfare. It was to remove poverty, promote, self-reliance through expert promotion and import substitution and import substitution. It was to promote efficiency in organisation. Resource mobilisation through public sector at 1984-85 prices was the to the extent of Rs. 1,80,000 crore. It envisaged a total investment of Rs. 3,22,366 crore, 40 per cent of which was to be financed from domestic sources, calling for tremendous effort at resource mobilization. The Plan sought to bring about a massive shift in favour of the poor. According to the mid-term appraisal available, for the Seventh Plan, the growth rate was 5 per cent, but the 1986-87 realisation was 4 per cent.

The Eighth Plan's clear-cut priorities were to expand employment, squeeze inflation and rein in the deficit in the country's account. Hence, the VIII Plan with employment as its central objective was different from the earlier Plans which had considered employment as a by-product of growth. The earlier plans were mainly related to the allocation of scarce domestic and foreign resources in various sectors. The Seventh Plan had projected a decline in poverty line to 29 per cent by 1988-89 but its level was 39 per cent in 1988.

In the VIII Plan, investment in small-scale industries was increased to give more direct employment. The basic objectives of theVIII Plan are:

— Revenue deficits of the Centre and the States should be reduced to nil by 31 march, 1995.

— The fiscal resources should be equally distributed.

— There should be fiscal discipline.

Further, revenue budget, both plan and non-plan should be considered as a whole. The monetary and fiscal policies should be effectively implemented to control excessive money creation. The mounting revenue expenditure which had grown at rate of 18.7 per cent during 1981-87 must be reduced. But these objectives remained only good intentions and nothing much was achieved. It, of course, had laid emphasis on human development and people's participation as had been the case in earlier plans as well.

The VIII Plan reflected the ideas of the government of the day. there were thus essential contradictions between planning as part of a long-term perspective and democratic elections as a result of which new government might come every five years. Thus, if different governments brought their new plan the whole concept of continuous long-term planning could be in jeopardy.

3

Member of Parliament Local Area Development Scheme

Background

The Members of Parliament are often approached by their constituents for taking up small developmental works of capital nature in their respective constituencies. The Members of Parliament, therefore, demanded that they should be able to recommend works to be done in their respective constituencies. After considering their suggestions, the Members of Parliament Local Area Development Scheme was announced in the Parliament on 23rd December, 1993 by the Prime Minister. The normal mechanism d planning is governed by a set of administrative guidelines with regard to cost norms, resource allocation and prioritisation of works to be undertaken. Consequently, it is not always possible to take care of some of the felt needs of the people In all circumstances. It was with a view to bridging this gap and also lending a certain degree of flexibility to the planning process that the scheme, which is expected to be an instrument for meeting the felt needs of the people, was thought of

The scheme was initially administered by the Ministry of Rural Areas and Employment. The subject was later on transferred to the Department of Programme Implementation, Ministry of Planning and Programme Implementation, with effect from October, 1994.

Objective

Under this Scheme, each MP will have the choice to suggest to the Head of the District works to the tune of Rs. 1 crore per year, to be taken up in his/her constituency. Elected Members of Rajya Sabha, representing the whole of the State as they do, may select works for implementation in one or more district(s) as they may choose. Nominated Members of the Lok Sabha and Rajya Sabha may also select works for implementation in one or more district(s), but within one state of their choice.

The salient features of the Scheme are :

- The works under the scheme shall be developmental in nature, based on the locally-felt needs and should lead to creation of durable assets.
- Purchase of inventory or stock of any type is not allowed Cinder this Scheme.
- The funds released under the scheme are non-lapsable.
- The normal financial and audit procedures would apply to all transactions under the Scheme.
- The release of funds under the Scheme is to be done twice a year on the basis of physical ẹ ncial progress.
- Office buildings, residential buildings and other buildings, relating to Central or State Governments, Departments, Agencies or Organisations are not permitted.

Detailed guidelines indicating the objectives of the Scheme, salient features of the Scheme, list of works that may be taken up, works which shall not be allowed under the Scheme, procedures for sanction and execution of works, monitoring arrangements, release of funds and special provisions were issued in February, 1994 by the Ministry of Rural Areas and Employment. After the Scheme was transferred to this Department, revised guidelines were issued in December, 1994.

The guidelines were further revised in February 1997 The new provisions inserted in the revised guidelines were:

- Funds can be used for partly meeting the cost of larger works.
- As far as possible all sanctions for works be accorded within 45 days.
- Decision making for technical and administrative sanction should be only at district level and for the purpose of implementing this Scheme, full and final powers should be delegated to the district technical and administrative functionaries.
- Implementing agencies may not collect any administrative charges, centage charges, etc., for their services.
- Allocation of MPLADS funds under the Scheme is for the consituency.
- Whenever there is a change in the Member of Parliament (MP), the works identified by the predecessor MP which are under execution should be completed. Also works identified by the predecessor MP .pending sanction due to administrative reasons beyond a period of 45days from the day of recommendation by the MP are also to be executed. Remaining unsanctioned works pending for less than 45 days to be executed subject to the confirmation by the successor MP.
- The district heads should also communicate information on the progress of works under the scheme on the INTERNET for which connectivity is available in the parliament.

- A senior Commissioner-level officer at the State headquarters should conduct an annual meeting involving the heads of districts and Members of Parliament to assess the progress once a year.
- The Bureau for Parliament Studies and Training (BPST) may arrange training of district officials in batches involving and bringing out interaction with MPs.

To promote awareness of computers among the students, a scheme for installation of computers in schools and other educational I institutions has been included under the guidelines on MPLADS. Apart from this, following four electronics schemes which can be implemented under MPLAD scheme are:

1. Information footpath,
2. HAM Club in High Schools,
3. Citizen Band Radio- and
4. Bibliographic Data Base Project.

The guidelines for implementation of 5 electronics schemes were issued by the Department of Electronics. With a view to streamline -the implementation of electronic schemes and to make them more attractive and useful for the student community especially, revision of the guidelines has been undertaken. For this purpose, a group was constituted under the Chairmanship of Hon'ble Dr. Shrikant R. Jichkar, MP (RS) with representative of Department of Electronics and Department of Programme Implementation as members. The Group could not submit its report due to the retirement of its Chairman from the seat of Rajya Sabha.

Recent decisions

As per statement laid on behalf of the Prime Minister in Lok Sabha and MOS (P&PI) in Rajya Sabha on 23.12.1998 the following decisions were announced :-

- The allocation of Rs. 1 crore per year per MP under the MPLAD Scheme stands increase to Rs.2 crores per year per MP.
- The interest accrued on MPLADS funds may be used for tile same purpose for which the basic amount has been allocated.
- In respect of Rajya Sabha Members, the unspent balance eft by the predecessor Rajya Sabha, MP in a particular State will be equally distributed amongst the successor Rajya Sabha Member from that particular State.

In addition, it was also decided to allow construction of manned Railway Level Crossings in place of unmanned level crossings to avoid railway accidents.

Funds released

As the scheme was announced in December, 1993 only a token amount of Rs. 5 lakhs per W was released by the then Ministry of Rural Development for the year 1993-94. These funds were released to the State Governments. The nominated Members of the Parliament were not covered in the release for this year.

The Ministry of Rural Areas and Employment released Rs. I crore per NW directly to the Collectors for the year 1994-95. Funds for this year were also released in respect of the nominated Members. In case of Lok Sabha constituency falling in more than one district, the District Collector, who receives the money, released by the Government of India, has to make available the necessary funds to other districts, in keeping with the MP's choice for the works proposed by the latter. Similarly, for elected Rajya Sabha Members and nominated Rajya Sabha and Lok Sabha Members selecting works for implementation in more than one district, the nodal Collector has to make available necessary funds to other districts.

During the year, 1995-96, two instalments of Rs.50 lakhs each per MP were released by this Department in July and December, 1995 respectively. For the year 1996-97, funds were released @ Rs. 1 crore per MP in December, 1996. For the year 1997-98 and 1998-99 funds have been released to those MPs whose unsanctioned balance was reported to be less than Rs.50 lakhs by the concerned Nodal Implementing Officer.

Year	Funds released per M.P.	Total funds released to the Collectors
1993-94	5 lakhs	37.8 crores
1994-95	1 crore	771. 0 crores
1995-96	1 crore	763. 0 crores
1996-97	1 crore (Rs.4.5 crores released from budget of 1997-98)	782.5 crores

Year	Funds released per M.P.	Total funds released to the Collectors
1997-98 *		483.5 crores (upto 31.03.98) + 206 crores from the Budget of 1998-99 (upto 31. 12.1998).
1998-99 *	316.6 crore upto 31.12.98	

1st and 2nd instalments of Rs.50 lakhs each for 1997-98 have been released in respect of 745 and 634 MPs respectively till 31. 12.1998 and 1st & 2nd instalments for the year 1998-99 have been released to 498 & 135 MPs respectively till 31.12.1998.

As per the information received from the various District Collectors an expenditure of Rs.2136.9 crores has been incurred against the total release of Rs.3359.8 crores, as on 31.12.1998

Statements indicating the releases made by the Government of India under the Scheme and the actual expenditure State-wise for Lok Sabha as well as Rajya Sabha are given in Annexures-I, II and III to this chapter.

The progress of expenditure under this Scheme remained rather slow during the initial years for various reasons but it gained momentum and as per the latest reports available about 64% of the amount released has actually been spent so far. Works to the extent of 84% have been sanctioned. It may not be out of context to mention h ere that during the year 1996-97 and 199798 the execution of MPLADS works received set-back due to declaration of general elections of Lok Sabha which affected starting of new works under MPLADS. The criteria adopted for release of funds in 1997-98 and . 1998-99 has improved the utilisation.

Implementation and monitoring

The District Collectors are responsible for the coordination and overall supervision of the works under the Scheme at the district level. The Deptt. of Programme Implementation, Government of India, has the nodal responsibility for the Scheme at the Centre.

For effective implementation of the works, each State Government/UT Administration is required to designate one nodal department for physical monitoring through field inspection and for coordination with the DPI. The revised guidelines specify the nature of monitoring and inspection of MPLADS works required to be undertaken by the District Head, officers of the District at Sub-division and block levels and stipulate the requirement of annual meetings at State headquarter by a senior Commissioner level officer with the Heads of the District and the MPs to assess the progress of works under the Scheme. For effective monitoring of the Scheme, formats have been designed by the DPI for network based monitoring system and sent to 38 Districts chosen for pilot testing. After the receipt of feedback of from these districts, this may be adopted in all other districts.

Review Meetings were organised with the MPs in Patna, Calcutta and Bhubneshwar in Sept. 1998, Jan. 1999 and Feb. 1999 respectively which were presided over by Minister of State for Planning and Programme Implementation and attended to by MPs, DCs and other Senior Level Officers from these States.

Impact of the scheme on development :

The Scheme has made a good impact on the development of various areas all over the country. Works of different varieties have come up for the benefit of general public at large. These works include construction of school buildings, libraries, provision of drinking water by drilling tubewells, approach roads, small bridges, sports stadiums, community centres, crematoriums and boundary walls around them, public toilets, drains, footpaths, bus stops and provision of electricity in rural areas. Construction of school buildings in remote areas and making provision of drinking water has fulfilled the basic requirements of the inhabitants of these areas to some extent. Implementation of electronic schemes at various places, especially the installation of computers in schools has been of great help to the student community. With the increase in allocation of MPLADS funds, it is expected that more & more works of public utility would be taken up for the benefit of general public at large.

4

Decentralisation and Planning

The concern for human poverty and its eradication to improve human environment have been the central focus of our development planning in the country since the inception of the planing era. Various schemes have been formulated and implemented with the sole objective of removing poverty and thereby increasing the quality of life of the people in the lower ranks of population. The explicit manifestation of the government's concern for poverty alleviation got its expression when the first 20-Point Programme was launched on 1 July 1975 under the connotation of Ganibi Hatao which was conceived by the late Prime Minister Smt Indira Gandhi. This programme was implemented with a pragmatic success during 1975-76 and 1976-77 Annual Plans. The Sixth Five Year Plan (1980-85)) incorporated these programmes as guiding factors in the planning process. Taking the past experience, the original 20-Point Programme was further re-defined, revitalized and announced to the Nation on 14 January 1982.

Increase irrigation potential, develop and dissemiinate technologies and imputs for dry land agriculture; make special efforts to increase production of pulses and vegetable oilseeds; strengthen and expand coverage of integrated rural development and national rural employment programmes; implement agricultural land ceilings, distribute surplus land and complete compilation of land records by removing all administrative and legal obstacles; review and effectively enforce minimum wages for agricultural labour; rehabilitate bonded labour; accelerate programmes for the development of scheduled castes and scheduled-tribes; supply drinking water to all problem villages; allot house sites to rural families who are without them and expand programmes for construction assistance to them; improve the environment of slums, implement programmes of house building for economically weaker sections and take measures to arrest unwarranted increase in land prices; maximise power generation, improve the functioning of electricity authorities and electrify all villages; pursue vigorously programmes of afforestation social and farm forestry and the development of bio-gas and other alternative energy sources; promote family planning on a voluntary basis as a people's movement; substantially augment universal primary health care facilities and control of leprosy, TB and blindness; accelerate programmes of welfare for women and children and nutrition programmes for pregnant women, nursing mothers and children, specially in tribal hill and backward areas; spread universal elementary education for the age group 6-14 with special emphasis on girls and simultaneously involve students and voluntary agencies in programmes for the removal of adult illiteracy; expand the public distribution system through more fair price shops, including mobile shops in far flung areas and shops, to cater to industrial workers, students' hostels, and make available to students textbooks and exercise books on a priority basis and to promote a strong consumer protection movement; liberalise investment procedures and streamline industrial policies to ensure timely completion of projects. Give handicrafts, handlooms, small and village industries all facilities to grow and to update their technology; continue strict

Table 1 Annual Growth rate of Industrial Infrastructure Sectors

(percentage)

Sector	*1985-86*	*1986-87*	*1987-88*	*1988-89*	*1989-90*	*1990-91*	*1991-92*	*1992-93*	*1993-94*	*1994-95*	*Actual Production/ performance during1994-95*
1. Power Generation (Thermal, Hydel and Nuclear)	8.6	10.3	7.6	9.5	10.8	7.8	8.5	5.0	7.4	8.5	351.020 (BU)
2. Coal Production	4.7	7.3	9.0	7.6	3.4	5.4	8.3	3.9	3.2	3.2	253.81 (MT)
3. Production at Integrated Steel Plants											
(i) Hot Metal	8.6	4.0	4.1	9.4	0.6	1.6	7.1	1.6	NA	NA	NA
(ii) Ingot Steel	9.2	0.3	7.4	10.5	–1.8	4.4	8.9	2.1	NA	NA	NA
(iii) Saleable Steel	11.2	5.7	4.5	7.2	–1.9	3.1	8.1	3.9	5.7	8.3	12841 (MT)
4. Railway revenue earning goods traffic	9.4	7.4	4.5	4.1	2.6	2.8	6.0	3.4	3.6	1.9	365.54 (MT)
5. Cargo handled at Major Ports	12.5	3.5	7.6	9.5	1.2	3.8	3.2	5.57.7	10.0		197.173 (MT)
6. Telecommunications Provision of new (net Tel. connections (monitored sector)		4.8	16.1	4.4	–1.8	23.2	11.6	47.0	19.420.5	52.0	701.383

										('000'Nos.)	
7. Cement Production	9.8	10.4	8.1	13.2	2.3	6.4	10.3	0.2	6.8	7.6	62.353 (MT)
8. Fertilizer Productionb											
(i) Nitrogen	10.4	25.0	1.0	22.8	0.4	3.7	4.1	1.8	–2.1	9.9	7.944 (MT)
(ii) Phosphate	13.3	16.2	0.3	35.3	–20.4	14.1	23.7	–10.5	–21.5	37.3	2.493 (MT)
9. Petroleum											
(i) Crude Oil Production	4.1	1.0	–0.4	5.5	6.4	–3.1	–8.1	–11.2	0.2	19.2	32.228 (MT)
(ii) Refinery throughput	20.7	6.5	4.5	2.2	6.4	–o.3	–0.7	4.0	1.6	3.9	56.440 (MT)

BU Billion Unit
MT Million Tonnes

action against smugglers, hoarders and tax evaders and tax evaders and check black money; and improve the working of the public enterprises by increasing efficiency, capacity utilisation and the generation of internal sources.

Various programmes were formulated to achieve the above objectives focussing mostly on the critical socio-economic constraints on development. The existence of human poverty was considered the single most adverse constraints to human development. Therefore, breaking the vicious circle of poverty which was both the cause and the effect of under development in the country was central to the formulation of 20-Point Programme. The Sixth Five Year Plan was designed taking note of the micro-objectives of 20-Point Programme in the critical sectors which were accorded high priority in the planning process. The emphasis on agricultural productivity, rural employment, provision of safe drinking water, allotment of houses sites to the rural families, improvement of slums, voluntary family planning, provision of basic health care, concern for environmental degradation, spread of elementary education, accelerating welfare programmes for the women and children were the most positive features of the revised 20-Point Programme which were spelt out keeping in view the basic objective of the development planning that the fruits of planning mustensure the 'basic needs' of human beings if development process is at all to be sustainable.

While the various evaluation reports indicate different positive impacts, the major impact of the 20-Point Programme in the country was the re—distribution of productive assets in favour of the less privileged who are the backbone of the economy. From the point of view of a sustainable growth, these programmes not only improve the productivity in the rural sector but also increased the overal quality of life in the villages to a perceptible degree.

Twenty-point economic programme

The Government was not content with mere re-establishment of law and order. It was keen that the new sense of national purpose should be harnessed to a speedier promotion of economic growth and social justice. On 1 July, 1975, the Prime Minister announced in a nationwide broadcast a "Twenty-Point Economic Programme" designed to achieve speedy development and to remove many of the evil practices which and persisted all these years, including bonded labour and rural indebtedness. It gave a further fillip to the official drive to contain inflation and root out black money. The programme was acclaimed by all sections of the people notably farmers and landless workers, industrial workers, representatives of trade and industry, and students and teachers. This meant:

1. Continuance of steps to bring down prices of essential commodities. Streamlined production, procurement and distribution of essential commodities. Strict economy in government expenditure.
2. Implementation of agricultural land ceilings and speedier distribution of surplus land compilation of land records.
3. Stepping up of provision of house sites for landless and weaker sections.
4. Bonded labour, wherever it exists, will be declared illegal.
5. Plan for liquidation of rural indebtedness. Legislation for moratorium on recovery of debt from landless labourers, small farmers and artisans.

6. Review of laws on minimum agricultural wages.
7. Five million more hectares to be brought under irrigation. National programme for use of underground water.
8. An accelerated power programme. Super thermal stations under central control.
9. New development plan for development of handloom sector.
10. Improvement in quality and supply of people's cloth.
11. Socialisation of urban and urbanisable land. Ceiling on ownership and possession of vacant land and on plinth area of new dwelling units.
12. Special squads for valuation of conspicuous construction and prevention of tax evasion. Summary trails and deterrent punishment of economic offenders.
13. Special legislation for confiscation of smugglers' properties.
14. Liberalisation of investment procedures. Action against misuse of import licences.
15. New schemes for workers' association of industry.
16. National permit schemes for road transport.
17. Income Tax relief to middle class; exemption limit placed at Rs. 8,000.
18. Essential commodities at controlled prices to students in hostels.
19. Books and stationery at contolled prices.
20. New apprenticeship scheme to enlarge employment and training, especially of weaker sections.

Transfer of technology

Involvement of all the 860 institutions and agencies of the Indian Council of Agricultural Research (ICAR), agricultural universities and voluntary agencies for the transfer of farm techniques to the field level with adoption of 50,000 agricultural families in the programme, has been recommended by the ICAE national workshop on transfer of technology programme for rural development.

The three-day workshop has also decided to prepare a "lab to land operational manual" providing information on all available technologies, besides embarking upon a continuous monitoring and evaluation of the implementation of the programme for making midcourse corrections. Such a manual will pay special attention to the small and marginal farmers and provide viable technology to them.

The workshop has decided that while ICAR and its agencies and the agricultural universities and their centres should adopt 20,000 farmers each, the voluntary organisations and affiliated agricultural college could be entrusted with the task of adopting 10,000 families.

The workshop felt that in selecting centres, preference should be given to institutions already involved in agricultural development and the selection of blocks, villages, farm families should also be preferably from the intensive agricultural development blocks already identified.

The approach for the transfer of technology should be on a cluster-village basis and proximity of the implementing agency should also be borne in mind for effective supervision.

Another important recommendation of the workshop was that related programmes for farm youth, farm women and children should be taken up simultaneously. It also strongly recommended creation of suitable marketing infrastructure and facilities well in advance to match the anticipated increased production.

The workshop recommended organisation of agricultural exhibitions at national, State, institute and university levels, during the national extension fortnight celebrations—inter—State and inter-regional exchanges, lectures by farm-professors organisation of debates and discussions special programmes and features on the radio, television, press and extension lectures should be taken up during the fortnight, it said.

In the light of the experience and achievements of the revised 20-Point Programme 1982 and the emerging new socio-economic problems during the Seventh Plan (1985-90) the programmes were restructured in 1986 with the directions given by the then Prime Minister Shri Rajiv Gandhi which was popularly known as 20-Point Programme 1986. The restructured programmes came into effect from 1 April 1987 along with Annual Plan of 1987-88. Briefly, the programmes are as under:

Attack on rural poverty: (i) ensure that poverty alleviation programmes reach all the poor in every village; (ii) dovetail wage employment programmes with programmes for area development and human resource development and create national and community assets like school buildings, roads, tanks, fuel and fodder reserves; (iii) correlate the various rural development productivity and production-expand rural employment; (iv) promote handlooms, handicrafts, village and small industries and improve skills for self-employment; and (v) Revitalise Panchayats, cooperatives and local bodies.

Strategy for rain-fed agriculture: (i) improve the technology for conserving moisture and ensure better management of land and water resources; (ii) develop and distribute appropriate and improved seeds; and (iii) reduce vulnerability to drought through suitable changes in droughtprone areas and drought-relief programmes.

Better use of irrigation water: (i) Develop the catchment areas and improve drainage in basins and deltas; (ii) improve irrigation management in command areas; (iii) prevent water logging, salinity and wasteful use; and (iv) coordinate the use of surface and ground water.

Bigger harvests: (i) revolutionise rice production in the eastern region and other areas of low productivity; (ii) achieve self-reliance in edible oils; (iii) secure greater production of pulses; (iv) intensify the cultivation of fruits and vegetables; (v) augment facilities for modern storage, processing and marketing of agricultural produce; (vi) help livestock and dairy framers to increase productivity; and (vii) develop fish farming and sea fishing.

Enfrocement of land reforms: (i) complete compilation of land records; (ii) implement agricultural land ceilings; and (iii) distribute surplus land to the landless.

Special programmes for rural labour: (i) enforce minimum wages for unorganised labour in agriculture and industry, (ii) fully implement laws abolishing bonded labour; and (iii) involve voluntary agencies in prigrammes for the rehabilitation of bonded labour.

Clean drinking water: (i) provide safe water all villages; (ii) assist local communities to maintain the sources of such water supply in good condition; (iii) pay special attention to water supply for SCs and STs.

Health for all: (i)Improve the quality of primary health care; (ii) fight leprosy, TB malaria, goitre, blindness and other major diseases; (iii) provide immunisation for all infants and children; (iv) improve sanitation facilities in rural areas, particularly for women; and (v) pay special attention to programmes for the rehabilitation of the handicapped.

Two child norm: (i) bring about voluntary acceptance ofthe two child norm; (ii) promote responsible parenthood; (iii) reduce infant mortality; and (iv) expand maternity and child care facilities.

Expansion of education: (i) universalise elementary education with special emphasis on girls' education; (ii) improve the content of education at all levels; (iii) promote non-formal education and functional literacy programmes, including promotion of skills; (iv) stimulate adult literacy programmes, with the participation of students and voluntary agencies; and (v) emphasis on national integration and social and moral values and instil pride in our heritage.

Justice to scheduled castes and scheduled tribes: (i) ensure compliance with the constitutional provisions and laws for the SCs and STs; (ii) ensure possession of land allotted to SCs and STs; (iii) revitalise the land allotment programme; ()iv) organise and assist special coaching programmes to immprove educational standards, (v) eradicate scavenging and undertake special programmes for the rehabilitation of Safai Karamcharis; (vi) provide better direction and adequate funds for the special component programmes; (vii) pursue programmes for the fuller integration of SCs and STs with the rest of the society; and (viii) ensure the rehabilitation of tribals displaced from their habitat.

Equality for women: (i) raise the status of women; (ii) enhance awareness of the problems of women; (iii) create mass consciousness about women's rights; (iv) implement a national programme of training and employment for women; (v) enable women to participate with equality in socio-economic development and nation-building; and (vi) rouse public opinion against dowry and ensure effective implementation of anti-dowry legislation.

New opportunities for youth: (i) enlarge opportunities for youth in sports, adventure and cultural activities; (ii) promote physical fitness; (iii) involve youth on a massive scale in projects of national development such as the cleaning of the Ganga, the conservation and enrichment of the environment and mass education; (iv) identify outstanding young persons in all fields to encourage and develop their talents; (v) involve youth in temper; (vi) expand the network of Nehru Yuvak Kendras; (vii) strengthen the National Service Scheme and the National Cadet Corps; and (viii) encourage voluntary agencies working for the welfare of rural youth.

Housing for the people: (i) make available house sites to the rural poor; (ii) expand programmes of house construction; (iii) lay special emphasis on construction of houses for SCs and STs; and (iv) develop low cost building materials.

Improvement of slums: (i) restrict the growth of slums; (ii) provide basic facilities in existing slum areas; and (iii) encourage planned house building in urban areas.

New strategy for forestry: (i) grow more trees and raise more firest, with the full involvement of the people; (ii) protect the traditional rights of tribal populations and local communities of access to fuel wood and forest produce; (iii) reclaim wastelands for productive use; and (iv) plant appropriate vegetation in hilly, desert and coastal areas.

Protection of the environment: (i) enhance public awareness of the dangers of environmental degradation;

(ii) mobilise popular support for environmental protection; (iii) promote recognition that enduring development demands preservation of the ecology; and (iv) ensure judicious site selection for projects and proper choice of technology.

Concern for the consumers: (i) bring essential consumption goods within easy reach of the poor; (ii) build a consumer protection movements; (iii) restructure the distribution system so that subsidies reach the most needy; and (iv) strengthen the public distribution system.

Energy for the villages: (i) expand the supply of electricity for productive use in the villages; (ii) develop alternative sources of energy, particularly biogas; and (iii) promote integrated area specific programmes for rural energy.

A responsive administration: (i) simplify procedures; (ii) delegate authority; (iii) enforce accountablility; (iv) evolve monitoring systems from block to national level; and (v) attend promptly and sympatherically to public grievances.

While the restructured 20-Point Programme renewed the nation's commitment to eradicate poverty, it laid balanced emphasis on how to raise overall procductivity, reduce income inequalties and remove social and economic disparities so that the ultimate fruits of development resulted in improvement of quality of life of human environment. The coverage of the programme was broadened to bring within its ambit a number of lmajor areas of social concern for fulfiling not only the 'basic needs' like adeauate provison of food, clean drinking water, housing and health facilities, it laid more emphasis on human dignity and individual rights by encouraging 'responsible' parenthood, equality for women, opportunities for the youth, rights of consumers, justice to scheduled castes and scheduled tribes, etc. The inherent philosophy behind the restructured programme was that the development has no real meaning without human dignity and individual rights.

The departments/ministries concerned on the subject of 20-Point Programme, 1986 set the annual targets in consultation with the states and the Department of Programme Implementation (DPI). DPI monitors the implementation of the 20-Point Programme. The management information system developed by this Department for implementation of the programmes consists of (i) Monthly Progress Report; (ii) Capsule Report; (iii) Half Yearly Progress Report; and (iv) Annual Report.

Under 20-Point Programme-1986, there are 119 items identified for monitoring. Of these, 54 are monitored on an evaluatory basis and 65 items are retained for physical targetting/monitoring. Again of the 65 items identified for quantitative assessment, 28 items have been identified for monitoring on a monthly basis. Only 19 items, out of the 28 items of the Monthly Report, are taken for the purpose of ranking. The Half Yearly Report covers majority of the items of 20-Point Programme indicating qualitative performance.

A three-tier system of monitoring has been established in the states/UTs, as follows: (a) at the agency level which are entrusted with the execution of the programmes in the field level; (b) at the state level which provides infrastructure and direction for programme execution; and (c) at the Central Government level not only by the sectoral ministries and departments but also by the Department of Programme Implementation under the Ministry of Planning and Programme Implementation, which oversees the monitoring and evaluation system on a contiuous basis

Table 2. All India Performance of Twenty Point Programme (1992-93 to 1994-94)

Sl. No.	Item Code	Item Description	Units	1992-93			1993-94			1994-95		
				Target	Achieved	Per cent	Target	Achieved	Per cent	Target	Achieved	Per cent
1.	01A	IRDP (Families)	Nos.	18,75,135	20,66,887	110	2,56,993	26,27,376	102	21,15,095	22,76,714	108
2.	01B	Jawahar Rozgar Yojana (Mandays)	Nos.	75,37,94,000	74,63,27,021	99	1,05,21,03,000	96,71,50,345	92	79,97,37,000	82,02,43,405	103
3.	01C	SSI Units (Regd.)	Nos.	40,270	1,72,221	123	1,48,234	1,72,110	116	89,834	1,20,823	134
4.	05A	Distribution of Surplus Land	Acres	1,50,720	1,11,024	74	5,98,563	70,887	12	5,63,860	61,927	11
5.	06	Bonded Labour Rehabilitation	Nos.	2,297	3,424	149	2,179	2,497	115	2,776	2,296	83

Sl. No.	Item Code	Item Description	Units	1992-93			1993-94			1994-95		
				Target	Achieved	Per cent	Target	Achieved	Per cent	Target	Achieved	Per cent
6.	07A	Drinking Water problem solved (Vlg.)	Nos.	33,453	33,618	100	40,187	35,730	89	58,891	74,201	126
7.	08A	Community Health Centres	Nos.	259	97	37	164	71	43	157	66	42

8.	08B	Primary Health Centres (PHC)	Nos.	759	314	41	640	174	27	780	296	38
9.	08D	Immunization of Children (DTP, Polio & BCG)	Nos.	2,42,89,660	2,16,40,778	89	2,47,89,635	2,22,21,933	90	2,47,65,000	2,26,28,328	91
10.	09A	FP Sterilization	Nos.	52,24,640	41,82,733	80	51,29,600	43,72,794	85	52,70,180	44,43,363	84
11.	09B	EQ Sterilization-IUD, CC & OP	Nos.	29,61,678	21,99,552	74	34,75,207	27,92,519	80	38,10,682	30,71,162	81
12.	09C	ICDS Blocks Operational (Cum.)	Nos.	2,595	2,601	100	2,760	2,766	100	3,066	3,066	100
13.	09D	Anganwadies (Cum.)	Nos.	2,82,849	2,73,994	97	2,99,830	2,78,423	93	3,31,869	2,90,655	88
14.	11A	SC Families Assisted	Nos.	25,95,568	19,95,877	77	25,24,800	23,23,722	92	25,83,500	26,96,412	104
15.	11B	ST Families Assisted	Nos.	8,95,862	8,56,837	96	9,00,000	10,24,798	114	10,12,175	10,51,806	104
16.	14A	House sites Alloted (Families)	Nos.	6,01,416	8,91,015	148	5,99,766	9,20,670	154	6,25,996	9,02,198	144
17.	14B	Construction Assistance (Families)	Nos.	3,30,352	3,99,879	121	3,21,950	4,41,094	137	3,63,541	4,31,986	119
18.	14C.	Indira Awaas Yojana (Houses)	Nos.	1,17,133	1,87,358	160	2,84,442	3,60,167	127	2,53,580	3,73,669	147
19.	14D	EWS Houses Provided	Nos.	1,15,122	1,23,908	108	83,577	1,23,099	147	89,940	1,16,816	130

20	14E	LIG Houses	Nos.	52,971	54,132	102	45,242	59,729	032	39,805	40,098	101
21.	15	Slum Improvement (Pop.)	Nos.	11,77,770	11,93,910	101	13,18,030	13,00,961	99	14,62,660	16,71,939	114
22A.	16A	Tree Plantation on Private Lands	Nos.	1,45,00,00,000	1,45,12,22,720	100	1,35,09,00,000	1,26,94,17,648	94	1,20.85,10,000	1,22,65,00,725	101
22B	16B	Area Covered-Public & Forest Lands	Hect.	10,64,000	10,24,595	96	11,65,300	9,75,213	84	10,31,320	10,28,007	100
23.	18	Fair Price Shops	Nos.	1,512	4,208	278	1,666	2,220	133	-	-	-
24.	19A	Villages Electrified	Nos.	4,240	3,726	88	3,218	3,337	104	2,897	3,540	122
25.	19B	Pumpsets Energised	Nos.	2,56,752	4,24,464	165	2,75,384	4,28,813	156	2,77,008	4,34,232	157
26.	19C	Improved Chullahs	Nos.	16,25,000	17,58,344	108	22,14,000	22,60,909	102	24,59,400	23,77,431	97
27.	19D	Bio-Gas Plants (States)	Nos.	1,14,400	1,56,761	137	1,39,200	1,81,446	130	1,64,750	1,58,095	96

and reports to the Cabinet Secretriat and the Prime Minister's Office.

Assessment of impact of 20-point programme

A statement showing the targets and achievements of major items of the 20-Point Programme on all India basis for the years 1992-93,1993-94 and 1994-95 is given in table 19.

Panchayati raj institutions

The introduction of PRIs was a revolutionary step to wards rural uplift in this country. Almost all the States have constituted Panchayati Raj bodies, with the exception of Bihar, Orissa, Lakshadweep. Pondicherry and the hill districts of Uttar Pradesh. The PRIs will function as effective institutions of local self-government and they would prepare plans for economic development and social justice and implement them. The PRIs will be the umbrella for integration of sectoral programmes. During the Ninth Plan, CAPART will continue to provide projectized financial assistance to voluntary organizations which will have to play a more dynamic role in empowering the poor through advocacy, awareness generation and formation of self-help groups. Decentralized planning will be made more effective through greater involvement of panchayats as also the voluntary organizations and people's self-managed institutions.

In the preceding pages we have discussed the objectives, strategies and various programmes which have been given priority in the approach to Ninth Five Year Plan. We all know that Rs. 30,000 crore had been earmarked for rural development in the Eighth Five Year Plan, even then we have not been able to achieve the desired success and the plan period is nearing completion. It has been proposed to spend RS. 90,000 crore on rural development during the Ninth Plan. But even then we cannot be sure that the whole objective and approach to the proposed plan will be moving smoothly and we shall be able to achieve our goals.

In this connection, it may be added that our policies in the past had hardly been in question so far as development objectives are concerned. At the implementation level there existed many bottlenecks which came in the way of proper implementation of the programme and achieving the real targets. The co-ordination problem had been so much chronic and the gap between plan formulation and its implementation so vast that we failed to achieve our goals. No doubt, the approach paper to the Ninth Five Year Plan makes a laudable attempt but the question still remains the same. Now we have effective Panchayati Raj system in our country and it is hoped that they will be capable of meeting the challenges at the implementation stage. But the question is whether the bureaucracy and State-level politicians will actually allow these institutions to take up the challenging task?

While concluding we may say that if there is real political will to achieve the objectives of approach to the Ninth Plan and the Panchayati Raj institutions are given real powers to implement, the objectives could really be achieved. However, keeping in view the hung nature of our Parliament and survival of the government on within and outside support by various political parties, it is still doubtful whether we will be able to achieve the objectives. A very pessimistic view suggests that it would be beyond the comprehension of the government. But an optimist student of rural development, may take a brighter view of the picture and hope that if not 100 per cent, at least 50 per cent of the objectives will be achieved.

Introduced in 1959, the Panchayati Raj is considered a political and administrative innovation of far-reaching importance. Initially, people envinced keen interest in the Panchayati Raj system and their representatives participated actively in local affairs. With passage of time, the initial enthusiasm and public participation gradually diminished. Again, after the enactment of the Constitution (73rd Amendment) Act 1992, there is a resurgence of rural local bodies in India. The objects of this amendment are:

(i) To place more powers in the hands of rural people to determine their own destiny and to build a society;

(ii) To enhance the capabilities of rural people to frame planning from below;

(iii) To decentralize execution of all kinds of development activities with the effective participation of the people; and

(iv) To alter the administrative methods in rural area.

The Panchayati Raj is the embodiment of rural local government with a three-tier system—village, intermediate and district levels—interconnected to provide for a community in experience as well as programme formulation and its implementation. To this system has been given powers and authority of governance as well as of plan formulation and execution. It has three roles to play simultaneously: (a) as a unit of rural local government; (b) as an instrument of community development; and (c) as an agency of the State government.

The Constitution Amendment Act 1992 has specified 29 items in the Eleventh Schedule which may be entrusted to the Panchayats in additon to any other schemes for economic development and social justice which may also be entrusted to them by the State governments. The following items from the Eleventh Schedule are important from environment protection and improvement point of view:

(i) Agriculture ;

(ii) Land improvement, implem-entation of land reforms, and soil conservation ;

(iii) Minor irrigation, Water management and watershed development ;

(iv) Social forestry and farm forestry ;

(v) Minor forest produce ;

(vi) Rural housing ;

(vii) Drinking water ;

(viii) Fuel and fooder ;

(ix) Non-conventional energy sources ;

(x) Health and sanitation.

If we compare the jurisdiction of Panchayati Raj with the aims of World Conservation Strategy, we find that Panchayati Raj is fully incorporating the aims in the following manner:

(i) To maintain essential ecological processes and life-support systems (such as soil regeneration and protection, the recycling of nutrients and cleaning of water) for human survival and development.

(ii) To ensure the sustainable utilization of species and ecosystems (notably fish and other wildlife, forests and grazing lands) which support millions of rural communities as well as major industries.

The role of PRIs is crucial for environment protection and improvement. Each tier is involved in the process of local planning about their jurisdiction. The plans are made at village Panchayat and then examined and compiled by the Panchayat at intermediate level (known as Block or Panchayat Samiti). After this, at district level as Zilla Pairshad) all plans from intermediae levels are considered. At the district level, there is a District Plan Committee which consolidates the plan looking to rational utilization of natural utilization of natural resources and environment conservation and forward it to the State Government. Such planning process takes care of local conditions, needs of the people, natural resources and geography of local areas.

The Panchayati Raj institutions have an effective role in the implementation of various policies and programmes contributing to environment protection and improvement, formulated by State and Central governments. In the Rajasthan Panchayati Raj Act, it is specifically mentioned that the State Government by its direction assigns the task of management and maintenance of forests in Panchayat area to Panchayat.

The PRIs also provide necessary assistance to the other agencies engaged in environment protection such as land allotment for forest and establishment of research centres. Besides this, the following roles of PRIs are also important:

— To create will and determination among the rural people to protect and improve the environment;

— To understand the local situation and to share the information about environment;

— To achieve integrated approach by co-ordinating the activities of various agencies interested in environment protection in rural areas;

— To provide a an open forum for discussion on environment protection;

— To give guidance and training to rural people; and

— To restrain the people from those activites which are harmful to environment, if necessary by imposing penalty and fine.

Backdrop

It is 1997. We are celebrating the 50th anniversary of our Independence. There could not be a better time to recap on what we have been able to achieve and how much we have been able to progress for the past five decades—economically, socially and politically.

At the time India became free, its economy was underdeveloped with abject poverty and an abysmally low quality of life. The two basic pillars of the economy were weak with agriculture in a very bad state and industrial growth almost nil. Our planners and leaders chose to improve the economy and hasten the development process through number of steps. The most significant among them was the initiation of five year plans with the launching of the First Plan in 1951. The main reason for the adoption of planning was that it was considered an effective way of developing the economy. This involved a vital role for the public sector and a strict control of the private sector and market. A large and pre-determined proportion of natural resources was devoted to the construction of infrastructural facilities (like roads, railways, communication, etc.) and capital-intensive industries (like machine tools etc.). As for the resultant problem of inadequate supplies of consumer goods was concerned it was decided to be tackled through an equitable distribution of the same (like PDS, rationing, etc.).

By this time, we have completed seven full five year plans and are on the verge of completing the Eighth. The approach paper (draft) to the Ninth Plan prepared by the

Planning Commission has already been endorsed by the National Development Council. If we examine the past plans, a significant common feature among them would be the dominance of centralized planning or planning from above. The direction of development and the problem of allocation of resources were decided by the administrators, so to say, from their central offices. Most of the times, such sensitive decisions were taken without considering the basic realities at the grass roots level which destroyed their practical viability.

Suggestions and corrections forwarded by experts, and other popular bodies were ignored by the bureaucrats resulting in most of the schemes and programmes getting aborted before reaching the really needy. Departmentalism, which is a child of concentration of power became the hallmark of Indian planning. This has been a major factor which has resulted in the uneven and imbalanced growth of our economy. Another serious consequence has been that whatever growth was achieved during the plan periods has benefited only a small minority while the majority remains in a state of poverty and insufficient necessities. This is the point where the Ninth Plan of Kerala gains significance where the other alternative, i.e. decentralized planning is given predominance.

Decentralization

The main reason for the failure of the past eight plans has been attributed by experts to the absence of people's participation in the planning and implementation of these plans and the consequent concentration of power. Although many commissions and groups have been formed to study in these governments to fill these lacunae. It was only belatedly that the idea of introducing Panchayati Raj institutions came up in the minds of our planners.

It is at the regional grass roots level that most of the resources required for development are created. Our failure for the past 45 years has been our inability to identify these resources and to utilize them collectively in the development process. This resulted in the absence of co-ordination in the working of different departments at the Panchayat level. Consequently, the pre-prepared plans/schemes handed down by the authorities became largely unsuitable for implementation as they did not conform with the realities at the lower level. We have wasted a big chunk of our valuable capital for such unyielding programmes. Hence the need for decentralization becomes more prominent than ever before. Any decentralization process should give emphasis to the following objectives:

— To fully exploit the resources and growth possibilities at the regional level and thus increase income and employment opportunities;

— To make sure that the fruits of development works reach the poorest of the poor in a better way;

— To help develop a balanced and even regional development culture;

— To make available to the people, the basic necessities of life like drinking water, health services, housing, educational facilities, etc.;

— To strengthen the social and economic factors that promote development;

— To restructure the existing rural development institutions and organizations in such a way that they serve the rural folk in a better way;

— To reach the benefits of improved technology to the people; and

— To curb corruption by making the people a part and parcel of the development process.

Constitution and composition of panchayats

Not giving membership to MPs and MLAs in Panchayats, not tampering with the VP and Block Panchayats (BPs) boundaries for the membership of the BPs and the District Panchayat, (DP) respectively and making the Chairpersons of the lower tier members of the immediate upper tier for establishing an organic link among them are welcome features of the State Act, which should also be emulated by other States. But there are certain features of the Act which need to be amended as they are against the spirit of the Central Act and participatory planning. These are:

—In Chapter II of the Act, reorganization of the boundaries of the wards of Panchayats has been vested in the State government, which is against the provisions of Articles 243 k and 243 O of the Constitution. All functions pertaining to the delimitation of boundaries, including disputes between or among Panchayats, should be performed by the State Election Commission.

— A provision for reservation of OBCs should also be made in the Act to enable them to participate effectively in decentralized governance.

— The election of the Chairperson of the VP should be made direct as is the case in most States. In this way, the Chairperson will be able to draw authority from the people. Besides making Chairpersons accountable to the people, this will also strengthen the institution of the GS.

— To provide more space for weaker sections to participate in planning and development, the reservation for SCs, STs, OBCs and women should be extended to include the post of Vice-Chairperson of different tiers. At present, Punjab is the only State where such a provision has been made at the intermediate and apex tiers. Kerala may do well to go one step further and provide reservation for these sections at all tiers of the Panchayats.

— As per Section 151 of the Act, if the government is satisfied that a Panchayat at any level cannot be constituted for certain reasons, like failure to elect the majority of the members, it can appoint an Administrative Committee consisting of at least the elected members and a President and Vice-President, or appoint a special officer for period not exceeding six months. This provision is against the spirit of the Constitution. If such an eventuality arises, only the elected representatives should govern the Panchayats for a specified period and not a special officer. Therefore, the provision of a special officer provided in this section should be deleted.

Devolving of adequate and clear-cut functions and powers to the Panchayats is very important for enabling them to function in a free environment. Let us examine the scope of Kerala Panchayat Raj Act (KPRA) in this regard.

— Under Section 164 (2), a provision has been made for constituting a Ward Committee for each constituency with the purpose of informing the VP on the needs of the constituency. But the GS will also be held at the ward level only, which among others, will list out its needs as is also envisaged as the role of the Ward Committee. The VP may also constitute a vigilance Committee as suggested earlier in this paper. Keeping these provisions in view, constitution of the Ward Committee is dispensable.

— The District panchayats, Block Panchayats and Village Panchayats shall perform their functions under the financial and technical guidance of the State government [Sections 166 (2), 172 (2) 173 (2)]. This is wrong in principle and operationally difficult as it does not put Panchayats on a firm foundation. Through provisions of this nature, the government can meddle with the functioning of the democratically elected institutions and deprive the people of freedom of action which is essential for participatory planing. These provisions in the State Act may have to be suitably amended so that the VP takes help from the BP which, in turn, takes help from the DP and the DP from the State government, if it is required. The State may be benefited from the Panchayati Raj Acts of States like Gujarat, Assam, Manipur and Madhaya Pradesh which have enabling provisions for consultation among the three tires without much intervention from the State.

— Functions to be performed by different tiers of Panchayats have been listed in Schedules 3,4 and 5 of the Act. Looking at their distribution among the three tiers, an hour glass picture emerges, because they have been concentrated either at the lowest level or at the apex. This shows that in deciding the distribution, proper thought has not been given. For example, functions relating to education do not figure in the list for the BP, which thus emerges as a weak tier of the PR system and, therefore, does not provide sufficient scope for its members to play a role in participatory planning. While participating in the Conference of Chief Ministers on basic minimum services 4-5, July, 1996 in Delhi, the Chief Minister of Kerala mentioned that less than one per cent of the total habitations in the State were fully covered as regards the availability of safe drinking water against the national coverage of 57 per cent. Shortage of clean drinking water is an important reason for the high morbidity in the State. This is one of the basic needs and could be handled effectively at Panchayat level. But very little responsibility to this basic necessity has been devolved to the Panchayats. It is suggested that in order to conserve water resources, construction of check dams in the rivers should be entrusted to the Panchayats. If this function is given lock stock and barrel to the Panchayats, it being a basic requirement, will enthuse the people to participate in water management.

— In inter-tier allocation of functions, the cardinal principle that what can be undertaken at a particular level should be entrusted to that level alone has been kept in mind. However, ample scope for improving the functional relationship between the three tiers is still there. Significantly, whatever functions have been allocated to the Panchayats in accordance with this principle have been taken away by Section 283, according to which the government may alter, amend or add to any of the entries made in the functions of the Panchayats. Hence this section should be repealed.

— To fully realize economic development and social justice, other functions like police powers and judicial powers should also be given to the Panchayats. Bihar, West Bengal, Punjab and Uttar Pradesh are the States which have given judicial functions to institutions at the grass roots level. Recently, the Madhya Pradesh State Assembly has also passed a legislation for constituting Gram Nyayalayas to administer justice in rural areas. The Karnataka government also proposes to introduce an amendment to the State's Panchayat Act in the coming session of the Assembly for setting up Nyaya

Panchayats. The kerala Panchayat Raj Act does not make provision for constituting Nyayalaya at grass roots levels for dispensing justice to the people. It is, therefore, suggested that police and judicial functions should be given to the Panchayats for meaningful decentralization.

Functional autonomy has not been given to the Panchayats, because provisions such as the schemes being contingent on the availability of resources and placing of performance of vital functions under the supervision and guidance of the government have circumscribed the role of participatory planning through the institutions. For ushering in an era of participatory planning for Panchayats, the State government should amend all the Acts pertaining to the subjects in the XIth Schedule of the Central Act, take out all relevant portions from the existing Subjects Acts and incorporate them in the Panchayat Act through an amendment by the State legislature.

Administrative autonomy

For enabling the people to participate effectively in planning and development of their areas through Panchayats, it is indispensable that these bodies should have their own officials. But this has not been provided for in the Kerala Panchayat Act.

— The secretaries of all the three tiers will be the government employees (Section 179) under the State Act. The power of transferring these employees is also vested in the government or in a prescribed authority if a resolution to that effect has been passed by the Panchayat by a simple majority. However, action on this resolution is not mandatory on the part of the government. This provision is objectionable, because this does not entail autonomy of the people in their actions. What is the rationale behind insisting on a simple majority for a resolution for transferring an official? It is practised at the State and the Central levels? Hence this provision may have to be repealed.

— The Chairpersons of the Panchayats have been empowered to exercise supervision and control over the officials of the Panchayats and prepare their confidential reports (Section 156 (4) (b). It is a welcome feature of the Act. But provisions in the Kerala Munidipal Act [Section 14 (3) (b)] which say that Chairpersons prepare the confidential report of the Secretary as well as review the confidential reports prepared by the Secretaries in respect of their employees should also be made applicable to the Panchayats.

— An enabling provision for constituting a separate Service or Cadre [Section 179 (3)] has been made in the Act. Other States which have some such provisions are Karnataka [Section 196 (5) and Punjab (Section 26). But the provision in the Kerala Act is not substantial in nature as it has not been clearly specified as has been done in the Gujarat Panchayati Raj Act. The provision under Section 179 (3) of the KPRA must be operationalized at once so that the Panchayats have their own officers and employees. Kerala may be benefited from Gujarat and Rajasthan Panchayati Raj Acts in which provisions for Panchayat cadre have already been incorporated. Under the Gujarat Panchayati Raj Act, there will be three cadres of Panchayat employees, namely the District cadre, the Taluk cadre and the Local cadre [Section 227 (3)]. For this purpose, a Gujarat Panchayat Service Selection Board shall be constituted. Besides this Board, a District Panchayat

Service Selection Committee shall also be constituted at the district-level to recruit the primary education staff (Section 236). In Rajasthan, a provision for establishing a District Establishment Committee under the chairpersonship of the President of the ZP has been made. This Committee shall make selections for the posts in different grades and categories for the Panchayats, prepare lists of the persons for promotion and deal with disciplinary matters affecting the officers and employee except officers of the State cadre.

Actually, a permanent solution of the cadre problem is to amend the Constitution, because the Panchayats after becoming local government must have their own employees as the State and the Centre have as per part XIV of the Constitution. But to begin with, the State government must invoke immediately the enabling provisions in the Panchayat Act.

Participatory planning denotes people's involvement from initiation to the completion of the Plan. It is an indivisible concept as it encompasses people's participation in decision-making, implementation of the decision, sharing of the benefits and evaluation and monitoring of the plan. Thus, people's particulation has to be threaded like warp and woof in every stage of planning.

According to the Working Group on District Planning (1984), participatory planning has three dimensions: nature of the participation, participants and the way of participation. The answers of the first two, i.e. the nature of the participation and who should participate, are based on the dictum "people plan and the government supports". The Panchayats are the institutions through which participation occurs. Thus, the whole concept of participatory planning depends on the extent of the autonomy of the people.

The objectives of the present paper are: (i) to review the role of the Panchayats in Kerala in a historical perspective with a view to examining the extent to which they have succeeded in ensuring people's participation in planning. (ii) to evaluate the role the community and the voluntary sectors have played in creating an environment for participatory planning in the State, and (iii) after critically reviewing the Kerala Panchayat Act, suggest changes in it so that it facilitates people's actions. While examining the last question, a comparison of the Kerala Act with other State Acts has also been made.

The State of Kerala was formed in November 1956 by merging the Travancore, Cochin and Malabar regions to create a single State. Since its formation, the State has had a chequered history in the sphere of democratic decentralization. In April 1957, the first leftist government led by E.M.S. Namboodiripad was installed in the State. It introduced the Kerala Panchayat and District Council Bills in the Assembly. But these Bills could not become law as the government was dismissed on 31 July, 1959 by the Centre. The succeeding government headed by Pattom Thanu Pillai, however, succeeded in enacting three Bills, the Kerala Panchayat Raj Act, 1960, the Kerala Municipalities Act, 1961. These Acts not only unified the laws in operation in the Malabar, Travancore and Cochin regions, but also enhanced the functional and financial autonomy of the local government institutions.

In 1964, the Kerala Panchayat Union Council and Zilla Parishad Bills, modelled on the recommendations of the Balwantray Mehta Committee report, were introduced in the State Assembly by the next government. These too could not be enacted due to the fall of the government. In March 1967, the CPI-M government headed by E.M.S. Namboodiripad again introduced a Bill called the Kerala Panchayati Raj Bill 1967 in the Assembly which envisaged a two-tier system of Panchayati Raj at the village and the district levels and induction of an organic link between the two tiers by putting the Gram Panchayat under the supervision and control of Zilla Panchayat. This Bill was referred to a Select Committee which recommended substantial amendments in it. It enabled the district level institution to function as the district government. But it could also not become law as the State Assembly was dissolved in August 1970.

In 1971, the government headed by C. Achutha Menon came forward with the Karala District Administration Bill the Select Committee set up in 1968 to consider the 1967 Bill. This Bill also could not become law. In August 1978, the A.K. Antony Ministry introduced the Kerala District Administration Bill in the Assembly. But this Bill was passed by the Legislature during the Chief Ministership of the CPI leader P.K. Vasudevan Nair and got the Presidential assent in May 1980 when the office had passed into the hands of the CPI-M leader, E.K. Nayanar, who incidentally holds the reins at present. But this could also not be implemented as the Ministry fell in 1981. The government however, commissioned a study on the shortcomings in the Act. This study was undertaken by a senior IAS officer, V. Ramachandran. In May 1982, a new government assumed office but it did not demonstrate the necessary political will to strengthen Panchayati Raj in the State. In 1987, the Left Democratic Front (LDF) government led by E.K. Nayanar again came to power. It implemented, although not fully, the recommendations of the Ramachandran report on the measures to be taken in democratic decentralization at the district and lower levels, which was submitted in July, 1988. This government also did very little for strengthening Panchayati Raj in the State, because at that time every political party was afraid of decentralization as V. Ramachandran (1995) had observed: "A fear has taken hold in the State that there was voodoo about decentralization in Kerala as every government, overcoming this fear showed political courage and announced elections to the District Councils in December, 1990. For the first time in the history of the State, District, Councils came into being in February 1991.

The provision of reservations for SCs, STs and women made in the Act enabled these marginalized sections of the society participate in the development process. The results of the elections held for the councils revealed that the share of SCs and STs in their total membership was 17 per cent. This was much higher than the ratio of their population in the State. The percentage of the SCs and STs in the total population in the State was 10.02 and 1.02, respectively. The LDF captured 13 out of the total 14 District Councils. The reservation for the marginalized sections of rural society in the District Councils gave them a Panchayat to enable them to participate in the system of decentralized governance and development.

But this welcome process could not be sustained for long as fresh elections to the State Assembly along with the parliamentary election were held in June 1991. In these elections, the LDF government law replaced by the United Democratic Front (UDF) regime led by K. Karunakaran. The first step this government took was to amend the District Administration Act, 1979. The amended Act made provision of appointing a junior officer as Secretary of the Council in place of the Collector who was its ex-officio Secretary under the original Act. The State government was also empowered to amend, delete or add to the powers and functions devolved to the Councils. In nutshell, the District Council was reduced merely to an agency of the State government.

The village Panchayats (VP) in the State also have a poor track record. It only in 1963 that had their first elections with the second after a long spell of more than one and a half decade in 1979 and the third in 1988. After the expiry of the term of the elected representatives, the government officials have been made their administrators. The latest elections to the Panchayats (i.e. VP, BP, DP) were held last year after an amendment of the State's Panchayat Acts in accordance with the Constitution (73rd Amendment) Act, 1992.

It can be seen that the Panchayats in the State have not yet become vibrant institutions for enabling the people to participate in local development. The factors responsible for this plight of these institutions, among others are the vested interests, i.e. the political leaders and bureaucrats who have not been interested in parting with powers in favour of the Panchayats. The LDF, which wanted to make the Panchayats the fulcrum for participatory planning could not succeed fully as its governments had fallen for one reason or the other. Otherwise, an enlightened and articulate public coupled with land reforms could have made panchayats a sound base for people's involvement in planning. That is why M.A. Oommen (1991) commented that "Kerala is probably on State where people's participation should be strong and successful given the level of literacy. However, the progress made, has been very poor".

People's participation

Development is the primary concern and responsibility of the people. They must prepare the plan and implement the same. This is much more true with the introduction of Panchayati Raj. The voluntary organizations may also be actively involved in this task. People are the primary concern. It is their confidence and credibility that needs to be obtained. It is mutual trust between government and the people that will repose faith in each other. There are three basic principles of people-centred development. First, sovereignty resides with the people. Second, to exercise their sovereignty and assume responsibility for their own development and that of their communities, people must control their own resources, have access to relevant information, and have the means to hold the officials of government and voluntary organizations accountable. Third, those who would assist people with their development must recognize that it is they who are participating in support of the people's agenda, not vice-versa. The value of the outsider's contribution will be measured in terms of the enhanced capacity of the people to determine their own future.

The Gandhian model of development requires active involvement and participation of man building his own "destiny". This is possible if some of us belonging to the so-called rich and middle class voluntarily, instead of dfrifting toward consumerism, are willing to sacrifice and share our pleasures in the interests of the downtrodden of our society. For rural India, time is running out and it must adopt strategies and methods to transform the socio-economic life of people to suit Indian ingenuity and culture. Integrated development sets forth a strategy of working with rural people—a strategy, in which participation by all is both the means and end itself.

In sum, the real wealth of a country lies in "human capital" and if you create conditions where human capital can flourish without being squashed by government controls, you can beat the rest of the countries of the Ninth Plan has to be very positive in building up "social capital" and infrastructure. Our social achievements are not outstanding despite our fifty years of Independence. Our literacy rate is 52 per cent; infant mortality 74 per thousand; access to sanitation is available to only 16 per cent of the people. Though life expectancy has gone up to 62, the fertility rate is still 3.3 which would double India's population in the next century. Just as the proof of the pudding is in the eating, similarly the success of the Ninth Plan will depend on as to how far it has raised "human capotal" of India.

We have to shift the paradigm of development from a right centred-economy to a duty motivated economy, from self-centredness to the love of our fellowmen, if we want to succeed in our planned development of rural society.

Community initiatives

It is evident from the above discussion that the Panchayats have been denied the possibility of carrying out participatory planning for local development at the grass roots level. This vacuum has been filled by the voluntary efforts of the people with the participation of intellectuals and voluntary network organizations like the Kerala Sastra Sahitya Parishad, Bharat Vigyan Samithi. The results of their efforts have been remarkable. In the field of literacy, the "Erankulam model" is acclaimed across the world and replicated elsewhere in India. The alphabet literacy has provided a sound base for a mass initiative in the field of environment protection, gender equality and women's empowerment. Thus social development in Kerala has been the contribution of an awakened and vigilant public. Majumdar (1995) rightly observed that "The enlightened and politically conscious electorate in Kerala closely monitors the functioning of schools, including those in the rural areas. Here, cases of shirking on the part of teachers evoke strong collection protest (e.g. many such cases are immediately publicised through posters in public places), and as a corollary, elicit appropriate policy responses.

The expansion of literacy has given a sound base for participatory planning which has successfully been operationalised in Kalliasseri Panchayat in Kannur district of the State.

The Community Development Society (CDS), with its thrift and credit activities, has improved the lot of poor women in urban Kerala. The Alappuzha CDS is an example, where "poor women have mobilized up to Rs. 37 lakh from their own savings. In two years, the Alappuzha CDS has generated more than 4,000 jobs ensuring 100 per cent loan recovery and repayment to banks as on date". Due to this exemplary work, the Alappuzha model has received "We the People Award" in 1994 from the United Nations.

Although Kerala could not provide a successful model for participatory planning through Panchayats due to political instability, its people, with the help of dedicated voluntary organizations have offered one. The other States could benefit from its success stories in participatory planning.

Environment protection

Even though India is one of the few Third World countries which has constitutionalized protection and improvement of environment, the various enactment suffer from several lacunae including the non-recognition of the crucial role that PRIs can play in the endeavour. The involvement of PRIs as the watch-dog of environmental protection at the grass roots level needs to be duty recognized. The Constitution (73rd Amendment) Act 1992 now provides these institutions an opportunity to play their legitimate role. Environment protection represents one of the more recent and yet one of the more profound aspects new public affairs dimension in public administration. Environmental issues have aroused too much intellectual and academic interest both in developing and underdeveloped nations. They include envioronmental degradation, deforestation and desertification, atmospheric pollution and imbalances as well as disertifications in ecology resulting from the way natural resources—land, water, forests, minerals, etc are harnessed for fulfilment of human needs. The UN Conference on Human Environment in 1972 proclaimed that the defence and improvement of human environment both natural and man-made had become an imperative good for mankind, to be pursued together with fundamental goals of peace and worldwide economic and social development. The achievement of these goals was the responsibility of citizens, communities, enterprises and institutions at every level. Later on, the World Conservation Strategy (1980) and the Brundthland Report also noted the irreversible destruction of ecosystems of the poor countries and the implicit threat to the world security and the consequent political instability and social problems. The problem of environmental crises of the developing countries is different from that of the developed countries. The establishment of viable community-based institutions for environment protection was suggested with full legal, administrative and technical support. These institutions should be empowered to plan, to work out the modality and to implement the various measures for environment protection and conservation. The Panchayati Raj as an institution of local rural government is the excellent model for it in rural India.

Among the developing countries, india is also facing environmental problems and crises. The enormous increase in population is the most potent cause for acceleration of the overutilization of productive resources and downgrading the quality of environment.

India has a domesticated animal population of nearly 500 million. Considering that only 3.5 per cent of the land area are under grass, the population is supported by the forest and agriculture residues which are thereby diverted from agricultural land. Out of the total cultivable land, 175 million ha are degraded needing special treatment to restore productivity. Of the 75 million ha designated as forest land, only 35 million ha are close forest. Despite all efforts, India has continued to lose forest cover. The deforestation causes loss in bivodiversity. Over 1,500 species of plants and animals are on the endangered list. Levels of air and water pollution are much beyond acceptable limits. These challenges disturb the environment equilibrium and the life of mankind. The basic aim of our National Forest Policy must be to ensure environmental stability and maintenance of ecological balance including atmospheric which are vital for the sustenance of all forms of life—human, animal and plant. Rural India has different kinds of environmental crises compared to other countries. The rapid growth of rural population has placed inexorable burden on farm as well as on other land resources, on forests, on water resources and worsened the quality of life of the rural poor in respect of housing, health, ecological surroundings and other essentials.

The Un Declaration on Human Environment in 1972 signalled India to initiate positive steps in the direction towards environment improvement. The Constitution of India has conceptualized its thinking on environment in the form of the Directive Principles of State Policy in favour of protection and improvement of environment, and safeguarding of forests and wildlife (Article 48A), a fundamental duty to protect and improve the natural environment including forests, lakes, rivers and wildlife and to have compassion for living creatures [Article 51A(g)], and a subject in the Consurrent List in its Seventh Schedule (Item 17A and 17B). Both the Directive principles and Fundamental Duty are non-justiciable, but these provide the necessary constitutional sanction if the State intends to adopt a law in the matter.

The other component of the infrastructure for environment improvement and protection is provided by the existing legislation. There are 30 major enactments such as Water Cess Act, Forest Act, Forest Conservation Act, Wildlife Protection Act, Environment Protection Act, of Union and State Governments. Administrative actions—regulatory, negotiational and persuasive—under these enactments are mainly taken by the Central and State administrative organizations—the Central Ministry of Environment and Forests, the Central Pollution Control Board and the State Departments of Environment and State Pollution Control Boards. Besides this, there also exist the other administrative mechanisms concerned with the implementation of policies on environment. The Panchayati Raj institutions have also become important instruments in rural India for environment protection and improvement.

Suggestive framework

We have seen that Panchayats in Kerala have not become a viable and pulsating institution for ensuring participatory planning. The prime mover in this sphere has been the voluntary sector, But after the 73rd Constitutional Amendment which, among other things, has ensured regular elections to the Panchayats and reservation of seats as well as of posts of Chairpersons for the weaker sections at all the tiers, they have to assume this role. The elections to these institutions were also held last year.

The People's Campaign for the formulation of the Ninth Plan has also been launched in the State for making decentralized Planning the key input in preparing the State Plan. All these efforts on the part of the State government are in the right direction. But the main question is whether the Panchayats have really emerged as institutions of self-government (as envisaged in Article 243 G of the Constitution) to help materialize participatory planning. As mentioned earlier, the two important dimensions of the people's participation are: who are the people and how would the participation occur. The answer to the first question is given by M.A. Oommen (1991) while discussing the formulation of a methodology for district planning with people's participation in Kannur district where he says, by people we mean those below the poverty line. The poor people, including other marginalized sections of society, have been statutorily given berth in Panchayats. The second question is also answered by constituting the Panchayats in the State.

But the most important question regarding realization of the objective of participatory planning is whether people enjoy autonomy in their actions. In other words, whether the various provisions of the State Panchayat Act establish Panchayats as an Institution of Self-government (ISG), i.e. whether they have institutional existence, institutional capacity and financial viability. Therefore, the question discussed in this part of the paper is whether the various provisions of the Kerala Panchayat Act enable Panchayats to usher in participatory planning. And if not, what amendments need to be made.

Like in other spheres, Indian women have proved their great potential as successful entrepreneurs. Some of Indian women entrepreneurs today lead the biggest shipping companies, trading and export houses, brewing industry, plastic & electronics establishment. Garment and handicrafts exports are primarily in the hands of women entrepreneurs. However, such achievement by about 100,000 women entrepreneurs in India touches just the fringe of vast future potential promised to Indian women.

Out of the total 761 million people in India, female comprise 360.74 million representing 47.7% of the total population. There are 99.4 million women workforce (representing 28% of the female population), but as per 1981 census, there are only 150,000 self-employed women accounting for only 5.2% of the total self-employed persons in the country. Majority of them are engaged in the unorganised sectors like agriculture, agrobased industries handicrafts, handlooms, and cottage based industries. Participation of women as industrial entrepreneurs, however, is comparatively a recent phenomena commencing from 70s onwards According to an estimate among 1.6 million SSI entrepreneurs in India during 1986-87, the total number of women entrepreneurs does not exceed 100,000.

Indian women's status in entrepreneurial terms

Item	Percentage
Women % to total population	47.7
Women % to total Workplace	36.4
Women % to total Unemployed	40.0
Women % to total Self-employed	5.2
Women % to total SSI Entrepreneurs	7.5

In late 70s, it became conspicuous that women offer great potential as entrepreneurs. Accordingly, besides encouraging more women to join regular EFP, a number of special programmes and strategies were thought out to ensure women to take up entrepreneurship as their career.

During 1978-87, Small Industry Development Organisation (SIDO) with its network of Small Industries Service Institutes (SISI) spread throughout the country conducted 248 Courses exclusively for women benefitting 8,904 potential women entrepreneurs.

During 1986, Industrial Development Bank of India (IDBI) launched a special Scheme for Women Entrepreneurs according to which the training support and counselling is offered in a package. The scheme emphasized the need to set up modern small scale units in electronics engineering, plastic and chemicals, etc. consistent with the knowledge, skills and personal background of trainees further suggests to include women entrepreneurs so far as possible and provide long lead time and the post-training escort services by the conducting agency until the projects taken up by women entrepreneurs generally reach their break-even stage. The success rate under this scheme has crossed the 50% mark of the national averag. Further, a this helped several new voluntary organisations in acquiring and improving their competencies and infrastructural facilities for conducting effective EDPs for Women. In September, 1986 the Government of India set up a National Level Standing Committee for Women Entrepreneurs under the Chairmanship of the Minister of State for Youth Affairs, Sports, Women & Child Development. The Standing Committee made suitable recommendations & suggestions to the Government regarding the problem of entrepreneurship amongst women.

In view of the growing importance of women entrepreneurship, several nationalised banks opened special Cells for women entrepreneurs. Many State

Financial Corporation have also developed special schemes for assisting the women entrepreneurs. Several entrepreneurs associations are very active in promoting and supporting the cause of entrepreneurship development. Most of them are now having a separate Women's Wing.

Only about a few year ago, an women entrepreneur, in India was visualised as a maker of pickles, papads, masala (spices) and other such household goods. But the recent EDPs have helped them in organising enterprises of complex type, bigger in size, with sophisticated technology involving higher managerial abilities. As such, the number of women entrepreneurs is increasing very fast. In order to further accelerate the process, it may be necessary to develop more man-power undertaking training and support to women entrepreneurs. Presently, two National Institutions, NIESBUD and EDII are organising half-a-dozen trainers training programme producing not more than 150 trainers in a year. To this even another 100 are added by other newly established institutions such as ICEW in Ahmedabad and IED in Lucknow hardly meeting the 50% of the total requirement.

Usually, it has been observed in the West that economic independence to women will increase the incidence of breaking of 'family tie'. Economic prosperity through entrepreneurial pursuits by Indian women has proved just the contrary. More often, women entrepreneurs have succeed in evolving other family members such as husband, father, mother etc. into her entrepreneurial folds. This is supported by the fact that majority of successful women entrepreneurs were married (85.5%), mostly between the age 36-45 year (56.2%) and most of them (81.7%) had children of about the age of 10 years. These empirical evidences raises a great of early entrepreneurisation of the whole society by promoting entrepreneurisation of the whole society by promoting entrepreneurship amongst women. Through women participation, the movement is bound to add momentum.

Safeguards

The Kerala Panchayat Act is full of provisions which empower the State government to interfere with impunity in the functioning of the Panchayats. These provisions have not created and enabling environment for participatory planning. They are as follows:

— Section 159 (1) of the Act empowers the State to remove the democratically elected Chairperson, and Vice-Chairpersons of the various Standing Committees on certain grounds.

— As per Section 161 (8) of the Act, the copies of the minutes of every meeting of a Panchayat shall be forwarded within 48 hours by the Secretary either to the government or its authorised officer. This is against the spirit of decentralization. What is the rationale for sending these minutes to the State authorities? This may be repealed as it will unnecessarily increase the burden of the secretary's work without any gain.

— Section 188 of the Act empowers the government and its officials to call for any record of Panchayats for verification, audit or examination. Section 190 empowers the government to direct the Panchayats to perform their responsibilities properly. The government can by an order fix a period for the performance of such duties. Similarly, Section 191 empowers the State government to cancel or suspend any resolution adopted by the Panchayat. The State government as per Section 193 can dismiss popularly elected Panchayats if they do not perform their duties properly.

— The Act empowers the State government to make rules and by-laws to carry out all or any purpose of this Act (Section 254). The State government, instead of making rules and bye-laws, may prepare model rules with flexibility which the Panchayats can modify keeping in view their requirements.

— The State government can delegate powers enjoyed by the VP, BP and DP to an authorized officer (Section 275). It means powers given to Panchayats by one hand can be taken back by another. Section 278 militates against Section 156 because as per the former, "executive functions of the President be construed as a reference to the Secretary of the village Panchayat," while as per the latter Section, the Chairperson is the executive head of the Panchayat. Thus Section 278 may have to be repealed.

— As per section 282, disputes between Panchayats will be referred to government officials. This Section should be amended to provide for referring disputes between Panchayats to the next higher tier of Panchayat.

Thus, a number of provisions in the Act are retrograde and reduce Panchayats to an agency of the State government. In order to ensure proper control with adequate safeguards over them, the following suggestions are made.

To establish an organic relation between and among the three tiers of the Panchayat Raj system for participatory planning, the VP should work under the direction of the BP and the BP should work under whose direction the DP. Now the question arises under whose direction the DP should work. Sometimes, due to political reasons, the upper tier of Panchayat may misuse its authority. The following measure is suggested to prevent such misuse.

A body under the chairpersonship of a person, qualified to be a judge of the High Court and comprising the representatives of the VP, BP and as members to be nominated by the government may be constituted. This body may handle all the cases relating to abuse accounts and other issues relating to decentralized governance. The idea here is that Panchayats should in real sense emerge as an institution of self-government without any threat of political onslaught.

The economy of Kerala today is in a really bad shape. The agricultural sector has not grown on expected lines. It is still a food deficient State and produces only 50 per cent of its total food requirement. Industrial growth has remained stagnant. As per the latest estimates, out of 108 lakh people who could be employed, about 28 lakhs are unemployed (zero working days/year but < 183 working days/year). This poses a big danger to the social structure of the State which has achieved 100 per cent literacy. The per capita income of the State is lower than the national average by about 15 per cent. Another major area of concern is the power sector. At present, Kerala is on the lowest rung of the national table of per capita availability of power. Power cuts and load shadings have become a matter of routine. Needless to say that this has stood in the path of industrial development in Kerala. All these point towards the absence as well as need for a strong base on which the growth of any economy can be planned.

The Ninth Plan of Kerala is unique in tow aspects. First, it removes a major drawback from the planning process—the absence of people's participation in planning. For the first time in any Indian State, the planning and implementation of government schemes and programmes will be decentralized thus taking the planning process to every village and every citizen. Secondly, the size of the Plan for the next five years would be higher than the total amount spent through eight five plans during the last 45 years. A rough estimate shows that the size of Kerala's Ninth Plan would be about Rs. 15,000 crore—higher than the total of Rs. 14,800 crore spent through the eight plans so far. The Ninth Plan aims at heavy investments in agriculture and industry in order to increase the production and productivity in every sector. These is no doubt that this will a milestone in the development process and planning in the State.

The whole of Panchayati Raj and other local bodies in the State will be part and parcel of the Ninth Plan. The State Planning Board has given shape to a massive campaign programme titled "Ninth Plan, People's plan" for its implementation. As part of this programme, nearly 35-40 per cent of the total outlay in the Ninth Plan will be set aside for the Panchayati Raj and other local bodies. This will include the scheme and plans put forward by Grama Sabhas of Panchayats, ward bodies of corporations and municipalities and the different block Panchayats and district Panchayats in different block Panchayats and district Panchayats in different stages. This should not be seen lightly. The allocation of 35-40 per cent of the total outlay would mean that a massive amount of Rs. 5,000-6,000 crore is to be set aside for the process of decentralization. This figure is higher than the total outlay of the Eighth Plan. The again means that and amount of about Rs. 1,200 crore would be available to the local bodies and about Rs. 85 crore for each district during each year of the Ninth Plan. In sum, every Panchayat is to be made available Rs. 1 crore approximately per year for development works.

Thus, Kerala's Ninth Plan aims at elimination the pitfalls in the previous planning programmes through a comprehensive, popular and decentralized planning process. This process starts from the grass root level of the Panchayats. Though it has to be recognized that every decision cannot be left to the discretion of the local bodies, whatever decisions and plans that can be undertaken at their levels should be allowed to be undertaken and implemented by them. The power in this regard will have to be handed over to them immediately. Besides, the suggestions forwarded from the grass roots level, regarding the planning and implementation of programmes by different State departments, should given proper weightage. People's participation should be ensured at every state of the Plan right from project formulation to the implementation stage. Only would we be able to identify and successfully utilize the resources including human resources to ensure regional development. This will also help in strengthening these institutions to serve the society in a better way.

New age planning

The formulation of the State's Ninth Plan has been divided into three stages.

The first stage begins with the convening of Gram Sabhas and Panchayat ward conventions. These conventions aim at listing out the problems in the development process of the corresponding regions and suggesting possible remedial measures. These will include all sectors like agriculture, irrigation, education, animal husbandry, industry, health, fisheries sanitation, drinking water, sports, etc. The participation of women in these programmes will be given predominance.

The second stage includes the Panchayat development seminar. This seminar will discuss a

"Development Report" prepared by specialists and experts after considering the different suggestions put forward by the Gram Sabhas and after collecting the required information from reliable sources regarding these suggestions. This seminar will pave the way for a more deep and detailed insight and discussion on different aspects of the problems. The seminar will be attended by elected representatives of the Gram Sabhas, Panchayat members, officials and subject matter specialists (SMS). Every sector should be opened up for separate and detailed discussions. Finally, every development problem is to be converted into separate development schemes after incorporating the different conclusions and suggestions emerging out of the seminar. The pros and cons of every such scheme is studied well and the economics of such schemes calculated. Out of the total expenditure, the amount that can be raised through voluntary services and organizations and through the utilization of locally available natural resources is also calculated.

The next stage includes the formulation of a "Panchayat development plan" which includes all the plans and schemes prepared by different Panchayat level seminars coming under each Panchayat. Such "Panchayat development plans" will be added up in each district by the corresponding district Panchayats. These reports are forwarded to the State Planning Board, which after detailed discussion on each plan, will suggest suitable development strategies and directions to each district. The sum total of all the district plans will take the lion's share of the State's Ninth Plan.

Whether it is fully realized or not, the Ninth Plan planning represents a new age planning of an age of management culture, economic restructuring, resource scarcity, economy, value for investment, global competition, MNCs, mega investments, free trade, intellectual property rights, R & D, productivity, quality, efficiency, hardware and software of production, human capital, strategic planning, economic vision, government-private sector partnership, value by results, international capital, regional economic groupings, delicensing, decentralization, lean taxation, FDI, foreign borrowings, JVs, market pricing, opening of the economies, public-private sector parity or equality, fiscal discipline, public-orientation, deregulations, budgetary imbalances, de-nationalisation, corporate takeovers, subsidy-cuts, commercialization of agriculture and free trade in agricultural goods, non-farm enterprises in rural areas, entrepreneurship, innovations, paid lunches, cutting down free rides, user-charges, gender equality and empowerment of women, and soon.

Break from the past: In spite of its not insignificant achievements, the bane of Indian planning has been poor implementation and results, viz operational shortcomings and 'targetism'. The Ninth Plan should and ought to make a break from it, to justify its nearly Rs. 1 m crore investment. It must have multiple effect, without which it is bad planning, though the plans do not work out the multipliers. The plan has to learn a leaf or two from corporate planning, particularly of MNCs which mean business of every dollar of investment. Not that the Plan should be devoid of human concerns and values, which it or for that matter any public planning anywhere should be responsive to, given the concern of planning with the have-nots. That is, the results of the planning need be measured not only, by the hard facts of growth rate but also by the light and laughter in the lives of the common people, visible to the naked eye. Otherwise, the purpose of the whole planning exercise would be much lost.

All said and done, the fact should be brought home to the planners in the Ninth Plan that it requires a lot of suffering and sacrifice to make the Plan operative with so much investment and it should yield commensurate returns in health, education, employment, social infrastructure, economic overheads, employment, enterprises, etc. for which the Plan is intended. India is one of the most poverty-ridden and low income countries. Our per capita income is not even $ 400 per annum. Millions and millions of people's daily concerns water, sanitation, medical aid, food and employment. Accordingly, the new age planning consists of making plan investments go as far as possible or maximum yielding. Planning must make the deserts bloom, not allow the forests to vanish so to say. If not, it is not proper planning.

Whether the plan size is optimal, suboptimal or overoptimal is irrelevant in the context of the plan. From plan-to-plan, planning efforts anyhow need to be raised. Considering This the plan is not at all oversized, considering the magnitude of the problems facing the economy and the efforts needed to overcome them. It is a different thing if the nation opts for a soft and small Ninth Plan. At no time, the plans had escaped the label of being ambitious and oversized. Notwithstanding plan size, the basic economic problems remain intact, if the poverty-line population increasing recently to 37 per cent is any indication.

Only, the Ninth Plan should be a new age planning or plan of operational efficiency, economy, efficiency, discipline, human and grass roots development, competitive, forward looking, co-ordinating and comprehensive. In addition, it must be time and cost bound. No doubt, it is a tall order of things but it is unavoidable if the Ninth Plan is to spell a success and make a dent into the thousand problems of the economy and the people. We have been lethargic with planning and it is time to be strictly business and management minded about planning and plan and the Ninth Plan is the right and opportune time to commence new age planning, without which it becomes increasingly difficult to sustain planning.

That is the law of diminishing returns which appears to have set in planning, since long, needs to be reversed in the Ninth Plan, failing which zero and even negative marginal productivities may set in for plan investments. There are increasing constraints on plan resources due to which the Ninth Plan should successfully go through its arithmetic of investments and returns in different lines of production and try to realize them for the first time in planning history of the country in tune with the new age stress on returns rather than or just investments. The Ninth Plan, in other words, should incorporate into its functioning strict business principles. The Plan thus should open a new chapter in planning not only in India but also the world over. Planning should assert itself and march ahead in the so-called market ruled economy and dispense its benefits to its large multitudes standing second to none in economy, efficiency and execution. It is the mandate of the populace. There is a national consensus behind planning, particularly the Ninth Plan, which promises to be a plan of action and of the people. It promises to give thrust to the thrust areas. Economy, productivity, returns and people should be the watchwords of new planning to commence with the Ninth Plan. There is no activity commensurate in importance with the Plan that should be No. 1 programmes, as nothing involves such a massive investment and the welfare and happiness of millions and millions of people and their living and natural environment.

One has to harp at length about the need for new planning because of the debris that is being left behind by improper planning, which is downward rather than upward. Rural development, for instance, is a greatly neglected aspect of our planning and the Ninth Plan promises to remove the whole backlog of it including human resource development and women and child development. Great challenges lay ahead of the new planning process.

Challenges

As said, formidable challenges lay before the Ninth Plan. In the first instance, it may be interpreted as the challenge of a seven per cent rate of GDP growth, which would be a break with the historical rate of growth of Indian planning of some 3.5 per cent to 6 per cent, depending on the moods of rain gods and the gods have been exceptionally kind to us consecutively for the last eight years, and let us hope and pray that they would be in the Ninth Plan also. It may seem an amazing assertion to say that the seven per cent growth rate is the least of the challenges of the Plan. Without exaggeration and bravado 8-10 per cent rate of growth is within the reach of the economy. What is seven per cent after all for a plan of nearly Rs. 1 m crore investment to which the plan investment should be rounded off. If a seven per cent rate of growth is not within the grasp of the economy, then what is all this liberalization, globalization, opening of the economy, etc. for? With improved management and evaluation and monitoring, an eight per cent rate of growth would be within easy reach.

That is, by all reckoning the seven per cent rate of growth appears to be a pessimistic rate of growth which in all likelihood would end up in an eight per cent rate of growth. That is the experience of the VIII Plan and there is no reason to believe that it won't repeat itself in the

Ninth Plan with the economic fundamentals of inflation, forex, FDI, etc. more in place. Like the export pessimism of the yester-years, the economy appears to be afflicted with growth pessimism bordering on defeatism and self-deprecation. This is evident in the panic reaction of the national industrial houses against MNCs and their threat of take-over. It is sorrowful if the Indian industry had not yet come of age. When would it? Never?

The whole planning debate is being expended on the rate of growth, the rate of saving (26.2%), the rate of investment (29.6%), ICOR (4.2%) and so, in a great exercise of not seeing the wood for the trees. There can be no doubt concerning the attainability and validity of these figures, which are the minor points of the plan. The economy in these respects appears to suffer from underestimates. The savings potential and rate of the Indian economy should not be underestimated, so also the size of the economy. There is a labyrinthine part of the economy which is quite formidable. There is no proper planning, strategy and foresight to utilized the economy's potential. In addition, there is an estimated 20 m Indian community abroad who still have their roots in the country. Their savings are estimated anywhere between $ 100 billion to $ 300 billion.

Triggering off rural economic revolution: The real challenges of the Ninth Plan are in the areas of rural development. The real planning and economic action must be planned in that vast rural sector. The strength as well as weakness of the economy is in the rural sector. Agriculture needs not just a 4.5 per cent rate of growth, which is most likely to be unattainable. There is no second Green Revolution in sight, even after nearly three decades of the first one. Economic revolution of the country, yet to take place, has to come about from the countryside or rural areas. One looks forward hopefully to an Indian economic miracle like the Japanese ad the South Korean ones. When is it likely to be? Not even after nearly 50 years of planning and planned economic development? Where are the millions of jobs to be created except in rural areas for quite some time? If urbanization of the 80s of less than five per cent is any indication, a lot of economic action ought to take place in the countryside from HRD to social economic infrastructure to environmental planning.

We have had enough of Malthusianism. It, without enough of rural development, is aggravating land wars. Only increased agricultural productivity, still a long way behind the world standards by about 60 per cent even in the 'developed' agricultural State, could considerably bring down the agrarian tensions. In other words, the Indian economic revolutions to be set from the countryside and it would be an indigenous revolution with all economic reforms and foreign capital participation confined to industry, services and urban areas. It must be the task of the Ninth Plan to trigger off the rural economic revolution and bring forth a second Green Revolution countrywide.

The economy, first, is suffering from improper house keeping and management on account of which it is caught in thick cobwebs. The first task of the Plan would be to clear the economy of these cobwebs, which are of social and economic overheads, infrastructural and improper and uneconomical plan and economy management.

The economy on the eve of the 21st century and the Ninth Plan is in need of stock-taking, spring cleaning, proper housekeeping and management, having grown without proper management and housekeeping over the last so many years. This is the first task and challenge of the Ninth Plan. Later on, it has challenges of proper housekeeping and management resources development.

Formidable tasks and challenges lay at the doorsteps of the Ninth Plan. The great task of rural development, fighting poverty employment generation, food security, HRD, population control, etc. The said thankless and profitless jobs would be the responsibility and challenges of the Plan, so also public enterprises profitability and viability.

Not that one is making too much of the Ninth Plan and trying to entrust with formidable tasks and challenges. They are very much there.

With the Ninth Five Year Plan (1997-2002), the Indian economy enters the 21st century and the this millennium, from which the formidable challenges facing the Plan can be guessed at. The Plan should be a turning point of the economy. In the first instance, it is good that notwithstanding a plethora of uncertainties facing the polity and the economy, the Plan could roll off setting to itself quite formidable tasks of a new century. And it augurs well for the Plan that it could muster a broad national consensus, over its approach and framework. The Plan is most likely to cheer all sections of the population with its massive investment and higher targets. Think big and act big, it seems, is the central message of the Plan, and it is incumbent on all to make a success of the Ninth Plan.

For, it must be said to the credit of Indian planning, quite an impressive one in the record of economic development and the annals of planning, that it could take the Indian economy from a small Rs. 10,000 crore GNP one to Rs. 1.2 m crore one in a span of some 45 years against all odds. What a country of diversities, pulls and pressures, size, populace, ideologies, interests, groups, divisions, threats, rebellions, riots, languor, storms and tempests! Yet, the caravan of planning moves on, pushing aside the forces of anti-development and democracy such as the zamindars and managing agents of the yester-years, to take the economy to the top brackets of the world economies, and in the process the Ninth Plan appears to be a great leap forward. It should set the trend for future unfailing planning of the country that goes a long way in alleviating the myriad economic problems facing the one billion strong Indian population growing at a Malthusian rate.

The Plan should draw lessons from the pitfalls of the previous plans and should establish proper input-output correlation and synergy. The expectations of the people are raised and they look forward to the Plan with many hopes and aspirations, particularly the common people or the masses. Marketism, to put things in proper perspective, need not come in the way of planning, as both can go hand-in-hand for common weal.. There in, so to say, nothing antagonistic between planning free enterprise.

Thus, with the decks cleared for the Ninth Plan, one may go about how it represents a new age spirit. It must be reflective of its times and must imbibe the spirit of the age, without which it cannot withstand its many challenges and steer the economy to greater heights and more satisfaction.

5

Common Minimum Programme

A document titled 'A Common Approach to Major Policy Matters and a Minimum Programme' commonly known as Common Minimum Programme (CMP) set out the United Front Government's agenda for action. Through the CMP, the United Front had presented an agenda for the Central Government founded on unity, secularism, stability, development and distributive justice. The commitment of the Government towards providing a stable Government at the Centre, empowerment of the underprivileged and deprived section and communities, secularism and democracy and growth with social justice had been brought out in the document. The document outlined the basic approach of the Government towards various socio-economic and political issues. The Department of Programme Implementation was the nodal Department to monitor the CMP which was being implemented by the concerned Ministries/Departments.

Implementation Reports from different nodal Ministries/Departments were received. Concrete steps to implement a number of items such as (i) Restoring democratic rights to the State of Jammu & Kashmir, (ii) Abolition of discretionary quotas of Ministers- (iii) Launching of a programme of Basic Minimum Services including roads, public distribution system, drinking water, health, primary education, mid-day meal and housing, (iv) Implementation of Prasar Bharati Act- (v) Preparation of draft 9th Five Year Plan, (vi) Preparation of draft 9th Five Year Plan; (vii) Special Economic Package Plan for all-round development of the north Eastern region; (viii) Revival of Inter-State Council, (ix) Initiation of process of consultation to arrive at consensus to prevent the misuse of Article 356 of the Constitution and many more measures to achieve socioeconomic objectives contained in the Common Minimum Programme were implemented.

In addition, many important steps were initiated in the fields of economic and financial administration, social justice, particularly in the interest of scheduled castes/ scheduled tribes, backward classes, and minorities-, international relations, particularly with neighbouring countries.

Due to dissolution of the 11 th Lok Sabha, many important bills such as Lokpal Bill, a Bill on freedom of information, a Bill on women's reservation in Parliament and State Assemblies, Agricultural workers' Bill etc., which were introduced in Parliament, remained pending.

6

Monitoring of Twenty Point Programme

Deviation of poverty and improving the quality of life of the people, specially of those who are below the poverty line, have been the prime objective of planned development in the country. In recent years, the, meaning of economic development has shifted from growth in per capita income to that of expansion of opportunities. Expansion of human capability can be, broadly, seen as the central features of the process of development. Government of India through different programmes/ schemes is helping its citizens to expand their capabilities. A package of programmes comprising schemes relating to poverty alleviation, employment generation, education and health, etc. called Twenty Point Programme (TPP) has been in operation since 1975. This package was restructured twice in 1982 and 1986. The present programme, known as TPP 1986, has been in operation since 1 st April 1987 in its present form. The details of TPP-86 in terms of its constituent points are given at Annexure-I. to this chapter. It Is to be noted that with globlisation of Indian economy and the adoption of market liberalisation process, the TPP - 86 provides much needed safety net to the deprived and adversely affected population. The Twenty Point Programme thus has a vital role to play to ensure growth with equity and social Justice.

Essence of twenty point programme - 86

The 20 - Point Programme forms an integral part of both the plan and non-plan Governments / UT Administrations and Central Ministries/ Departments. The outlays for different items under the programme are derived from the relevant plan heads under State Governments/UT Administrations and Nodal Ministries/ Departments at the Centre. Some schemes like family welfare programme are funded entirely by the Central Government while other programmes like IRDP, JRY and Indira Awas Yojana are jointly financed by the Centre and the States.

The Departments/Ministries concerned with the subject of TPP-86 set the annual target in consultation with the States. The Department of Programme Implementation monitors the implementation of 20-Point Programme. Under TPP - 86 there are 119 items identified for monitoring; 54 items are monitored on the basis of evaluatory criteria and 65 items are amenable to physical targeting/ monitoring. Out of 65 items, 20 items are being monitored on monthly basis during the current year.

Monitoring design at the centre

At the Central Governments level, the progress is monitored and reviewed both by the concerned Departments/Ministries and finally by the Department of Programme Implementation which monitors and evaluates the progress on a macro-basis. These monitoring bodies review the progress of TPP-86 and provide feedback for removing bottlenecks in effective implementation of the programmes.

The Management Information System developed by, this Department on the Implementation of the programme consists of (i) Monthly Progress Report (MPR) and (ii) Half-Yearly Progress Report (HYPR). The

Monthly Progress Report covers achievement during each month against pre-set physical targets of carefully selects 20 items which have a direct and crucial bearing on the deprived and under-preveleged classes and those living below the poverty-line. Based upon the performance of TPP, the States are ranked every month. Only 14 items out of 20 items of monthly report are taken for the purpose of ranking. Besides, a half yearly report on all items is brought out by the Department indicating the qualitative aspect of performance.

Performance review in brief

The TPP-86 is monitored on Monthly, Half Yearly and Annual basis. In case of 20 items, physical targets are set and achievements are monitored each month. When the achievements is more than 90 per cent of the target, the performance is categorised as 'very good'. Performance is I good' if the achievement is between 80 to 90 per cent. Performance is 'poor' if the achievements is below 80 percent of the targets. Targets and achievements under TPP-86 during 1996-97, 1997-98 and April 1998 to November 1998 are provided in Annexure II to this chapter. Performance under TPP-86 at Macro level is discussed briefly below.

In the year 1997-98, 'very good' performance was achieved in case of employment creation under Jawahar Rozgar Yojana (JRY). Provisioning of Drinking water In villages and habitations, immunisation of children, Integrated Child Development Services (ICDS) Blocks, Assistance to Scheduled Tribes, Indira Awaas Yojana for SC/ST, slum improvements, tree plantation, village electrification, pumpsets energisation and installation of bio-gas plants. Performance was 'good' in case of opening of Anganwadies, assistance to Scheduled Caste families and installation of improved chullahs. But, in case of distribution of surplus land, opening of community health centres, primary health centres, provisioning of Economically Weaker Section (EWS) and Low Income Group (LIG) houses, and area covered under tree plantation the performance is below 80 per cent of the target and these were identified as areas of concern.

During the period April to November, 1998 'very good' performance was achieved in case of primary health centres, Integrated Child Development Services (ICDS) blocks, opening of Aganwadies, construction of LIG house, slum Improvements, village electrification and pumpsets energisation and area covered under tree plantation. Performance was good in case of employment creation through JRY and immunisation of Children. In case of rest of the items, the achievement was below 80 per cent of the targets.

7

Monitoring of Performance of Infrastructure Sectors

Monitoring of the production performance of the infrastructure sectors was aimed at removing the bottlenecks in the way of their accelerated growth. In the existing scheme, the Infrastructure Monitoring Division (IMD) is collecting relevant statistics of Production and productivity and compiling it in the form of Monthly Reports. This division is entrusted with the monthly performance monitoring of the country's eleven industrial infrastructure sectors viz. Power, Coal, Steel, Railways, Telecommunications, Ports, Fertilizers, Cement, Petroleum & Natural Gas, Roads and Civil Aviation for submission, inter-alia, to the Prime Minister's Office (PMO) and the Cabinet Secretariat. Certain identified parameters of production and productivity relevant to each of the 11 sectors are monitored with reference to their Physical targets along with the achievements in the corresponding period of previous year.

Since every Ministry/Department is concurrently undertaking its own in-depth monitoring, IMD is expected to play a qualitatively different role. The DPI's concern is to bring to the notice of the Administrative Ministries/Departments any slippages or short-comings in the implementation of the schemes/programmes to enable them to take remedial measures for effective and meaningful implementation of the schemes/programmes.

Moreover, being independent of the Planning Commission as well as the implementing agencies, the DPI alone is in a position to look at the entire system and to suggest improvements in a more objective manner.

The following reports are prepared and submitted to the Government by the IMD - (i) Capsule Report on infrastructure Performance, and (ii) Review Report on infrastructure performance.

Overall performance of infrastructure sectors

The economic growth of the country depends considerably upon the performance of the infrastructure sectors. The production performance during the year 1997-98 and for the current year (April-November, 1998) is given in Annexure-I.

Infrastructure performance during April' 1998 -November, 1998

The actual production in respect of all the sectors remained below the target during April-November, 1998. As compared with the achievement of April-November, 1997, the performance in all the sectors except Finished Steel, Railways, Crude Oil and net (new) village public telephones, registered positive growth. The trend in the overall infrastructure performance during April-November, 1998 vis-a-vis the target for the period and the performance of April-November, 1997 is at Annexure-I to tills chapter. The sector-wise performance has been as follows:

Power

The overall power generation during April-November, 1998 at 290.452 BU (Billion Units) represents 98.5% of the target of 294.91 BU. Thermal power generation was below the target by 2.7%. However nuclear and hydro power generation exceeded the target by 14.8% & 1.3%

respectively. The total power generation during the period achieved a growth of 6. 1% over the generation of 273.632 BU during the corresponding period of last year.

Thermal generation

The thermal generation during April - November, 1998 at 225.387 BU remained below the target by 2.7%, but registered a growth of 4.3% over the corresponding period of previous year. The generation in central and private sectors was more than the target by 7.8%, but the generation in state and private sectors was below the target by 8. 1 % and 8.4% respectively. The three central, state and private sectors have achieved a growth of 1 .8, 3.6% and 22.4% respectively over the corresponding period of previous year. The shortfall from the target in the state sector was mainly due to lower contribution from most of the State Electricity Boards.

Plant Load Factors (PLF)

The Plant Load Factor (PLF) of the Thermal Power Stations during April-November, 1998 at 61.9% was lower than the target of 63.0% and the achievement of 62.5% during the corresponding period of last year. During

April - November, 1998, expect Eastern region, the PLF in all other regions were lower than the target.

Hydro generation

The hydro generation during April-November, 1998 at 57.624 BU exceeded target by 1.3% and represented a growth of 13.5% over the achievement of 50.766 BU during the corresponding period of previous year. However, except Northern region, all the regions showed shortfall from the target.

Nuclear generation

The nuclear generation during April-November, 1998 at 7.441 BU was 14.8% higher than the target of 6.484 BU and recorded a growth of 10.7% over the same period last year. However, Narora Atomic Power Station (NAPS) recorded a shortfall from target and the achievement during the corresponding period of last year by 3.1% and 13.7% respectively. RAPS generation at 0.88 BU exceeded the target by 125.6% and recorded a growth of 174.1%.

The overall power supply position in the country during April-November, 1998 showed improvement as compared to the corresponding period of previous year. As against the requirement of 288.81 BU, the availability remained at 2,73.69 BU which was 5.2% short as compared to the shortfall of 8.9% during April-Nov., 1997.

Coal production

The total coal production during April-November, 1998 at 179.68 MT indicated a shortfall from target by 3.0% but achieved a marginal growth of 0.9% over the production of 178.08 MT during the corresponding period of last year. Tile production of Coal India Ltd. (CIL) at 160,12 MT was 1.3% lower than the target of 162.19 MT but it was 1.6% more than the production of corresponding period of previous year. The production of the Singareni Collieries Company Ltd. (SCCL) was less than the target and the production of the corresponding period of last year by 16.7% and 5.0% respectively.

The daily coal loading by Rail during November, 1998 averaged 15,484 wagons per day (wpd) as compared to the target of 20,122 wpd and the loading of 18,545 wpd during the corresponding period of last year by Coal India Ltd.

The overall Coal despatches during April-November, 1998 at 181.00 MT showed a decline of 3.2% against the despatches of 187.03) MT during the corresponding period of last year.

The pithead stock as on 30. 11.98 at 24.54 MT was higher than the stock level of 17.59 MT on 30.11.97.

Finished steel

The overall production of Finished Steel during April-November, 1998 at 15.392 MT remained less than the target of 17.656 MT and the achievement of 15.701 MT during the corresponding period of last year by 12.8% & 2.0% respectively. The production of Finished Steel by Steel Authority of India Ltd. (SAIL) during the period at 4.122 MT remained lower than the target of 4.709 MT and the production of corresponding period of previous year by 12.5% and 11.6% respectively. All the major producers & small producers failed to achieve the target during the period.

Tata iron & steel company

During April-November, 1998 TISCO's production of Finished steel at 1.444 MT was 11.0% lower than the target but it was 18.0 higher than the production of corresponding period of last year.

Visakhapatnam steel plant

During April-November, 1998 VSP's production of Finished Steel at 0.922 MT was 30.4% less than the target of 1.325 MT. It was also 11.0% lower than the production of corresponding period of last year.

Coking coal receipts: steel authority of india limited

The receipt of coking coal including imports at SAIL steel plants during November, 1998 at 38,167 tonnes per day was 3.9% lower than the programme of 39,707 tonnes per day. However, it was 3.0% higher than the receipt of corresponding month of last year.

Coking coal stock: steel authority of india limited

The stock of coking coal (imported + indigenous) at SAIL steel plants at the end of November, 1998 was 3.37 lakh tonnes as against the stock of 3.27 lakh tonnes at the end of November, 1997.

Railways

The revenue earning freight traffic moved by the Railways during April-November, 1998 at 270.53 MT was 6.7% lower than the target of 289.85 MT. It was also 2.2% lower than the actuals of 276.69 NIT during April-November, 1997. The loading of all commodities except iron ore for export, fertilizers and other goods was lower than their respective targets.

Roads

During the period April-September, 1998, a sum of Rs. 306 crores has been spent on repair and maintenance of National Highways as against the annual target of Rs. 496 crores. A sum of Rs. 110 crores has been sanctioned for upgradation of National Highways during April-September, 1998 as against the annual target of Rs.962 crores. 124 Kms National Highways were widened /strengthened during April-September, 1998 against the annual target of 3227 Kms.

Shipping and ports

The total cargo handled at major ports in the country during April-November, 1998 at 162.225 MT was 3.5% lower than the target of 168.086 MT and it was equal to the achievement of the corresponding period of the previous year. The performance of most of the ports was less than the target and the achievement during the corresponding period of last year.

Coastal shipment of coal to the south via Haldia, Paradeep and Vizag ports of Tamil Nadu Electricity Board (TNEB) and the cement plants, aggregating to 10.000 MT was 2.9% higher than the target of 9.72 MT and it was 9.7% more than the achievement of corresponding period of previous year,

As on 30.11.98, 25 vessels were waiting for berth at major ports.

Civil aviation

During April-November, 1998, Mumbai, Calcutta, Delhi and Chennai airports handled 78,100 MT, 10,357 MT, 73,619 MT and 26,070 MT export cargo respectively. The import cargo handled by these airports during the same period was 42,357 MT, 4,713 MT, 29,931 MT and 11,888 NIT respectively. The number of passengers carried at the domestic terminals of Mumbai, Calcutta, Delhi, Madras and Trivandrum together was at 94.23 lakhs as against the capacity of 216.00 lakhs. The number of passengers carried at these International terminals was at 77.47 lakhs as against the total capacity of 104.70 lakhs.

Telecommunications

The net addition in switching capacity during April-November, 1998 at 13.79 lakh lines was 49.4% higher than the corresponding period of previous year.

A total of 13.29 lakh new (net) telephone connections provided during April-November, 1998 represented an increase of 25.5% over the achievement of the corresponding period of last year.

8205 Nos. of Public Telephones provided at village level during April-November, 1998 was 36.4% lower than 12,911 Nos. provided during the corresponding period of previous year.

Fertilisers

During April-November, 1998, the total production of fertilisers (nitrogen and phosphate) at 8.821 MT was 1.8% lower than the target of 8.984 MT but achieved a growth of 4.6% over the production of 8.430 MT during the same period of last year.

Nitrogenous fertilisers production during April-November, 1998 at 6.845 MT was 1.9% lower than the target of 6.98 MT but recorded a growth of 6.1% over the production of 6.45 MT during April-November, 1997. The public sector plants and private sector plants produced less than their respective target by 2.6% & 3.9% respectively. The capacity utilisation remained 97.6% as compared to 99.0% during corresponding period of last year.

The phosphatic fertilisers production at 1.976 MT was 1.4% lower than the target of 2.005 MT. The phosphatic fertilisers' production in the public sector and coop. sector was 2.5% and 20.1% higher than their respective targets for the period but private sector recorded a shortfall of 7.4%. Capacity utilisation was 93.5% as against 102.0% achieved during the corresponding period of last year.

Cement

The total production of cement (including Mini/white) during April-November, 1998 at 54.53 NIT was 5.7% lower than the target of 57.82 MT but achieved a growth of 2.8% over the production of corresponding period of previous year.

The production In Public Sector plants during April-November, 1998 at 2.02 MT was 35.0% less than the target of 3.11 MT but this was 8.1% higher than the production of 1.96 MT during the corresponding period of last year. The capacity utilisation at 77% was the same as recorded during corresponding period of previous year.

Petroleum

Crude Oil: The production of crude oil during April-November, 1998 at 21.666 MT was 5.8% lower than the target of 22.999 MT and it was also 4.0% lower than the production of 22.576 MT during the corresponding period of previous year.

Refinery Production: The refinery production (in terms of crude throughput) during April-November, 1998 at 44.411 MT was slightly lower (0.2%) than the target of 44.509 MT. However, as compared to the achievement in the corresponding period of last year it was 3.0% higher. The performance of Indian Oil Corporation, Guwahati, Hindustan Petroleum Corporation Limited, Vizag,, Madras Refineries Limited, Manali, Indian Oil Corporation, Panipat and Bongaigaon Refinery & Petrochemicals Limited, Assam was less than the target by 15.9%, 29.5%, 7.2% 52. 1% and 15.8% respectively.

The overall capacity utilisation at 98.4% was lower than the achievement of 104.8% in the corresponding period of last year.

Natural Gas Supplies: The supplies of natural gas during April-November, 1998 was 13,146 million cubic metres (MCM) which was 1.3% higher than 12,979 MCM supplied during the corresponding period of last year.

Follow up

The role, as perceived, by the Government includes the presentation for a holistic picture to be placed before the top management of the Government through the process of analytical reports of the achievements or otherwise of the different sectors being monitored was well played by the IMD. This enabled a close interaction with the Ministries/Departments and implementing agencies in order to suggest remedial measures for the consideration of the administrative Ministries/Departments as well as the Cabinet Secretariat and the PMO. Concerted focus made by the Division on the potential constraints and bottlenecks affecting the smooth performance of the infrastructure sectors helped in providing timely signals for applying corrective measures.

8

Management of Projects Implementation

An overview

The Project Monitoring Division (PMD) monitors and facilitates the implementation of projects costing Rs.20 crores and above in the Central sector.

The related important activities of the PMD are as follows:-

- To bring out periodical reports, review notes, suggest remedial measures and facilitate its solution of the problems of projects under Implementation.
- To assist the Public Investment Board. In the case of new projects, the main job of the PMD as one of the board member is critical appraisal of the state of preparedness with respect to the project inputs In terms of land availability, equipment deliveries, feedstock and other linkages necessary for the project completion and its commissioning, and the strength of the organisation/management team for implementation within the stipulated time and cost. In the case of revised cost estimates, the main Job of the PMD is to analyse the causes of time and cost overruns with a view to learning lessons for future and, if necessary, fixing responsibility for time and cost overrun;

- To assist the Committee of Secretaries (COS) headed by Cabinet Secretary which reviews the on-going projects and gives direction for remedial action. The PMD continuously apprises the COS on the constraints in implementation and action taken or initiated by various agencies on its directions;
- To assist the Cabinet Committee oil Infrastructure (CCI), set up under the chairmanship of the Finance Minister. The Minister of State (Independent Charge), Ministry of Planning & Programme Implementation, is a member of this committee,
- To monitor irrigation projects covered under the Accelerated Irrigation Benefit Programme (AIBP).
- To monitor private and joint sector infrastructure projects in Civil Aviation, Coal, Power, Petroleum & Natural Gas, Mines, Ports, Roads and Telecommunication sectors costing Rs. 100 crores and above.
- visit the project sites to identify critical and important milestones for monitoring the project, review the progress of implementation of projects, and hold in depth discussions with the Public Sector Undertakings (PSUs) and administrative ministries/ departments in order to get first hand knowledge of the problems and to initiate facilitative action for resolving them,
- To assist the ministries/departments/public sector undertakings in evolving suitable monitoring system for keeping a close watch oil the projects under their control and timely flow of information;
- To analyse the draft Memoranda of Understanding (MOU) between the Public Sector Undertakings and the Government of India and also assist the Adhoc Task Force and the High Power Committee to make

the MOU system, particularly with respect to the implementation of projects, more effective.

- To motivate the project implementation agencies to strive for excellence in the implementation of projects;
- To carry out evaluation of the on-going projects and expost evaluation of the completed projects, on the basis of completion reports submitted by the PSUs with a view to drawing lessons for the future;
- To organise training programmes in the areas of Project Management, Computerised MIS, etc., for the managers of the PSUs and the Government officers engaged in the implementation of the Public Sector projects;
- To conduct seminars/workshops on various topics in the areas of Project Management & related activities and to make use of the feedback from such seminars and workshops for .strengthening the art of project management in the Country.
- To continuously review project formulation, appraisal, monitoring and implementation system and initiate action to bring improvements; and
- To facilitate development of project management profession by encouraging institutions working in the concerned areas.

Monthly monitoring of major and mega projects

A two tier system of monitoring is adopted. While all projects are monitored on a quarterly basis, the Major projects costing between Rs. 100 and Rs. 1000 crores and Mega projects costing over Rs. 1000 crores are monitored on a monthly basis through Flash Report System. The project records are fully computerised.

A summary Flash Report, together with an analysis of the report, is sent to the Prime Minister's Office/Cabinet Secretariat and to the concerned Ministries/Departments (in respect of their projects for information and requisite action).

Each Ministry/Departments is required to analyse the, reasons for slippage of the critical milestones and send a report to the PMD indicating action taken/proposed to be taken to tackle different problems reported by the project authorities. The reports received from the Ministries/Departments are scrutinised and a consolidated "Exception Report" for all the projects costing above Rs. 100 crores is drawn Lip before the end of the month.

The Exception Report concentrates on the exceptional issues and problems of the projects causing further delays in the commissioning schedule and non-achievement of the milestones in the preceding month. The critical and chronic issues requiring action at the higher levels are also brought into focus repeatedly. The emphasis is on exceptions and problems that need to be tackled without delay.

Quarterly monitoring of all projects

The Division prepares Quarterly Project Implementation Status Reports (QPISR) in respect of all projects, costing Rs.20 crores and more, in each sector. Each QPISR covers salient features of the projects in the sectors and indicates, among other things, the latest commissioning date, cumulative expenditure on the project upto the end of the quarter reported on and the time and cost over-runs. This Report is also kept in the Parliament library for reference. The report is also forwarded to the Minister incharge of the concerned Ministries by the Minister of State for Planning and Programme Implementation.

Scenario of project implementation in 1998-99

As on 01.04.98 there were 461 projects on the monitor of the DPI. During the period April to Dec.98, 5 7 projects were dropped and 17 new projects were added to the monitor. Thus, there were 421 projects on the monitor of DPI as on 1.1.1999 involving an estimated investment of Rs. 1,61,585 crores.

Status of projects during the ninth plan

At the beginning of the Ninth Plan (as on 0 1.04.1997) there were 415 Projects on the monitor, of DPI. Out of these 17 number of projects were dropped/frozen, 96 projects completed till the end of 2nd quarter of 1998-99. This includes 37 projects completed during the year 1998-99 (upto December, 98), the details of which are given is Annexure-IV. In addition 112 projects are scheduled to be completed by March, 1999. This will make a total of 149 projects to be completed in 1998-99.

Causes of time and cost overrun

As an apex-monitoring agency, the DPI provides management services to the Government. It is not only providing information on the Implementation of projects but also on system improvements. These could be at any stage from conception to completion. The DPI suggests project/sector specific as well as systemic changes/ improvements required overcoming constraints. Project Monitoring Division also acts as a coordinator and facilitator within its limitations of manpower and other resources in resolving various critical problems in the implementation of projects.

The PMD's analysis shows that the time overrun is the most serious problem because apart from upsetting the plan targets, it also leads to cost overrun. With time overrun, cost goes up on account of inflationary pressure, exchange rate variations, higher incidence of interest during construction,, higher incidence of administrative overheads, etc. The major causes of time overrun include sanction of projects without firming Lip of techno-economic parameters, sanction in excess of financial resources, uncertainty about the availability of forest and non-forest land, contractual problems, Inadequate delegation of power to the field level executives and poor performance of consultants, vendors and contractors. The other factors include delay in obtaining clearances, court cases, inadequate infrastructure support, and poor law & order situation in certain parts of the country.

Remedial measures

On the basis of the analysis of problems carried Out by the DPI, reports of Group of Ministers and Committees of Secretaries, a number of specific measures have been initiated to cut delays in project implementation, These include more strict appraisal and sanction of projects, weeding out/transfer to the private/joint sector projects which are unable to make progress, re-prioritisation of projects in the light of resource constraints, filling the board level vacancies in the PSUs, appointment of a nodal officer for each project with long tenure and accountability for implementation, formation of Empowered Committees in the administrative Ministries for constant review of status and constraints in respect of Government-owned projects, quarterly performance review of the projects being implemented by the PSUs, delegation of power to the field level executives, strengthening of the monitoring system including introduction of on-line computerised monitoring system for updated information about the status and giving advance warning for remedial measures, yearly updating of sanctioned cost, improvement in contract management system, higher weightage to project implementation in the Memorandum of Understanding signed between the administrative Ministries and PSUs, etc.

The DPI's analysis shows that if time overrun Could be checked nearly 75 per cent of the cost overrun could be checked. Therefore DPI's future strategy is largely to control time overrun in projects. As advised by the Planning Commission, action has already been taken by various Ministries to constitute Standing Committees for analysing the reasons for time and cost overruns and fixing responsibilities for the same, while examining the RCEs of various projects.

Each Ministry, Department has set up a task force to review the Contract Management System and other project management procedures with view to draw up transparent contract management system which would be applicable nation wide.

Other important activities of the department during 1998-99

As an integral part of the monitoring exercise, various problem solving initiatives were taken by the PMD during the year. The main activities were as follows:

The Division took follow up action on the specific measures approved by the Government. These measures are being implemented in consultation with the concerned Ministries/Departments.

During the year upto Dec.'98, the PMD carried out in-depth analysis of 7 new projects and assisted the PIB in approval of these projects. The PMD also carried out analysis of the revised cost estimates of 4 projects with a view to identifying the major factors responsible for time and cost overrun. The following reports/RCE were examined by the PMD during 1998-99 (till Dec.98)

- PIB note on ULDC for Eastern Region.
- PIB note on Inter Regional Line between Eastern & Northern Region.
- RCE-Kayamkulam Transmission line.

- RCE-Kopili HEP Expansion.
- PIB note on SCI acquisition of 2 vessels of 4500 DMT each.
- PIB note on Udham open cost project.
- PIB note on ULDC for Western Region.
- PIB note on Talchar STPS-II Transmission scheme.
- Examined the proposal of the Dredging Corporation of India to acquire two dredgers of 6500 cubic meter each.
- RCE-II of Nathpa Jhakri HEP.
- RCE of Koel Karo HEP.

During the year upto Dec.'98 following projects were inspected and reviewed at the sites at different levels. Some of the Projects visited and reviewed by the officers of PMD are listed below:-

- HPCL of Mumbai, Panipat & Mathura Refinery, Cochin Refinery, Visakh Refinery.
- IOC's Refineries at Panipat, Mathura, Koyali & Haldia.
- BPCL's Bombay Refinery.
- Madras Refinery at Chennai of CRL.
- Mumbai Manmad pipe line of BPCL at Mumbai.
- Visakh-Vijaywada pipeline for review and the status of SCDA Ultra-Ferric Oxide Project of NMDC
- Reviewed the Visakh Refinery of HPCL for equipment supply problem.
- Construction of Terminal Ph-III at Mumbai Airport.
- Modernisation of Air Traffic System at Mumbai, Airport.

- Construction of 2nd hanger, AI at Mumbai.
- 4 Modernisation/replacement projects of Mumbai Ports.
- Halida - Barauni Crude Oil pipeline terminal at Haldia.
- Uranium Mill Expansion at Narwaphar of UCIL..

The following important notes/reports were prepared during the year (upto Dec. 1998):

- Prepared a note on the 7 selected projects for review by the Secretary(Expenditure).
- Revised guide lines for the formation and functioning of the "Empowered Committee" in the Ministries Implementing Projects departmentally and other matters relating to project management were finalised and issued.
- A note for COS was prepared on the status of the implementation of various specific measures approved by CCEA and COS and also along with other the suggestions and remedial measures to improve Project Implementation and cut down time and cost overrun in projects.
- The proposal for new railway projects were examined and comments sent to the Ministry of Railways to facilitate discussion in the meeting of the Expanded Board.
- For the Monitoring of the Projects in the Joint/ Private sector based on the format designed by the DPI and instructions issued by the Cabinet Secretariat the concerned Ministries were followed up to provide basic information to the DPI.
- Provided assistance to the Govt. of U.P. in preparing the Technology Mission and in designing a suitable Monitoring and evaluation system for the UP Govt.

and the Chief Minister.

- A system of review by the Prime Minister's Office was introduced in May, 1998. The PMD prepared Special Monitoring Reports for review by the PMO.
- A brief report on the implementation of projects in the North-Eastern Region was prepared and forwarded to the Ministry of Home Affairs for the information of the Standing Committee of that Ministry.
- The Interim Report on the restructuring for the Department of Programme Implementation submitted by the S.M.G. was examined and commented upon to include full facts on the work handled by the PMD.
- A brief note on the problem of Mega and major projects relating to the clearances and land accusation by the Govt. of Bihar was prepared and submitted for the consideration of the Minister of State to take up with the C.M. of Bihar.
- A note for the COS on the specific measures and other measures to fill the gap in the guidelines issued by the Govt. to cut delays in implementation was prepared and submitted
- A note for COS on the on-line monitoring system was prepared and submitted for the consideration of the COS.
- A detailed note has been prepared on the four major projects one each in power, petroleum, road and ports for review by the FM. These were reviewed by the Finance Secretary In the initial stages.
- A note on the implementation of projects in the NE Region was prepared for the consideration of the

High Level Committee and attended the Meeting at Agartala.

- A note was prepared on the 15th Expanded Board Meeting of Railways for project costing Rs. 50 crores and more. The meeting was attended by the Secretary.
- Note was prepared to consider setting up of Indian Railway Catering and Tourism Corporation.
- The Draft MOU of 35 enterprises were examined in detail, comments prepared and issued for the consideration of Adhoc Task Force and attended the negotiation meetings.
- A note for COS on the private/Joint Sector projects in the mining/non-ferrous sector was prepared highlighting the status of projects which are In the process of implementation / in the process of approval/obtaining clearances and Submitted for consideration of the COS.

The officers of the PMD attended various meetings during the year. Some of the important meetings attended are listed below:-

- Attended the meeting of the Standing Committee of the MHA to examine time & cost overrun for Regional Institute of Medical Sciences and Rokhia Gas Power station stage-II
- Attended PIB meeting and discussed the Joint venture proposal of 9 MMTPA, grass root refinery at Bhatinda Punjab (HPCL)
- Attended the meeting of Standing Committee for fixing responsibility for time & cost overrun for. Madras Fertiliser Ltd. (MFL), Nathpha Jhakri HEP, Rangit HEP and Fertiliser Projects in private sector.
- Attended PIB Meeting of RCE of Nathpha Jhakri HEP.

- Attended meeting of the Empowered Committee of Ministry of Power to review progress of Tehri HEP and Naphtha Jhakri HEP
- Attended Pre-PIB Meeting on Koel Karo HEP.
- Attended the PIB Meeting to acquire two dredgers of 6500 cubic metre by Dredging Corporation of India.
- Attended PIB/Pre-PIB meeting on Transmission System associated with Talcher STPS Stage II and on RCE of Visakh Refinery Expansion Project.

The officer of the PMD also attended the performance review meetings of the PSUs for the quarter ending June and September chaired by the Secretaries of the concerned Ministries/Departments.

Future strategy for better project implementation

The Implementation of projects on schedule can be ensured only through constant monitoring, evaluation of activities and constantly highlighting the slippages in project implementation and taking initiatives in problem solving. With this view in mind the PMD is constantly reviewing existing system of monitoring and suggesting improvements to be made in the system to make it more effective and result oriented. Some of the strategic Action Points drawn out by the PMD are as follows:

- Analysis of investment proposals from the point of view of the state of preparedness, organisational and managerial capabilities of the project management, Availability of funds and linkages.
- Persuading the project enterprises to prepare the detailed project plan with full consultation of all agencies including State Governments for providing necessary land, infrastructure and clearances.
- Increasing the awareness of latest project

management techniques including computerisation of PERT programmes for project planning, implementation and monitoring.

- To constantly review the effectiveness of the specific measures recommended by the CCEA and the Committee of the Secretaries to cut delays in the implementation of projects and suggest improvement from time to time.
- Introduce an On-line Computerised Monitoring System (OCMS), restructure the input and output reports and, if necessary, redefine the role of the DPI in regard to the Project Management as a whole. The OCMS is aimed to strengthen the DPI in timely reporting, flagging of problem for resolving and giving warning signals if a project is going out of track leading-to time and cost overruns.

Sectorial analysis of projects under implementation

The Sectorwise analysis of projects under implementation with brief details of all mega and some selected major projects In each sector and the problem solving initiatives taken by the Department in respect of these projects is outlined in the following paragraphs.

Atomic energy

As on 1st April, 1998 there were 6 projects on the monitor Out of these 6 projects, 4 projects are directly connected with power generation. There are 3 mega projects pertaining to Nuclear Power with a total anticipated cost of Rs 10803 Crores. The fourth project (Coolant tube replacement at Rajasthan Atomic Power Station's unit II) is in the category of revamp of an existing nuclear power reactor. The other two, are projects belonging to the Nuclear Fuel Complex, Hyderabad, for manufacturing fuel for commercial power reactors and Uranium Ore Extraction.

The total anticipated cost of these 6 projects on the DPI's Monitors Rs. 11462.27 crores. The two nuclear power projects have suffered high cost and time overruns due to reasons peculiar to this sector. The escalation in cost reported by the Rajasthan and Kaiga Atomic Power Projects with respect to original cost were, 196 percent and 211 percent respectively. Another nuclear power project recently taken on the monitor, was the 2x500 MWe Tarapur Atomic Power Project, at an initial cost of Rs. 3447.06 Crores, approved earlier by the GOI in Jan '1991.

However permission has been granted by the Govt. recently in December, 1997 to start implementing the project. Its latest approved cost is Rs. 6421 crores and an expenditure of Rs. 90 crores has been incurred on purchase of long delivery items Stricter safety conditions, as required by the Atomic Energy Regulatory Board (AERB), is one of the features of Nuclear Power Project Implementation. Contractors must be prequalified to undertake work pertaining to the Nuclear power station. General inflation, change in scope and higher safety norms as stipulated by AERB, are the main reasons for cost and also time overrun. There is a need to reduce time overrun in Nuclear Power Projects through faster pace of civil construction as also expediting resolution of problems by AERB. Fund flow to the site should be expedited. The consequent delays, due to the non-availability of funds, and other technical reasons (mainly slow pace of civil works and continuous slippage of equipment deliveries and its erection at site), lead to the large increase in cost, of which an increasing component is that of the interest during construction (IDC). It is now around 32% of the total cost of the projects. Shorter gestation period is one of the solution to reduce IDC. Firming up designs / specifications for equipment, stations & civil works and also duplication of, similar capacity power reactor units with minimal changes, is essential to have faster pace of construction.

Atomic power projects

In the case of Kaiga Atomic Power Project, major civil works for Reactor Buildings 1 & 2, Turbine Buildings 1 & 2, Service building, Reactor Auxiliary Buildings 1 & 2 and control buildings are complete. The major items of equipment (calandria vessel for the two reactors, Primary Heat Transport System, Active Process Cooling System, erection of condenser upto top neck in Reactor 2, Steam generator header and Turbo Generator for Unit I etc.) are already being erected. In Reactor Building-1, all construction work pertaining to inner & outer containment dome was at a stand still for the last 40 months. The AERB has approved the design and the basis for construction of the new IC dome for the reactor No. 1 at Kaiga, but complete drawings were provided by AERB to the construction authorities at Kaiga, during the middle of the year 98. The dome has been dismantled and a new dome based on AERB approved design will be constructed. The erection of Induced Draft Cooling Tower at both the reactor sites is proceeding as per schedule. The erection of compressors, Active Process Water (APW) pumps/pipings, erection of moderator pumps and piping are complete. Fueling machine head & Fueling Transfer System for Unit 2 completed & unit I is not complete. Air hold helium leak test and flushing, for Unit primary heat transport systems hydrotest and logic test, earlier scheduled for 1997-98 for both the reactors at Kaiga have now been further rescheduled to 1998-99 & for Unit 2 these tests have been completed. In the case of Rajasthan Atomic Power Project, some works such as active process water pumps and associated piping installation of fueling machine head, fuel transport system and the PHT Hydro test are behind schedule and are now expected to be completed in 1998-99. In the other areas of the Reactor construction, progress is satisfactory. Criticality for both Kaiga & Rajasthan projects is now scheduled for the latter part of 1999-2000. Commercial power will be generated 6 months - 8 months latter to the criticality date. Cooling channel replacement project for RAPP-II has been completed ahead of schedule and the reactor has been made critical , in May 1998. Civil works has started on the 2x500 MW Tarapur Atomic Power Project 3&4 & and it is expected to go critical by 2007-08.

Nuclear fuel projects

Three projects at Nuclear Fuel Complex (NFC) at Hyderabad, namely, setting up of a 80 TPY (Phase-I) New Zircalloy Fabrication project, New Uranium Oxide Fuel Project (capacity 670 TPY), New Uranium Fuel Assembly Project (capacity 600 TPY) are all linked to the Nuclear Power Stations projects under implementation. Two of these projects (i.e. New Zircalloy Fabrication facility and New Uranium fuel assembly project) have been commissioned by the end of 1996 - 97 and made fully operational in 1997-98. There has, however, been a delay of more than 29 months in the case of Uranium Oxide plant with respect to the original schedule, mainly due to delays in the supply of equipment and their erection at site. This project has been commissioned during the 3rd quarter of year 1998-99.

Atomic mineral project

The Narwa Pahar-Jaduguda Uranium Mill expansion project was approved by the Government in April, 1989 at a cost of Rs. 495.54 crores (January, 1988 base) to be financed entirely by the Government. This project now comprises of the mining facility at Narwa Pahar and expansion of the existing Uranium mill at Jaduguda. This will supply Ammonium Di Uranate which is the raw material for the new Uranium oxide plant at NFC Hyderabad. Project comprises underground mines at Narwa Pahar, for which, entry is through a series of declines. The vertical mine shaft is complete and shaft head equipment has been installed. Ore extraction on a commercial basis is on. Uranium Mill expansion project at Jaduguda, delayed due to late delivery of equipment, is now complete and is to get AERB clearance for full commercial operation. This project will be made operational on a commercial basis during the year 1998-99. The cost of this project, has been scaled down to Rs. 311.41, crores due to the change in scope.

Civil aviation

There were total 10 projects (3 major and 7 medium) costing Rs. 949.27 crores on the monitoring system upto September, 1998. The project implementation status of important major projects is as under:

Modernisation of air traffic services at Bombay and Delhi airport by national airport authority

The project was approved in June, 90 with date of completion as Oct., 92 and cost Rs. 210 crores. However, the anticipated date of completion was June, 1998 and estimated cost Rs. 351.87 crores. The main features of the project are (i) enhancement of the present handling capacity of 10 to 12 aircrafts per hour to 35 to 40 aircrafts per hour. (ii) More safe landing and take off facilities, and (iii). Reduction in approach and landing phase of flying time resulting in substantial saving in fuel And time. The scope of work includes construction of new control and technical building and installation of latest radars. The NBCC and EIL are the project managers for civil works at Delhi and Bombay respectively. The Raytheon of USA is turnnkey contractor for all equipment including the Radar.

The project was mechanically completed by 9/98. Trial runs have been completed. Modifications and system optimization are in progress.

Terminal complex phase-III at Mumbai (AAI)

The proposal for the construction of Phase-III of the International terminal Complex at Bombay Airport is a part of master plan for the Bombay Airport. The Phase-I was commissioned in 1980 and Phase -II in March 1986 The combined Phase-I and II capacity in peak hour handling is 4200 pax., and annual handling capacity of 50 Lakh pax. The existing international terminal , (Phase I & II) is likely to be saturated during the year 1993-94 when the traffic would be 51.66 lakh. To cater the additional traffic, Phase-III is planned which will have additional area of 55000 sq.m. with the addition of Phase - III, the resultant capacity of the international terminal (peak hour : 6300 pax-, annual 75 lakh pax) will suffice upto the year 2000-2001.

Foreign Exchange Components: Rs. 5.72 crores (incl. In Rs. 84.12 crores for 8 aerobridges) Finance: The entire expenditure on the project is financed from the internal resources of AAI.

In order to utilise the land area to the maximum extent, the design of the building was modified to 70, 865 sqm. With an estimated cost of Rs. 142.32 crores and date of completion as 12/97 which was shifted to May 1998 due to enrichment of specifications to bring it at par with the international standards. The building is two and a half level terminal and is being provided with 4 in-contact bays for B747 type of aircrafts.

The work is in advanced stage of completion on all fronts. Some delays have taken place due to increase in cost and scope of additional work and fire protection regulation requirements. The project is likely to be completed by 8/99. The project is being closely monitored by the DPI to keep the latest schedule.

Coal

In the beginning of the year 1998-99, there were 71 projects costing Rs.20 crores and above on the monitoring system. During the course of the first two quarters of the year, 12 projects were dropped from system and 2 were added to the monitoring system.

Thus, there are 61 projects 4 mega, 16 major and 41 medium on the monitoring system, with a total cost of Rs. 12598.02 crores. 25 projects are for opencast mines, 33 for underground mines and 3 other projects belong to non-mining sector such as CPP, Workshop and other allied facilities required for existing and new mines.

Out of 61 projects, 10 projects had cost overrun aggregating to Rs. 900 crores. 28 projects are showing time overrun, ranging between 2-120 months with reference to the latest approved schedule.

The problems of land acquisition, supply of equipment, fund constraints and Geo-mining problems have delayed a large number of coal projects. The analysis of projects on the monitoring system shows that 7 mega and major projects are suffering from land acquisition problems. 5 are having equipment supply problem, 1 each is delayed due to civil works and funds problem. Overall, 15 Mega and Major projects out of 20 are reporting one or the other problem.

The implementation status of some of the mega/major projects are summarised as follows:

Life extension of TPS-I (NLC)

Life Extension of TPS-I of Neyveli Lignite Corporation was taken up to renovate the existing units of Stage-I which have completed almost 27 years of service. The scheme is to carry on renovation of Units-9. This would increase the life of the plants by another 15 years. The contract had been signed with M/s. Technopromenom export (TPE Moscow) and their Indian associates ACC Bobcock Ltd. ABL on 3.5.92. The latest anticipated cost of project is Rs. 259.56 crores as against the original cost of Rs. 315.23 crores (for all the nine units). Unit-I was completed on 23rd April, 1994 and unit-9 m 19.11.94 respectively Unit -4 was completed in 1996. There has been a delay of about one year in the implementation of the contract by TPE and ABL due to delay in receipt of certain equipment. The work on Unit-1 and 9 were completed on 23rd July, 1994 and 29 November, 1994 respectively. The time taken was 29 months against the schedule of 12 months. Unit 3,5 and Unit 7 were planned to be completed by March, 1998 but delayed due to delay in delivery of equipment and have since been completed. For Unit-2 and 8, the work is in advanced stage and unit 6 was released recently for LEP works. The project is likely to be completed by March, 1999.

Mine I expansion project

This project was sanctioned by the Government in March '92 at a total cost of Rs. 1336.93 crores with a foreign exchange component of Rs. 278.28 crores at 7/91 base. The Completion schedule of the project is 55 months from the date of project sanctioned. The project was sanctioned to step up the lignite output from 6.5 MT to 10.5 MT per annum. The project envisages the step up of lignite production by deployment of additional Specialised Mining Equipments, supported by other conventional Mining and ancillary equipments and also by creation of one or more overburden system of higher capacity for tackling the increased overburden cover. KFW loan signed in March, 1997 only and funding arrangement for rupee portion is yet to be signed. The sanction for the linked Thermal Power Station-I Expansion Scheme (2x210 MW) was given in February, 1996 and scheduled for completion by March, 2001. M/s. ISEC have been appointed as Trusted Financial Adviser to help NLC in mobilising the funds required for implementing both Mine-I and TPS-I Expansion projects. Loan agreement for funding Foreign Exchange portion was signed on 13.03.1997 only. LOI has been issued on 10.08.1998.

Dhudichua (NLC)

The project was sanctioned by Government in February, 1984 for an investment of Rs. 289.68 crores and for an annual output of capacity of 5 MTY to be reached by 3/94. The implementation of the project was taken up with the World Bank assistance of US$ 151 m and the construction of the project has been completed one year ahead of schedule i.e. in March, 1991.

In original proposal for development of Dudhichua project, NCL had presented a developmental plan for an ultimate output of 10 MTY. However, when the project was discussed in the meeting of IMG on 11th January, 1982, it was decided that project may be developed in 2 stages i.e. Stage-I of 5 MTY and ultimate Stage of 10 MTY. Accordingly, the Govt. had approved the first Stage of 5 MTY which was implemented. With the increasing demand of coal for power sector during 8th & 9th Plan period it had become necessary to augment the production capacity to 10 MTY. The Govt. had sanctioned expansion of the project for 10 MTY at a capital cost of Rs. 868.93 crores on 25.08.92 including the Foreign exchange component of Rs. 163.13 crs. (increased from Rs. 147.29 crs.) out of which US (S 108.36 m) is committed. As per the CMPDI estimate of April, 1995, the anticipated cost is Rs. 1149.04 crs. Due to delay of project CMPDIL has been requested to prepare RCE. Land required for the purpose is 1748 Ha. Possession till date is 1470, ha. The investment is substantially lagging due to fund constraints. However, the project has been posed to World Bank for funding. The loan became effective only in June, 1998. Major activities including procurement of HEMM, suffered due to delay in arranging loan, are now progressing.

The Jhanjra underground project of ECL

The Jhanjra Under Ground project of ECL was sanctioned by Government in December, 1982 for a targeted capacity of 3.5 MT and a capital investment of Rs. 184.55 crores. The completion of project was scheduled for 3/94. Jhanjra is a deep underground mine which was designed by the experts of erstwhile USSR. Project was implemented in initial years in collaboration with Soviet Union for sinking of shafts and drivage of main coal clearance incline. Two shafts A & B and main coal clearance incline were driven by erstwhile USSR as per agreement. Two sets of power supports longwall equipment were also procured from USSR. Subsequently due to disintegration of erstwhile USSR serious difficulties were faced in procurement of further longwall equipment as well as spares for the equipment already procured. Components and spares for longwall were manufactured in 4 different states of erstwhile USSR. There were serious bottlenecks in shipping facilities and coordination. The major critical activity was the sinking of shafts A & B which was delayed by 34 months and consequently the other activities were held up. M/s. HEC had delayed supply of winders for the shaft A by 14 months. M/s. Triveni structure delayed the erection of head gear by 21 months. The resultant effect of all these factors accounted for the overall delay of 48 months from its original schedule (3/94 to 3/98).

Committee of Secretaries reviewed the project and suggested that project should be taken up in two phases. Phase-I for 2 MT capacity and from 2 to 3.5 MTY capacity should be taken up as Phase II. In August, 1994 Govt. sanctioned Phase I of the project (2.0 MTY) with the capital cost of Rs. 403.9 crores. (inclusive of Rs. 17.72 crores for advance action activities for phase II).

The project completion was envisaged by March, 1998. The increase in the project's cost was mainly on account of delay of 4 years during which the normal escalation was Rs. 58.69 crores, taxes and duties variation by 79.14 crores and financing and other charges Rs. 51.65 crores (Total Rs. 189.48 crores). Change in scope etc. account for the net increase of Rs. 31.45 crores. The major problems coming in the way of speedy implementation of the project are:

- Procurement of longwall spares from CIS countries.
- Supply of extensible belt conveyor from MAMC.
- Installation of 4th Longwal set from Churcha project after refurbishing etc.

The project is now expected to be completed by March, 2002.

Finance (deptt. of expenditure)

At present, there is only one project under implementation.. The scope of the project is to modernise the mints situated at Bombay, Hyderabad and Calcutta in March 1989 with date of completion as March 1992 and estimated cost Rs. 118.28 crores. However, now the anticipated date of completion is March, 1999 and cost Rs.348.80 crores. The project envisages shifting of Hyderabad Mint to a new location at Cheerlapalli (an industrial area at the outskirts of Hyderabad city) and for other 2 mints, modernisation in the existing premises. The project activities at Bombay and Calcutta are far behind schedule due to delay in Civil works. The Hyderabad Mint has been commissioned.

Fertilizer

There are 3 projects on the monitoring system in the beginning of the year. One project, namely the Haldia Fertilizer Project, of the HFC continues to be in the frozen stage and it will be taken off the list of active fertilizer projects under implementation once the final decision is taken by the CCEA. During the year 1998-99, Ammonia Plant Replacement Project of FACT was commissioned. With this commissioning, there is only one project namely Kandla Phase-II DAP- NPK of IFFCO under implementation.

Kandla phase-II DAP-NPK project (IFFCO)

This project, approved by the Government of India in January, 1997 at a cost of Rs. 212.2 crores with a foreign exchange component of Rs. 18.1 crores, involves setting up a DAP-NPK plant with a capacity of 2 lakh tonne per annum. For the main plant and the offsites, Indian consultants M/s Hindustan Dorr Oliver and M/s PDIL have been employed. The progress so far in the case of main plant is 87.55% and in the case of offsites, progress is 75.85%. Commitments till date is Rs. 166.2 crores. with Rs. 95.76 crores expenditure already incurred. 100% detailed engineering has been completed. The purchase requisitions, technical specifications and engineering drawings have been finalised.

Information & broadcasting

As on 30.12.98 there were 7 projects (5 of AIR and 2 of Doordarshan). The total anticipated cost of these project was Rs. 316.91 crs. Implementation of AIR projects was slow, particularly in the project of setting up of studios at Borivilli, Bombay (the Short Wave Transmission facilities at Goa for these Studios had been set up more than two years back). Civil works of construction of Doordarshan Bhavan at Delhi progressed during the year. Most of the equipment installation projects have been redesigned in view of latest developments in transmission technology.

It was reported by the All India Radio that implementation of its projects at times was delayed mainly due to delay in the procurement of equipment /material etc. One of the Doordarshan project at Bombay is nearing completion.

Mines

As on 1st April 1998, there were three projects, with a total anticipated cost of Rs. 3884.08 Crores. Two of them, are mega projects, costing Rs. 3726.58 Crores. One of the projects, namely, Expansion of NALCO's Bauxite Mines from 2.4 MTPY to 4.8 MTPY, with an associated Alumina Refinery, to be expanded from 0.8 to 1.575 MTPY, costing Rs. 1664.60 crores, is to be set up at Damanjodi, Orissa with a gestation period of 36 months, & will be operational by March, 2001. The other mega project, also belonging to NALCO, involves setting up of an Aluminium smelter for increasing the capacity of the existing smelter from 2,30,000 tonnes to 324000 tonnes along with a captive power unit of 110 MW capacity. The third project, belonging to BALCO, involves installation of a cold rolling mill at its Korba Smelter Complex in Madhya Pradesh with an anticipated cost of Rs. 157.5 crores including a foreign exchange component of Rs. 103.11 crores. All the basic engineering packages for the Bauxite mine and Alumina project has been received and major orders for equipment and also civil / mechanical contracts placed. The Aluminium smelter project is still in the initial stage of implementation and agreement has been signed with the foreign collaborator for knowhow. In this project placement of order for 120 MWe Steam Turbine Generator is yet to be placed. In the case of BALCO's cold rolling mill, orders for all major equipment such as strip casting machine and cold rolling mill, as also nitrogen plant have been placed.

Steel

As on 1st April, 1998, there were 9 projects on the DPI Monitoring System. The anticipated cost of these 9 projects was Rs. 8871.90 Crores. This included two mega projects, whose anticipated cost is Rs. 7347.58 Crores. The other projects on the monitor include Coke dust injection project at Bokaro & Bhilai Steel Plants, third sinter plant at Bhilai Steel Plant all belonging to SAIL and development of iron ore deposit of 10/11A at Bailadila in M.P & Ultra Pure Feric Oxide plant, at Visakh in A.P. by NMDC. During the year major global packages in Bokaro & four out of five global packages in Raurkela modernisation project have been fully commissioned. The long delay and high cost escalation suffered by the projects in the steel sector are mainly due to under estimation in the initial stages, change of scope when the project is being executed and exchange rate variation affecting the Indian rupee, which resulted in high cost of those packages having large import content in terms of equipment and also other services. The time overrun is also due to poor resource mobilisation by the local contractors, due mainly to the poor state of finance of some of the contractors. Other locally based major and medium sized fabricators/ contractors employed in turn by turnkey contractors for global packages in the private sector have also contributed to of slippages. The delayed delivery of equipments is, the other main problem, affecting this sector. It is also observed that PSUs like Heavy Engineering Corporation, Ranchi, Triveni structurals Ltd., Hindustan Steel Construction Ltd. as also capital equipment manufacturers in the private sector do not generally adhere to the delivery schedule for equipment.

Rourkela steel plant modernisation project (SAIL)

This project with anticipated cost of Rs. 4938.01 crores was approved in July, 1988. The original date of commissioning was April, 1995 and now anticipated date of commissioning (all packages) is October, 1998 and has already suffered a delay of 42 months. This project is divided in two phases with Phase-I scheduled for commissioning in July, 1993) and Phase-II consisting of 5 global & 10 indigenous packages. The Phase I and most of the Phase 2 package have been commissioned. Out of 5 global packages, Concast Plant package, Basic Oxygen furnace, Sinter plant II, plate mill and reheating furnace No.6 have been commissioned. Work on reheating furnace No. 5 have been delayed and it will be completed by October '99. For all practical purposes, modernisation project of Raurkela Steel Plant is complete in all respects. The expenditure, as on December, 1998 is Rs. 4163.86 crores. The now anticipated cost of this project is Rs. 5112.13 crores. The main constraints in the execution of this project are the lack of full mobilisation of resources by contractors and late delivery of equipment at site, and need to plan shutdowns, for carrying out project work in a functioning plant.

Modernisation of stage I of Bokaro Steel Plant (SAIL)

The present project costing Rs. 1625.79 crores (FE Rs. 283 crores) approved by GOI in July '1993 involves reconstruction of the existing Steel Melting Shop No.II (to increase its liquid steel capacity from 1.84 MTPA to 2.25 MTPA), installation of 2 double strand slab casters, partial upgradation of 2000 MM Hot strip mill &.Related service facilities. Detailed Engg. have been completed. Reheating Furnace No.3 which is part of the modernisation project (reheating furnace package) is to be commissioned by March '99. Operation of Reheating Furnace No.4 has been stabilised. The civil works in hot strip are nearing completion. Work oil coiler No. 2&3 has been completed. Hot trials of coiler No.2 has been completed in June '98 and subsequently commissioned. Coiler No.3 was completed in October '98 and expected to be commissioned by the end of the year. Automation, instrumentation & mill electrics for Hot Strip mill global package No.3 has been completed. As against the anticipated cost of Rs. 1792.90 crores, the expenditure as on Dec., 1998 is Rs. 1956.82 crores. The project is expected to be completed fully by the first quarter of 1999 -2000.

Bailadila iron ore deposit 10 & 11A project and ultra pure ferric oxide project at Visakhapatanam, (NMDC)

This project costing Rs. 430.50 crores with a foreign exchange component of Rs. 18.61 crores was approved by the Govt. in August 1995. The gestation period for this project is 48 months. All major (process and Crushing equipment) equipment for execution of this project have been ordered. Major constraint in the implementation of the project is delay in obtaining the mining lease and forest clearance. The mining lease, given by the M.P. Government on the basis of final clearance of MOEF communication dated 29-07-1998, in respect of Bailadila deposit NO 10 ML and Bld no. deposit 11, is of temporary nature and they have been advised to Continue working only in already broken area till formal renewal of Mining Lease is granted. MP govt. have advised the NMDC to follow the orders of the Supreme Court that no trees are to be felled in the forest of Bastar District even under any permission granted by the local administration until further orders. MP Govt, has advised the NMDC to approach the Supreme Court for tree cutting clearance in Bastar District. The project is making satisfactory progress till now but in the absence of full clearance, work in block 11 will suffer and it may lead to slippages such as in the construction of process plant. Structural fabrication work, is in progress (4731 MT out of a total scope of 7275 MT) and erection going on in areas where statutory clearances are not required. In the case of Ultra pure ferric oxide plant at Visakhapatanam (capital cost Rs. 47.93) Crores with a cumulative expenditure of Rs. 36.99 crores and commitment of Rs. 46 crores till date), plant erection is complete and trial runs are expected to start in Dec '98 and plant fully commissioned by March 1999.

Chemicals & petro-chemicals

As on 1st April, 1998, there were 3 projects of the IPCL on the monitoring system of the DPI, with the total anticipated cost being Rs. 3852.6 Crores. Of these 3 projects, Gandhar Petro-chemical complex, located at Dahej in District Bharuch, Gujarat, is a mega project costing Rs. 3505.00 crores. The other 2 major projects, approved in May 1992, are down-stream units of the Maharashtra Gas Cracker Complex (MGCC) at Nagothane, Maharashtra.

Gandhar petro-chemical complex

This project with 3 lakh TPA capacity of Ethylene and associated down stream conversion units with a capacity of 1.5 lakh TPA of Poly Vinyl Chloride (PVC) & one lakh TPA of Alpha Olefins was approved by the Government of India in March, 1992. The project authorities are now executing the project in two phases. Phase I (first phase consists of putting up a 1.5 lakh TPA, PVC Plant based on import of liquified Ethylene & liquid salt) of the project has been commissioned on April 1997. A separate product slate in place of Alfa olefin has been formulated. This is necessary to utilize the excess ethylene from the proposed gas cracker. The second phase consisting of Gas Cracking of ethane feedstock, for production of ethylene is being executed at present. Over 99% of detailed engineering in the gas cracker and Ethylene oxide/Ethylene Glycol package is complete. Reactors, columns, Column internals, VHP drums/ vessels has been received and progressively erected at site. Site assembly/erection of fabrications is going on. Cracker furnace has been erected and hydrotesting of radiant coils remains to be completed. Pressure Swing Absorption system is under final stages of erection and hookup. C2, C3, Cracked gas, expander and Recycle gas compressor has been received and erected, with final hook up remaining as the balance job. Feedstock for the cracker would be supplied from a gas processing facility to be put up near the Gandhar Field development project. The gas processing facility - i.e. LPG recovery plant based on the firm availabiiity of 5 MMSCMD of gas from ONGCL's fields, is to be put up by another PSU (GAIL) and will supply rich gas for extraction of feedstock Ethane-propane (C2C3) at the separation plant inside the petro complex. Lean gas will be returned back. This facility is yet to be approved by the Government, and, in case of delay, this may lead to uncertainty in supplies to the cracker complex.

Expansion of ethylene & HDPE capacity at MGCC, nagothane

Expansion of additional Ethylene capacity by one lakh TPA involves an investment of Rs. 177.58 crores. The project has been completed by June, 98 and subsequently integrated with the existing separation facility of the existing cracker on a continuous basis. Work on the down-stream High Density Poly Ethylene (HDPE) project, which was also approved in May, 1992 at cost of Rs. 158.78 crores, has been completed in the second quarter of 1998 - 99. This project has been executed on an EPC basis by M/s Samsung Engg. Co. The project is based on Rationalisation and optimization of existing HDPE capacity at MGCC, by modification of polymerisation process, based on Degassification technology. This has been implemented, at a fraction of a green field plant cost, instead of a new plant as approved originally.

Petroleum & natural gas

As on 1st April, 1998, there were 49 projects on the monitoring system of the DPI with total anticipated cost of Rs. 32,021.2 crores & cost overrun of 3.8 percent with respect to the original approved cost of Rs. 30846.3

crores. The time overrun ranges from I month to 64 months. Of these, 33 projects are on the Flash Report System of Monitoring (of which 11 are mega projects, with a total anticipated cost of Rs. 20,472.18 crores). This includes 9, environment related, Diesel Hydro Desulfurisation Projects at the existing refineries, all approved by the GOI in June 1997, to be commissioned by April 1999. The project completed/commissioned are Catalytic Reformer Unit at Mathura, Kandla-Bhatinda petroleum product pipeline & Gas rehabilitation and expansion of Pipeline Project (i.e. Augmentation HBJ pipeline), POL pipeline between Vijayawada and Visakh as also Mumbai and Manmad, LPG recovery plants at Usar in Maharashtra, and at Lakwa, in Assam, UP petrochemicals complex at Auraiya in Etawaha district of UP, Gandhar Development Phase II, B-173 and B-55 offshore oil field development, Heera Development Phase III The projects making satisfactory progress are Numaligarh Refinery Project of NRL, Panipat Refinery Project of IOC, and Visakh Refinery expansion project of HPCL. All DHDS projects at refineries require greater effort to complete and commission the project by the first quarter of 1999 - 2000.

The projects in the Petroleum Sector involve exploration, development and production of oil and gas from offshore and inland fields, refining and processing of oil/gas and transportation of products to consuming centers. These activities are not only capital intensive but also import intensive. The cost overrun, is mainly due to currency devaluation. It is necessary that once a project is approved by the Government for investment, the projects authorities should draw project completion schedule backed by PERT network expedite selection of Process licensers, sign agreements to start the flow of data and other technical information, evaluate tenders speedily and place orders for equipment fabrication and other services. Unless the gap (which is now between 6 to 18 months) between the date of Government approval and actual start of work at site by project authorities, is reduced considerably, time overrun will continue to occur. Many items of equipment for petroleum exploration & drilling, production and processing of oil and gas are being made within the country, but, there is some delay in delivery by local suppliers. Free import of some critical, high pressure equipment, boiler quality and stainless steel plates for fabrications, and semi-finished materials forgings should be resorted to for bringing down the cost of locally fabricated equipment and shorter delivery schedules. Advance action regarding long delivery items from local fabricators, and supply of steel plates, pipes etc. by project authorities, has reduced uncertainty to a great extent in many projects. It is also observed that those projects authorities that take early action regarding detailed engineering and place orders for long delivery equipment in time, have better able to control slippages. This is all the more necessary in the case of Diesel Hydro Delsulfurisation projects in 9 refineries, taken on the monitor during the year, which have a predetermined commissioning date of April, 1999.

Visakh refinery expansion, Visakhapatanam (HPCL)

This project, costing Rs. 998.26 crores with foreign exchange component of Rs. 79.85 crores was approved in September, 1995. It envisages expansion of the Refinery from existing 4.5 MTPA to 7.5 MTPA by installing a separate crude/ vacuum distillation units, vis breaker units,, augmentation of the existing - Fluidised Catalytic Cracker Unit (FCCU-I), bitumen blowing unit, sulfur recovery unit and LPG/gasoline units. Foreign technology tie ups are envisaged for FCCU, LPG/ Gasoline/ Merox units, and sulfur recovery units. This project has an implementation schedule of 3.6 months from the date of govt. approval. Advance action has been taken for placing orders on all long delivery items and most of the items of fabrications such as FCCU regenerator & reactor, Gas Turbine generator and HRSG package have been progressively received and being erected. Progress achieved in the area of equipment erection and piping is 40 % and the work is expected to be completed by March 1999. Packagewise progress in the Crude distillation and. Fluidised cracker unit is 88.3% and 65.6% respectively. There was some setback due to fire accident in Sep. 97 and project work was suspended for a few months. This has led to slippage in commissioning by a further nine months to September, 1999. However it is understood that the CDU and other associated units would be ready by April 1999- i.e. capacity expansion of 3MMTPA to be ready and available by April, 1999. However, secondary units such as FCCU etc. will be operational by Sept. 1999.

Numaligarh refinery project, Numaligarh (NRL)

This project with a throughput of 3 MMTPA was approved by the Government in July, 1992 at cost of Rs. 1830 crores with the original date of commissioning being October, 1997. This project will process Assam crude. The project has suffered fifteen months delay, in the early period of its implementation, due to delay in finalising the technology for the Hydro Cracker and Hydrogen Units. The detailed engineering for crude distillation unit (CDU) and vacuum distillation unit (VDU), Delayed Coker Unit (DCU), Catalytic Cracking Unit (CCU) & Utilities/offsite is being undertaken by the local engineering consultant, Engineers India Ltd. (EIL). Total commitment on the project till date is Rs. 2100.0 crores and expenditure is . Rs. 1787 crores against an anticipated cost of Rs. 2489.12 crores for the refinery. Overall physical progress is 94.7% against a schedule of 98.2% till mid Dec 1998. Cogeneration and HRSG plant is ready for commissioning and Pipe/tankage/ other systems are getting readied for receiving crude oil for the refinery. All columns for CDU/VDU, HCU Reactor, Coke 'Chambers etc. have been received at site. The project is expected to be mechanically completed by March, 99.

Haldia-barauni crude oil pipeline

To ensure uninterrupted supply of 4.2 million TPA of imported Crude to the Barauni Oil refinery of IOCL, the Govt. of India in Jan., 1996 sanctioned the Haldia-Barauni Pipeline project at an estimated cost of Rs. 953 crores, (at Dec. 1994 prices). Gestation period for the project is 42 months. Work of main pipe laying commenced on 25.9.97. All ordered mainline pipes/pumps and mainline engines has been received and erected at various intermediate booster stations. Entire length of the pipeline route has been laid and activities are in hand to make pipeline and station ready for pumping oil. Laying of the pipeline across the River Gail a completed. All crude oil storage tanks at Haldia erected along with piping hook up with Haldia port. Civil works for various plant buildings at Haldia and Bolpur approaching completion. Completion of this project by the end of 1998-99 is necessary as crude from Assam Oil fields would be directed to Numaligarh Oil Refinery, now expected to be operational by the first quarter of 1999-2000. As against the original commissioning date of July 1999 and cost of Rs. 952.95 Crores, commissioning will be 5 months ahead of schedule and estimated cost is expected to be around Rs. 660 crores.

Crude distillation unit & revamp of FCCU, Koyali refinery

This project will process 3 MMTPA of crude from western onshore area. The project involves revamping of existing feed preparation unit (from 1.67 to 2.37 MMTPA), and fluidised catalytic cracking unit (FCCU- from I to 1.5 MMTPA), alongwith offsite facilities (7 Nos. crude tank and 4 No. product tankages) to convert heavier ends into distillate products. The cost of this project approved in December, 1996 is Rs. 748.88 crores for distillation unit/ FCCU etc. and Rs. 304.12 crores for augmentation of SVK crude oil pipeline of existing Salaya - Mathura Pipeline. The gestation period is 36 months, with scheduled commissioning in December, 1999. Construction progress in CDU is 44.5% as against a schedule of 26.4%. In Crude charge heater, 49% of work completed with the completion of stack fabrication and alignment. As per present indication, this project may not suffer any slippages.

U.P. petro-chemical complex (GAIL)

This Gas Cracker Unit, designed to produce 3 lakh TPA of Ethylene from feedstock Ethane separated from Natural Gas supplied through HBJ Pipeline, was approved by the Government in October, 1992 at cost of Rs. 2941.48 crores. The original scheduled date of commissioning for this project was December, 1996. There was delay mainly due to late receipt of equipment from local and foreign suppliers. It may however be mentioned that this project, situated as it is in a backward area had a very tight erection and commissioning schedule. The delay of 24 months with respect to the original date, need to take this factor into account. Gas processing unit and Gas cracker unit have been commissioned and ethylene of polymer grade has been produced. LLDPE and HDPE Units have been mechanically completed. Both the polymer units are expected to be commissioned by the end of the fourth quarter of 1998-99.

Panipat refinery project (IOC)

This project consisting of 6 MTPA crude throughput Refinery, Second Submarine Mooring Buoy at Salaya in Gujarat Oil Pipeline Augmentation along the Viramgam

-Chaksu - Panipat route, & Panipat Marketing Terminal was approved by the Government in October, 1992 at cost of Rs. 3868 crores with the scheduled date of commissioning as August, 1997. Some of the equipment deliveries from local suppliers in public and private sector have been badly delayed, resulting in postponement to the completion date of the project (i.e. refinery portion) by 18 months with respect to the original completion date of April, 1997. Many orders had to be off loaded from the failing vendors at their risk and cost. But for Amine regeneration unit (ARU), all other units including Hydro cracker unit, FCCU and Sour Water Unit are ready for commissioning. Revamp of Sulfur Recovery unit is also to be got ready for integration with the Diesel Hydro De-Sulfurisation Unit, now under implementation, and targeted for operation by 31 st March 1999. Other major reason for delay has been overall poor management by package vendors like Ms. Bridge & Roof Ms. ATV, Ms. BHPV, Ms. Kaveri etc. Linked project such as 2nd SBM at Salaya and Viramgam - Chaksu - Panipat pipeline is ready for receiving oil for pumping to the Panipat Refinery. Panipat Marketing Centre has been commissioned & 1 million tonne of oil refined . Actual progress on refinery portion is 99.8%. As per latest progress Report, crude distillation units, vacuum distillation unit, and catalytic reformer unit have already been commissioned. Balance units (FCC, Hydro cracker) are expected to be commissioned by the first quarter of 1999 -2000.

Matching secondary processing facility, mathura refinery, (IOC)

This project was approved at estimated cost of Rs. 1041 crores, in May 1996. This will provide facilities commensurate with the crude processing capacity of the

Mathura Refinery and also keep SO2 emission under check. On implementation of this project, there will be upgradation of heavy oil to the extent of 626000 TPA to SK/HSD and 33000 TPA of LPG. Process package for Hydro Cracker Unit has been received. Engineering & procurement is in an advance stage. Out of 3 units of sulphur recovery unit, one train is exclusively for DHDS Unit and is expected to be completed by April, 99. Hydrogen unit is in an advanced stage of fabrication. This project is expected to be commissioned by Feb, 2000.

Diesel hydro de-sulfurisation project at 9 refineries of HPCL, BPCL, IOCL, CRL & MRL

In order to reduce environmental pollution due to vehicular emissions, the oil companies have been ordered to supply high speed diesel with maximum sulfur content of 0.25% by the Honourable Supreme Court by April, 1999. As the DHDS Project proposals of all the above 9 refineries are technologically similar in nature and since all the projects are to be completed expeditiously, a consolidated proposal was approved by the Govt. in June, 1997 at a cost of Rs. 556831 crores with a 'foreign exchange component of Rs. 966.86 crores. Govt. of India approved setting up of DHDS facilities at 9 refineries viz., IOC (at 4 refineries), HPCL (at 2 refineries), BPCL , CRL and MRL. The total value of equipment to be procured is put at Rs. 4000 crores. As the project has a- very short gestation period, it was ensured, that, only vendors with capability to adhere to contractual delivery schedule for equipment and fabrication have only been considered. Of the 9 DHDS projects approved, 2 are to be implemented on a conventional basis and others on the basis of Lump Sum Turnkey (LSTK) contract for different packages. LSTK contracts have been awarded on the basis of competitive bids for packages such as, DHDS, Hydrogen Generation, Reformer, Sulphur Recovery Units (SRU), Offsites &

Captive Power Plants. LSTK contractors have inturn awarded the orders for all major equipments and fabrications on a competitive basis taking into consideration the delivery schedule and also price competitiveness Full mobilisation of erection teams at various sites started by April-May, 1998. MRL & BPCL are implementing the project on a conventional basis for DHDS package offsites etc. They have awarded LSTK package for Hydrogen Generation (MRL & BPCL) & Sulphur Recovery Packages. Overall progress of MRL & BPCL projects are 84.35% and 89.2% respectively. These two DHDS projects may get completed by April-May'99. In the case of DHDS, HPCL-Visakh, overall progress for SRU & DHDS is 48,9% & 69% respectively, and this may result in 2-33 months slippage (i.e. commissioning by June'99), In the case of DHDS, HPCL - Mumbai, progress of DHDS/Hydrogen/Sulphur block is 48.4%, 65% & 40.2% respectively. This may also suffer 4 months slippage w.r.t. original commissioning date. Progress in the case of DHDS-CRL is 72.9% and they have been able to make up w.r.t. their projected commissioning date of Nov. 1999 by 4 months i.e. July, 1999. In the case of DHDS project of IOC at Mathura & Panipat, overall progress is 79.4 1% & 85.71% respectively. They may be commissioned with a slippage of about 1 month, i.e., by April-May'1999. In the case of DHDS - IOC Gujarat, progress is 84.81% & 67.67% respectively, They may slip by 2 months w.r.t. original commissioning date of 31 st March, 1999. DHDS project at IOC's Haldia Refinery may suffer three months slippage (overall progress 67,67%) as they have to do extensive piling work at site due to soil liquefaction factor. These projects as per present indication may be commissioned with a slight slippage of 2-6 months with respect to the scheduled commissioning date of April, 1999. As the delivery period is very short expeditious action is required to ensure delivery and erection of equipment at site. Receipt of 90% of equipment by Jan - Feb. '99 is crucial to the projects completion by 2nd quarter of 1999-2000 as per latest indication of construction status.

There were 38 projects on the monitoring system at the beginning of the year 199899 with anticipated cost of Rs. 42379.77crores. Of these, 14 were mega projects costing Rs. 34334.52 crores. Among the projects completed during the first two quarters of 1998 99 are Kathalguri Gas based power project, Gandhar Transmission and Kopili Transmission Project. In addition one unit of Kayamkulam GT has been commissioned in Nov. '98 and Coal firing has been achieved for the 3rd unit of 210 MW at Mejia. Also the projects likely to be completed by the end of March, 1999 are Mejia TPP (balance works), Rangit HEP (60 MW), Kayamkulam (GT-2nd unit), Kathalguri Transmission System, HVDC back to back at Jeypore, Kaiga-Sirsi Transmission System, Augmentation of Transmission System in NER and Kayamkulam Transmission System. 19 projects are under Transmission which include Unified Load Despatch and Communication System in Northern, Southern and North-Eastern regions, an HVDC back to back station at Jeypore and Transmission Systems associated with Nathpa Jhakri, Vindhyachal Stage II, Unchahar Stage II and Kayamkulam CCPP. One project has been added during the year -Tuirial HE Project (60 MW) to be executed by NEEPCO. Thus there are 36 projects oil the monitor of DPI at the end of Sept., 98.

During the Ninth Plan, upto September, 98, a generating capacity of 1265 MW has been added under the Central sector. Regarding Transmission projects, about 3000 ckm of 400 M 82 ckm of 220 kV and 184 ckm of 132 kV transmission lines have been added during the period. The status of the Mega and some of the Major projects has been highlighted in the following paragraphs.

The projects in the power sector face a variety of problems in their implementation. At the beginning of the project formulation itself, demand pattern, linkage of coal mines to the specific project and the availability of transport for movement of coal/ gas pipeline, acquisition of land, availability of adequate amount of gas/coal and cooling water for running the plants, and sources of funding for projects need to be identified clearly. This is not done in all the cases and is usually left to be sorted Out by the project authorities after the project is finally cleared by the government. These parameters which are not specifically cleared continue to haunt the project implementation process. In the case of hydro electric power projects, survey of the site should be thorough from geological and environment angle. This is not done or left for later investigation as and when the problem recurs. Along with these problems, the other constraints are slow mobilisation of resources by the contractors, slow rate of equipment erection, delay in deliveries of equipment and their non sequential supplies. From a survey of projects under implementation, major problems reported by various projects are pending of Environmental clearance (Doyang HEP) and Funds (for e.g. 3 mega & major projects) have this problem. Some projects report delay either in contract finalisation or in supply of local/ imported equipment. This problem is affecting implementation of Dulhasti arid Dhauliganga projects of NHPC. Other problems are inadequate supply of gas to projects which are already commissioned, Coal linkage and non completion of coal handling plant, Railway line -specifically merry go round system (Mejia TPP), inadequate transmission capacity (specifically in eastern region), Law & Order problem (Tehri HEP, Kathalguri Transmission project and Augmentation of Transmission System in NER) and land acquisition problems (Dhauliganga and Koel Karo H.E. projects).

Mejia thermal power project (DVC)

Sanction was accorded for this 3x210 MW coal fired thermal power project on 20.3.1986 at an estimated cost of Rs.641.42 crores (3rd Qtr. 1983 price level). Revised project cost of Rs. 1989.14 crores (3rd Qtr 1995 price level) has been approved by the Govt. in October '97. There was some initial delay in the acquisition of land (2502 acres of land out of 2594 acres has been acquired). The project has been delayed mainly due to fund constraints, low productivity of workers on various fronts, mismanagement at all levels and also contractors not adhering to schedule, and instrasigent labour unions supported by politicians of the area. The first unit has been commissioned on a commercial basis from March '96 and the second unit synchronised with oil in March' 97 and with Coal on 31.3.98. The third unit achieved Synchronisation with oil in March, 98 and with coal on 17.10.98. The delay was due to slow erection of Boiler and TG by BHEL. With this all the three units of the project have been commissioned., and only some balance works are going on.

Tehri hydro electric project (THDC)

Tehri Hydro power complex was transferred to THDC by the State Govt. of UP in June, 1989. The Government of India have accorded approval in March, 1994 for execution of Tehri Dam and Hydropower project of 4x250 MW Stage-I alongwith the compulsory and committed works of Tehri Pumped storage plant and Koteshwer dam project at a cost of Rs.2963.66 crores at March, 1993 price level. Various infrastructure works have been completed at the project site. All four diversion tunnels completed. Excavation work of dam, power house and Transformer hall is in progress and for machine hall, it has been completed.. About 60% excavation for TRT has been done. Much of the rehabilitation work for urban and rural rehabilitation has been completed and the balance land for the purpose is being acquired. Expenditure as in Nov. '98 was around Rs. 1775 crores. The rate of progress is slow and the project commissioning has been rescheduled to March, 2002,

Dulhasti hydro electric project (NHPC)

The 390 MW Dulhasti Hydroelectric Project is located in Kishtwar Tehsil of District Doda in Jammu & Kashmir on the Chenab River to generate 1928 MU of energy annually in a 90% dependable year. Initial investment approval for the project was accorded in Nov. 1982 at an estimated cost of Rs. 183.45 crores including IDC of Rs. 21.733 crores. It could not be executed for want of funds. A project proposal at a cost of Rs. 1262.97 crores (October 1988 price level) including an IDC of Rs. 96.20 crores, for turnkey execution by French Consortium was sanctioned on 12.7.89. The total off-shore cost of the project is to be met through French treasury grant of FF 190 million treasury loan of FF 987 million and & commercial loan of FF 1405.6 million, The order to commence work was issued on 11.10.89 and was scheduled for completion by 7/94 i.e. In a period of 57 months. The revised cost at Nov., 1996 price level, at Rs. 3) 559.77 crores with completion of the project by March, 2001 has also been approved by the Govt. in Oct. '97. Right in the beginning, the approach has been for turnkey execution of the project by French Consortium led by M/s CGEE Alsthom. The civil works contractor (M/s DSB a French Firm) suspended work from 24.8.92 due to disturbed law and order conditions at the project site. The physical progress of various works achieved till then was completion of diversion channel, cofferdam, access tunnel to powerhouse and excavation and partial completion of Concrete Dam (18%), Head Race Tunnel (HRT) - 12% Power House - 52% Hydro mech. & Electro mech works - 50% Tail Race Tunnel (TRT) - 50% the overall progress was 27%. The NHPC had invited bids for balance civil works, The LOI was issued to successful bidder in September '96 and contract awarded to M/s JSAJV on 9.4.97. Diversion Channel, Çoffer Dam and Dam excavation has been completed, The work of HRT - U/S with Tunnel Boring Machine has been started and a progress of 2190 meters has been achieved. Work on HRT - D/S with conventional method is going on and 2571 meters out of 3026 meters has been completed. Excavation in transformer gallery and powerhouse has been completed and concreting is in progress. Progress of work in HRT suffered due to poor rock conditions and breakdown of TBM. The commissioning schedule indicated by THDC as March, 2001 may not be possible.

Rangit hydro electric project (NHPC)

Rangit Hydro Electric Project with a capacity of 3x20 MW was originally approved in April '90 at an estimated cost of Rs. 181.15 crores with the date of commissioning of Sept '95. The estimated cost now anticipated is Rs. 361.86 crores with the date of completion of March '96 It is a run of the river project on Rangit river and consists of diversion tunnel of 6 meter dia 358 meters long 45 meter high dam, 3 km long 4.5 meter dia HRT and an overground powerhouse. The diversion tunnel and adit to HRT downstream has been completed. The work of river diversion has been completed. The powerhouse excavation is going on. 100% of main tunnel has been completed. The concreting in the dam started in March '96 and 48% has been completed. The work on the dam concreting needs to be speeded up by mobilising additional tower crane. Most of the equipment has been received at site and EOT crane erected and commissioned. The commissioning schedule of March, 1999 appears to be very tight and all out efforts are needed to adhere to the schedule.

Nathpa jhakri hydro electric project (NJPC)

The project was sanctioned in 4/89 at an estimated cost of Rs. 1678.02 crores. The project was initially in the state sector which was later on taken over by the NHPC. The project cost has been further revised to Rs. 4337.95 crores (i.e. $1377 million at March 1993 price level). Now anticipated cost Rs. 7179.64 crores. World Bank is aiding this project to the tune of Rs. 1376 crores (around Rs. 582.63) crores has already been utilised). M/s EUCONA (consisting of ABB, Siemens, Sulzer & BHEL) has been awarded the main contract of supply and erection of electrical generating unit in March '94. Dam and desilting chamber works contract (value Rs. 439 crores), contract for Head Race Tunnel (length 16.05 kms) costing Rs. 5 10 crores, contract for Power House complex (value Rs. 475 crores) have all been awarded along with the other minor contracts, the infrastructural facilities required for the project are Augmentation works on National Highway -22, Shimla Bye Pass road, Rampur Bye Pass road. They are not fully complete and need to be expedited in the interest of the project. Construction is in full swing though not as per schedule due to under performance by the contractors. The progress has suffered due to delay in mobilisation, rock slide on the river Satluj at Nathpa Darn, geological problems in Daj adit, non-availability of adequate construction power and flash floods and land slides in July '97 caused extensive damage to the works and equipments. The expected schedule for synchronising Unit I - 12/2001, Unit II - 1/2002, Unit III - 2/2002, Unit IV - 2/2002 and Unit V & VI - 3/2002.

Vindhyachal STPP-II (2x500) MW & Kayamkulam combined cycle power project (400 MW) (NTPC)

Vindhyachal STPP II project approved in Feb '95 is subsequent to the Vindhyachal STPP II advance action sanctioned in March '90 for preliminary studies and other works. Presently the project is anticipated to cost Rs. 2858 crores. All major orders have been placed and work is proceeding as per schedule. The first unit is likely to be commissioned by Feb. '2000 and the second unit by Feb. '2001.

Kayamkulam CCPP was sanctioned in Sept '96 and is to be financed by World Bank loan) Orders for main plant on turnkey basis has been placed on BHEL in Sept. '96. First unit of GT has been commissioned by NTPC in November, 1998 ahead of schedule. The second unit is expected by March, 1999 and the Steam Turbine (ST) by March, 2000.

Unchahar TPP stage II (NTPC)

Unchahar TPP Stage II with an installed capacity of 2x210 MW being executed by NTPC was approved in April, 1995 at an estimated cost of Rs. 1279.51 crores with the commissioning date of July, 2000. All orders have been placed including the C&I package which was delayed by about 15 months due to retendering and has since been awarded to BHEL in August, 97. The supply and erection of steam generator and TG are going on. The project is oil schedule.

Doyang HEP (NEEPCO)

The 3x25 MW Doyang Hydro Electric Project oil the Doyang river is situated in the Wokha district of Nagaland, 105 km North East of Kohima. The project will utilise the discharge from the Doyang river, a sub tributary of the river Brahamputra and is capable of generating 227 MU in 90% dependable year and 364 MU oil average after completion. The dam has height of 87.5 M with impervious core. Entire land is acquired. As per the latest indications, commissioning dates for different units are Unit I 3/00, Unit II 3/99, and Unit III 12/99 (original date of commissioning for the entire project was

06/92 and revised date-sanctioned in 7/1989-of commissioning of the project was 7/1995). The major civil works of the project are diversion tunnel, approach channel, and spillway, water conductor system, power house building and rock fill dam. Orders for TG, diversion tunnel, dam, P.H. excavation, spillway, power channel and PH (civil works) have been placed in 9/88, 3/89, 6/89, 6/92 and 6/92 respectively. Diversion tunnel has been completed and water diverted through this in Dec. '96. Boring of water conductor system has been completed and steel lining is in progress. Excavation and rock filling of Coffer dam has been completed.. Civil works of Powerhouse are running satisfactorily, 100% turbine parts and generator items have been received. Erection of TG units is in progress. EOT crane has been erected. Switchyard erection work has also been completed. Perennial law and order problem in the area is working against the smooth Implementation of this project.

Ranganadi HEP (NEEPCO)

The project, (3x135 MW), is located on the Ranganadi, a tributary of river Brahamputra, in the lower Subansiri district of Arunachal Pardesh. The main feature of this project is 68 meter high concrete dam with 6.75 m. dia, 9145 metre long horse shoe type Head Race Tunnel for supplying water to generate 405 MW power. Design head is 300 meter with a surface power house. This project will generate 1874 MU in 90% dependable year. HRT is being bored in a geologically unpredictable rock formation. Of the 282.12 Ha of land, 271.07 Ha has already been acquired. As against the original commissioning date of August 1994 for all the three units, now anticipated date is Unit I-3/00, Unit II - 1/01, and Unit III - 3/01. Diversion tunnel has been completed. HRT is the critical item of the project, the boring of 10.27 kms. long tunnel has been taken up at 8 faces with 2 adits for entry and exit. Boring for about

99% of length has been completed and concreting of about 90% done. The excavation for main darn is in progress. So far about 80% excavation has been completed. Concreting in river bed portion has started from Feb. '97 and the work suffered due to submergence of river bed by flood water during May '97. The excavation of powerhouse pit is completed. In regard to supply of TG units, BHEL has dispatched most of the turbine parts and some of them have been received and erected. The erection work of generating plant and equipment for all the units is progressing satisfactorily. All GTs have been received at Guwahati and further transportation to project site is being taken up. Erection of EOT crane in service bay has been completed.

Simhadri TPP stage I (2x500 MW) and Faridabad CCPP (400 MW) (NTPC)

Simhadri TPP Stage-I to be executed by NTPC at Vizag district of Andhra Pardesh, envisages installation of two units of 500 MW each. The project has been approved in July '97 at an estimated cost of Rs. 3650.79 Crores with the completion schedule of December, 2002. Though the executing agency is NTPC, the total output will be utilised by Andhra Pradesh only. The financing of the project is through OECF. The project is in its initial stages and the main plant award is expected by May, 98. The soil investigation and land acquisition is in progress and the bid documents for main plant package are under approval by OECF.

Faridabad CCPP, with an installed capacity of 400 MW has been approved in July, 97 at an estimated cost of Rs. 1163 crores with date of completion as January, 2001. The project is being executed by NTPC, though the only beneficiary is Haryana. OECF are financing the project. The project is in the initial stages and infrastructure works and land acquisition are going on. Land for critical main plant area has been acquired. The LOI for Main Plant turnkey package has been placed on BHEL oil 23.11.98.

Power transmission, load despatch and communication facilities (Power grid corporation)

There are 19 projects on the monitor which mainly deal with the power evacuation and load despatch in the Power sector. For interregional power transmission, an HVDC back to back station at Gazuwaka in AP alongwith associated transmission line is under execution. The 400 KV Line has been completed and the HVDC portion is likely to be completed by 2/99. In addition, one HVDC back to back station and a 400KV tie between Northern and Eastern region and Load Despatch Scheme for Eastern region have recently been approved by the Government and have been put on the monitor w.e.f. Nov., 98. Five transmission projects are likely to be completed by the end of March '99. The rate of implementation of some of the associated transmission lines which are being implemented by the Powergrid in North Eastern states is not satisfactory mainly due to law and order problems in the regions. The progress of Unified Load Dispatch centres for the Northern, Southern and North Eastern region are far from satisfactory. The limitations of grid operation in the Eastern region may pose problems in evacuation of power from the existing/new projects in the area.

On the overall, the implementation of thermal power projects and some of the Transmission projects has been satisfactory during the year 1998-99, whereas implementation of hydro projects was delayed due to various reasons. Some of the transmission projects are also delayed mainly due to law and order or contractual problem or due to deferring the associated generation projects.

Railways

During the period April - September '98, 13 projects already frozen / dropped by Railway Board (mainly due to reasons like fund constraints, lower operating priority and/or other reasons) continued to be out of the effective list of monitoring of DPI and placed in a separate list of frozen/dropped projects. The projects on the monitoring system include 3 mega projects costing Rs. 408 crores, 72 major projects costing Rs. 19,113 crore and 99 medium projects costing Rs. 4113 crore.

The 174 projects of the Railways (after excluding 10 projects completed during the Quarter ending September, 1998) on the monitoring system comprise Line Doubling projects (45 Nos.), New Line projects (40 Nos.), Workshops and Production Units (9 Nos.), Gauge Conversion Projects (339 Nos.), Traffic Facilities Projects (6 Nos.), Railway Electrification projects (12 Nos.) Metropolitan Transport Projects (8 Nos.), Signalling & Telecommunications Projects (7 Nos.), Freight Operation Information System Project (1 No.). Bridges & Structures Project (4 Nos.) and projects relating to setting up of New Railway Zones (3 Nos.). The present status and problems of some of the mega/major projects are outlined below.

During the period April-December, 1998, 14 new projects (costing Rs. 50 crores and more) have been examined in-depth by PMD of DPI for the Expanded Board. Out of 14 projects, 9 projects were approved and remaining 5 projects were cancelled and/or deferred.

Some of the common problems being faced by the projects of Railway Sector are : frequent sanctioning of the projects without fully completing certain essential pre-project activities (like detailed estimates etc.) and also without due regard to the availability of adequate funds. This has resulted in a large number of projects remaining non-starters and/or making slow progress, as well as thin dispersal of limited resources over a large number of projects. The other factors affecting the path of implementation are delays in acquisition of land, award of contracts, civil work etc. Further, often large number of new projects are sanctioned, while old and continuing projects are remaining starved of funds. Some times this also leads to frequent freezing and de-freezing of existing projects.

Freight operation information system (FOIS) project

The Freight Operation Information System (FOIS), a mega project originally approved in November, 1989 with - its revised scope and cost of Rs. 1098.00 crores is now under implementation by the Centre for Railway Information System (CRIS). The original objective of the project is to reduce the wagon turn around time by 15% and improve the quality of service to the customers. The original project provides for the installation of data input system at 700 locations called Area Reporting Centres.. These will be hooked up to 5 zonal processing centres at Delhi, Bombay, Calcutta, Secunderabad and Madras. The main centre will be at Delhi. The date of commissioning for the Northern Railway Centre (at Delhi) was tentatively fixed as March, 1994, and that of the entire project as March, 1995. However, due to funds constraints, the scope of the project was later reduced to implementation in Northern Railway zone Initially at a cost of Rs. 267.20 cr. This consists of commissioning of over 12400 on-line terminals at over '32 locations, using railway owned or leased DOT line or Satellite telecom circuits, wherever necessary by December, 1995. At present, pre-implementation trials with available hardware are in progress. But, recently, it has been reported that there are problems in customizing the software and IIT, Delhi has been assigned by the project authorities, with the task of evaluating the software and advising on the future course of action to make it functional and acceptable to the user. The IIT-committee has, among other things, recommended stoppage of further software development work alongwith trials and adoption of a modified approach to the development of software and then taking up software development in line with their recommendations. The report of the IIT has been considered and it has been decided in principle to award a consultancy contract to Computer Maintenance Corporation Ltd. (CMC) for suggesting ways and means of implementing the IIT Committee's recommendations and helping CRIS in developing prototype of some modules of FOIS and test the same in actual field condition.

Jogighopa-Guwahati (New line) (North eastern frontier railway)

For the Jogighopa-Guwahati New Line Project (142,15 kms), expected to provide an alternative route for the Assam area, besides the Railways, there are two other funding agencies namely, Ministry of Surface Transport (MOST) and NEC (North Eastern Council). The latest estimated cost of the project is Rs. 641.95 Cr. Rail-cum-road bridge along with railway line upto Goalpara (20 kms.) was opened for goods traffic / passenger traffic on 15th April, 1998. Finishing works on the Project are likely to be completed shortly. Balance Section between Goalpara to Kamakhya (125 kms.) is likely to be completed by March '99.

Guna-Etawah (New line) (Central railway)

The Guna-Etawah New Line (348.25 Kms.) with an anticipated cost of Rs. 256 cr., has been divided into 3 phases out of which Phase-I between Guna-Shivpur (102.40 Kms) has been completed. In phase-II between Shivpuri-Gwalior (124.55 Kms.), so far 2 sections viz. Gwalior -Panihar (24.85 Kms) and Shivpuri-Khajuri (15.9 Kms) have been completed. In Phase-II, Panihar-Mohana

Section was opened for traffic In July, 1998. For the Section between Mohana-Khajurl (46 Kms.), earth work and bridges are 98% and 99% complete respectively. The Section is likely to be completed by December, 1998. In Phase-III between Gwalior-Itava (117 Kms.), Birlanagar-Sanichera (15.6 Kms.) was opened for goods traffic in March, 1993.

For Nonera-Bhind (50 Kms.), contracts for earth work and bridges have been finalised and earth work is in progress. For Bhind-Etawah (36.44 Kms.) Section, construction of 3 major bridges on Chambal, Yamuna and Konwari rivers is being planned for which approval of Inland Water Way Authorities is awaited. Overall physical progress is 62% till November '98. Anticipated dates of commissioning for Nonera-Soni and Soni-Bhind Sections are Feb. 99 and June '99 respectively.

Rail coach factory (RCF), Kapurthala (Northern railway)

The Phase-I of the project has been completed as per schedule in March '88 and manufacture of ICF (Integral Coach Factory, Perambur) design coach has commenced in March '88. While RCF manufactured 1025 coaches in 1993-94 based on old design against the planned capacity of 1000 coaches per annum. The implementation of the new coach design has been delayed due to failure of the Ministry of Railways to obtain the least cost option. Project Report for manufacture of new design coaches has since been submitted to the Railway Board for approval.

Jammu Tawi-Udhampur (New line) (53 Kms.) (Northern railway)

This project was originally sanctioned in March '1991 at a cost of Rs. 50 crore with the original date of commissioning March, 1994. Presently, the cost of the project is Rs. 350 crore and the anticipated date of commissioning is December, 1999. Overall physical progress is 73%. Land acquisition was completed. Work relating to the longest tunnel in the Section is held up due to the failure of two contractual agencies. Ministry of Railways has directed that fresh tenders may be invited for this Section. Likely anticipated date of commissioning is December '99.

Bagaha-Chitauni (New line) (28 kms) (North eastern railway)

This project was originally sanctioned in April, 1994 at estimated cost of Rs. 6.74 crores, with the objective of restoring the rail link between Bagaha & Chitauni. The project remained suspended for several years and is now estimated to cost Rs. 184.68 crores The project is being jointly funded by the Ministry of Railways, Govt. of U.P., Govt. of Bihar and Ministry of Water Resources. The work on rail bridge has been completed and work on road bridge has been awarded to M/s IRCON which is yet to start. Date of commissioning is not known.

Delhi-Ambala-Ludhiana (Railway electrification) project (314 kms.)

This project was originally sanctioned in March' 1992 at a cost of Rs. 136.32 crore with a date of commissioning of December '1996. The entire section has been energised. The scope of the project has been enhanced by including electrification to more branch lines namely Sirhind-Nangal Dam and Ambala-Kalka and electrification of these branch lines Is likely to be completed by March, 2000.

Gondia-Chandafort (Gauge conversion)(242 kms.) (South eastern railway)

This project was originally sanctioned in December '1992 at a cost of Rs. 158.83 crores with a date of commissioning of December' 1996. The revised cost of the project is 232.82 crore and anticipated date of commissioning is December '98. Gondia-Wadsa-Nagbhir (132 Kms.) has been completed and opened to traffic.

Work on balance Section from Nagbhir to Chanda Fort (110 Kms.) is in progress. Overall progress is 75% as on September, 1998.

Lumding-Dibrugarh (Gauge conversion) (628 kms.) (North eastern frontier railway)

The project was approved in October, 1993 at a cost of Rs. 300 crore. Revised cost is Rs. 700 crore. The Section between Lumding to Dimapur was opened for goods traffic in June, 1995 and for passenger traffic in October, 1995, Passenger services between Dimapur to Tinsukhia started in May '97. Passenger services on Furkating - Mariani (85 Kms.) and Simaluguri and Moranhat (54 Kms.) have started from August '98. Residual works in yards and blasting are in progress.

The project sanctioned in June '1995 is presently costing Rs. 266 Crores and its anticipated date of commissioning is December, 2000. This project is divided into 3 parts viz., Part-I (Hotgi-Bijapur) (94 Kms.), Part-II (Bijapur-Bagalkot)(97 Kms.) and Part-III (Bagalkot-Gadag) (95 Kms) out of which Part-II& III are being implemented under Build, Operate, Lease & Transfer (BOLT) scheme.

Udhampur-Srinagar-Baramulla (New line) (290 kms) (Northern railway)

The project has been sanctioned in March '1995 at a cost of Rs. 2500 crore. This project was sanctioned as a project of national importance which would be funded outside the Railway's plan budget. Design Consultancy for all major bridges awarded. Final location survey from Kaba to Baramulla was to be completed by August, 1998. Technical bids for 6 tunnels out of 7 tunnels and major bridge Nos. 2 and 3 have been finalised. Progress on the project was hampered by Snowfall in the valley. Overall physical progress is only 1%. The project has funds constraint.

Brahmaputra bridge at Bogibeel and link line (54.30 kms.) (North eastern frontier railway)

This project was sanctioned in April, 1996. The major objectives of this project are construction of rail bridge across the river Brahamputra at Bogibeel (in Assam) and link lines between Dibrugarh and North Bank line. Presently, final location survey and the detailed investigation for the bridge and approaches by M/s RITES are in progress. RITES submitted an Interim Report to Railway Board. A Technical Advisory Group was appointed which met on 1.12.97 to consider design of the bridge. Final Report by RITES was to be submitted by September, 1998.

Madras Beach - Chengalpattu - Trichy (401 Kms) (Gauge Conversion)

The project was approved in April, 1992 at an original cost of Rs. 200 Crore revised to Rs. 467.20 crore. Original date of commissioning was December, 1995. Phase-I was commissioned in August, 1998. Phase-II work is in progress.

Arsikere - Hassan - Mangalore (Gauge conversion) (236 kms.) (Southern railway)

Tenders for supply of ballast and earth work have been finalised and work started. Presently, various activities like earthwork, construction of major and minor bridges etc. are in progress. The progress of Arsikere - Hassan is 98% and it has

Erode - Ernakulam (Railway electrification) (324 kms.)

Erode- Palghat - Shoranur (217 RKM) has been energised. The section Shoranur -Ernakulam which was earlier proposed to be done under BOLT scheme has been discharged from BOLT and approved under Railway funding. The overall progress is 70%. Against original date of commissioning of March, 1.998, anticipated date is March, 2000.

Nangal Dam - Talwara (New line) (113 Kms.)

The original cost of the project was Rs. 37.60 crore (March, 1981) which was revised to Rs. 150 Crore. Original/Revised dates of commissioning are not fixed. Nangal darn - Una Section (17 Km) was opened to passenger traffic in January, 1991. Estimate for Una (Himachal Pradesh) to Chuaru Takaila (Rs. 38.63 Crore) was submitted to Railway Board for sanction . Work frozen in 1992-93 after Nangal Dam - Una Section was opened was restarted in 1997-98. After follow-up, Himachal Pradesh Government handed over a part of land for the section beyond Una and balance land acquisition Is going on. Overall progress is 22%.

Surface transport

There were 44 projects on the monitoring system during the year (upto December, 98). These includes 2 Inland Water Transport Projects, 19 Port Projects, 20 National Highway and bridges and 3) shipping projects. During the year for the period April, 1998 upto December, 1998, 4 projects were completed and 12 projects are expected to be completed by March, 1999. The projects were regularly monitored, reviewed by the DPI, Committee of Secretaries and the Prime Minister's office. The status of some of the major projects has been highlighted below:

Major ports Construction of a new port at Ennore (near Madras) :

The new port at Ennore (near Madras) is being built to receive 6,500 DNV Geared/Self-Loading Coal Vessels from Paradip Port. The Coal is required for existing power station of Tamil Nadu Electricity Board and for future coal based power plant to be setup in the coastal region of South India. The proposed port at Ennore will have an enclosed harbour basin surrounded by northern and southern backwaters. The entrance to the port will be in the eastern side and would be about 250 meters wide, around 9 million cubic capital dredging will be done. The dredging will be carried out by combined application of cutter trailing and hopper suction dredgers. Coal from the port berth to the stock yard of northern Madras thermal power station will be transported by suitable conveyor system. To mitigate the possibility of erosion on the northern side of the Ennore port due to construction of breakwaters, suitable coastal protection measures would be provided. The offshore civil works include construction of staff quarters, office building, road and bridges, etc. The scope of the project also includes procurement of 4 nos. Tug boats of 30 ton bollard pull, 2 nos. of Pilot Launches, 4 nos. of Mooring Launches and I no. of Survey Launch and provision of suitable Navigational Aids. The project is funded by Asian Dev. Bank (ADB). The project consultants are M/s HASKONING (Netherlands) and RITES (India). The project consultants were appointed on 17.8.94. The anticipated date of completion of the project is Sept. '2000 against the original date of commissioning of April , 1998. A close monitoring is being done with the help of a High Powered Committee. The project has made significant progress in 1998-99. All the orders have been placed and construction work is in full swing.

Creation of mechanised coal handling facilities and two coalberths at Paradip port, Orissa (Paradip port trust):

The Tamilnadu State Electricity Board (TNEB) is setting up 2130MW Coal Fires Thermal Power Station at Ennore in 3) stages and the project is referred as "North Madras Thermal Power (NMTPP)". The Coal demand of NMTPP along with the coal requirements of the already existing power stations of TNEB at Ennore and also at Mettur are to be handled at the new port at Ennore. The coal will be supplied from the Kalinga Block of Thalchar Coal Fields (Orissa) located about 200 kms. West of Paradip Port. The existing facilities at Paradip Port are not adequate to handle the bulk movement of coal, accordingly the govt. had sanctioned this project in April 1993. The project is financed by the Asian Development Bank. The contract for detailed engineering, design and supervision was award in April '1994. The contract has been divided in 3) phases (i) Concept Development (ii) Detailed Engg. (iii) Construction. The following works are being carried out departmentally (i) Survey & Soil Testing (ii) Housing & necessary infrastructure (iii) Rehabilitation (iv) Power supply (v) Reclamation of stockyard; and (vi) Procurement of equipment. The orders for equipment and construction of jettie have been placed. The work has started in full swing. The work is reviewed regularly by a Highpowered Committee headed by ex-Secretary of the Ministry of Surface Transport.

Mumbai port-replacement of the very old band of seven submarine pipelines connecting the Marine Oil Terminal at Jawahar Dweep and the Pir Pan manifold

The Marine Oil Terminal at Jawahar Dweep was developed in the mid 1950's to cater to the needs of the two refineries of BPCL & HPCL set up at Trombay. The terminal at Jawahar Dweep will three oil jetties is connected to the main land by set of seven submarine pipelines. These pipelines are now 40 years old (C.E. to accounting life of 20 years) and need urgent replacement. As measure of safety, the operating pressure in the lines are reduced from 150 psi (Pounds per square inch) to 120 psi. Apart from the oil pipelines are very old., the sizes are also inadequate to handle the present parcel size resulting low pumping rates which increase the service time of the tankers, and pre-berthing detention. It was, therefore, decided to replace the 40 years old submarine portion of the six oil pipelines and one fresh water pipeline connecting the Marine Oil Terminal at Jawahar Dweep and Pir Pau Manifold. Detailed project report for the project was prepared by the Consultants M/S Engineers India Ltd. In June '1993 and estimate amounting to Rs. 165.15 crores was sanctioned by Government in March '1995 M/S KRJ Browns was appointed on 24.4.97 for detailed engineering. There has been very little physical progress during the last 30 months due to delay in award of contract. The project as anticipated may be delayed beyond the present date of commissioning of 12/99. The estimated cost of the project at Rs. 272 crores is yet to be approved.

Bombay port-modernisation of MOT berths 1,2 & 3 at Jawahar Island

The project forms the second part of the improvement of oil handling facilities in Mumbai Port. The scope of the works covers replacement of the on shore pipe lines from JD manifold upto MOT jetties replacing the present ship shore transfer using flexible hoses by marine loading arms, upgrading the fire finghting facilities, examining the adequacy of ballast water treatment plant based on IMO requirements and safety audit & review of environmental safeguard. Detailed Project report for the project was prepared by the consultant M/s Engineers India Ltd. In October 1994 and estimate amounting to Rs. 167.99 crores was sanctioned by Govt. in August 1997. Consultant M/s K.R.J. Brown Ltd. Were appointed on 26.9.97.

Ahmedabad -Vadodara expressway

This project is the first high speed toll express in the Country and has reported maximum time and cost overrun due to the failure of the road contract twice. The balance road work is to be implemented by NHAI. The Bridge package has achieved 86.8 percent progress. The progress of the road package is about 50.9%.

Varanasi bypass and bridge across the river Ganges

This was the most badly delayed project in the road sector. The work, if completed by the now anticipated will have more than 10 years gestation period against 4 years indicated initially. The bridge portion has been completed and that of road work is in advanced stage. This project has seen the light of the day only after active campaigning by the DPI. The project is likely to be completed by 3/99.

Calcutta-Palsit section of Durgapur express way (West Bengal PWD)

The work of six lane Calcutta Durgapur Expressway was originally started in early 60s but it was shelved after land acquisition, partial embankment construction and construction of cross drainage work due to meagre fund mobilisation. In 1975, Ministry of Surface Transport declared this project as a National Highway project. In 1984 a proposal for 4 laning Calcutta-Durgapur Expressway over existing lining constructed embankment with interchange for cross roads was submitted to Ministry Of Surface Transport with provision of service roads on either sides throughout the entire expressway to segregate the slow moving and local traffic for inclusion in the World Bank aided expressway project. Ultimately two lane road at grade interaction was sanctioned in Jan '86 at an estimated cost of Rs. 48.60 crores with completion date of June '90. It was a World Bank aided project but due to extremely slow pace of work, the aid from the World Bank was discontinued 64.5 km stretch of road was originally divided into 6 road and bridge packages. The main reasons for extremely slow progress of the work are, (a) poor contract management of the project by the Bengal PWD and (B) litigation between the State Govt. and its contractors. The work in package VIII (Bridge) has been completed, The packages being executed by M/S L&T were completed. But the packages being executed by Central Concrete & Allied Products Ltd. (CCPA) and Bridge & Roof were to be completed by 1998. The progress of overall road work was 98%. Work in respect of bridge position has been completed. The Phase I of Calcutta-Durgapur Expressway opened to traffic for 48 kms. Out of 65 kms. Total length in August '97. With introduction of toll and balance portion of the road is likely to be opened 3/99. The project along with service lanes is now expected completion by 3/99.

Lane widening on NH-3 Indore dewas section and construction of Indore bypass

The project of 4-lane widening on NH-3 on Indore-Dewas Section and Indore Bypass in the State of Madhya Pradesh were sanctioned In February 1992 and January 1992 respectively. The work could not be taken up due to delay In award of contract. Final Bid documents for the project have been Submitted to World Bank for approval. Approval of World bank has been received. Prequalification of contractors is complete. Notice for bidding issued on 5.8.96. Tenders received, Evaluated and sent for the concurrence of the World Bank. The work has been awarded in August, 1997 and is in progress. Physical progress upto 12/98 is about 7%. Contractor to be persuaded to accelerate the pace of work as the progress till 3/98 was negligible.

Lane widening of Cuttack-Jagatpur, Orissa

The Ministry of Surface Transport (MOST) communicated a provisional administrative approval of the project in June '92 at an estimated cost of 126.7 crores which was later on revised as Rs. 133.982 crores in April '93. The sanctioned gestation period of the project is 5 years from April '92 e.g. to be completed by March 1997. The work is supervised by an international consultant (CEC) for quick transfer of technical knowhow. The State PWD agency charges are restricted to 3% instead of the usual 9%.

Four laning of Alwaye to Vytalla-Aroor to Sharthalai NH-47 in Kerala (ADM.II)

The project is sanctioned with the Asian Development Bank (Package-II). The estimate for these works was sanctioned for Rs 60.59 crores in March '93) Revised estimate is for Rs. 134.00 crores. The project has been delayed by 1 year and is now expected to be completed by 3/99. The project suffered additional delay due to change of design of the Edapally Bride required by the Greater Cochin Development Authority (GCDA). The present physical progress is over 94%.

4-Lanning & strengthening of NH-1 km 132.675 to 212.161 from Karnal to Haryana/Punjab border

The project is sanctioned with the assistance of World Batik (Project Package-II). The estimate for the works for Rs. 166.71 crores was sanctioned oil 31st March' 1993. Revised estimate is 28777.22 crores. The project has been divided into two lots. Lot HR-I and Lot HR-II. Due to lack of efficient forward planning and site management leading to problem in material supply and equipment failure, redesign of elevated highway and grade separate interchange with associated retaining walls and structures and poor mobilisation by the contractors the project has been delayed. The present physical progress is about 60%. Unless the contractors increase the rate, the project, may slip beyond the present date of completion of 12/98.

4-Lanning of Mathura-Agra section of NH2

The project was originally approved in November, 1993) at an estimated cost of Rs. 103.21 crores with completion date of April 1999. The 4 Laning of 51.33 km length between Mathura and Agra is marginally delayed due to initial delay in start of road and asphalt work and delay in taking up of Flyover work. The project completion is expected by December, 1999 (contract date) at an anticipated cost of Rs. 125.75 crores. The project is being executed under the Supervision of UP, PWD from Km. 148.33) to Kms. 199.06. Due to initial delay in award and start of road and asphalt work and delay in taking up flyover work. The project has made over 60% progress Upto 12/98. The project is likely to make substantial progress in 1998-99. The UP, PWD may have to keep a close watch to ensure implementation of the approved programme. They have also to ensure that the obstruction are removed so that the fronts are available. The contractor must put adequate supervision/technical staff and mobilise resources to remove the front line constraints.

4-Laning of NH-I from km 212.20 to km 252.25 in Punjab

The project was approved in August '93 at an estimated cost of Rs. 166.71 crores with completion schedule of 7/98. The present estimated cost of Rs. 240.00 crores and completion date 9/99. It is a World Batik aided project. The project is being executed under the supervision of Punjab, PWD. The road will have four lane divided carriage way and the existing road pavement will be strengthened. The project has been divided into two packages (Lot PB-I 212 to 228 kills. & Lot PB -II 228 to 252.25 kms.). The work was awarded on 4.1.199 5 to M/S Som Dutt Builders for Lot PB- I and to M/S L & T Ltd. For Lot PB- II. The work commenced on 25th March 1995 oil both the contracts with schedule completion date of

24th September 1998 and defect removal liability up to 24.9.99. Work is in progress in all the sections. The overall physical progress of the project is 69.04% (6/98) (Lot I-53.46% and Lot II-65.58%).

Improvement of NH-2 Bihar

The project was sanctioned in early 1995 and is funded by the Asian Development Bank under Loan Scheme No.III. The project is strengthening, and widening of existing 2 lane road to 4 lane road. The total length of the road being strengthened and widened to 4 lane is 42.69 kms 398 to Km 441.44). There is no physical and financial work progress reported by the NHAI since the approval of the project by the Government in March '1995. NHAI had called the tenders for the Civil work and after evaluation, the work has been awarded. Establishment of a field unit is still to be done by the NHAI. The project is scheduled for completion by 6/2000. The overall physical progress is about 14 percent

Improvement of NH-2 in West Bengal (NHAI)

The project was sanctioned in early 1995 at an original estimated cost of Rs. 143.35 crores. The project is strengthening and widening of 42 kms (Kill 474 to 516) length of road. The project is funded by the Asian Development Bank under Loan Scheme No.III. The anticipated cost of the project is Rs 2316 00 crores The physical progress till 12/98 is only 6% since the approval of the project by the Government in March '1995. The NHAI had invited tenders for the civil works and before the issue of the letter of intent by the NHAI for the contract one of the tenders appealed to the Delhi High Court and the Delhi High Court in August, 1996 had cancelled the award as decided by the NHAI. The Delhi High Court also directed the NHAI to retender the work. The work has been awarded (24.7.97). The Project Director had been appointed by the NHAI in February

'1996 and the project office is being set up at Durgapur. The expected completion date is January, 2001.

Improvement of NH-8 in Haryana & Rajasthan

Mobilisation The project was sanctioned in early 1995 and is funded by the Asian Development Bank under Loan Scheme No.III, As per the original estimate, the cost of the project in the State of Haryana is Rs. 177.86 crores and in the State of Rajasthan is Rs. 120.06 crores (total Rs. 298.50 crores). However, as reported by the NHAI as the cost of the project has gone up and is now anticipated to cost Rs. 304.12 crores. The project now expected completion by March, 2001. The physical progress was 50% (12/98) after the sanction of the project by the Government in March '1995. The NHAI had issued the Letter of Intent (LOI) on one of the tenderers for the civil construction work oil July 1, 1996. The agreement was signed in August '1996. However, one of the unsuccessful tenderers had gone to the Delhi High Court appealing against the decision of the NHAI. Though, the Delhi High Court has not set aside the award of contract by the NHAI, but it has made execution of the work of the present contractor condition to the final award by it, NHAI has appointed a Project Director in January '1996 and he has set Lip a field office at Gurgaon. The letter of acceptance issued oil 1.7.96. Agreement signed on 19.8.96. But the work could not be taken up. It has been communicated by MOST that the work had to retendered. The new contract was signed oil 27.8.97.

NH2 4 laning between 438-474 kms. West Bengal (WBPWD)

The project was sanctioned in early 1995 at an original estimated cost of Rs. 88.21 crores. The project is strengthening and widening of 42 kms (Km 438 to 474) length of road, The project is funded by the Asian Development Batik under Loan Scheme No.III. The physical progress till 12/98 about 7% since the approval of the project by the Government in March '1995.

The NHAI had invited tenders for the civil works and before the issue of the letter of intent by the NHAI for the contract one for the tenderers appealed to the Delhi High Court in August, 1996 had cancelled the award as decided by the NHAI. The Delhi High Court also directed the NHAI to retender the work. Further action in the matter is to be taken by NHAI. The Project Director had been appointed by the NHAI in February '1996 and the project office is being set up at Durgapur. The work was finally awarded in September, 97. The expected completion date is 9/2000.

Telecommunications

There are 14 projects on the monitor including one project of Department of Telecommunications and 13 projects of Videsh Sanchar Nigam (VSNL). Out of these, two projects namely, International Gateways at Ernakulam and Jullundhur under VSNL were commissioned in March '98 and April, 1998 respectively, Others are in advanced stage of implementation.

Urban development (others)

There are 13 civil construction projects which are being implemented by the CPWD of the Department of Urban Development. Of these only four projects belong to the Deptt. of Urban Development and 4 others belong to other organisations. The estimated cost of these projects is Rs. 5810.55 crores. Three projects namely, Bhasa Bhavan at Calcutta, IGNOU campus and General Pool Residential Accommodation at Bombay were originally due for completion in the VIII Plan have slipped to IX Plan for various reasons like delay in tendering and mobilisation, delay In award of contract, fund constraints, court cases and delay in obtaining approval from various civil bodies. A review meeting was held under the Chairmanship of Minister of State in October 1997 to avoid further slippages. The construction for the Parliament Library is progressing as per the revised schedule. Three projects are nearing completion. The General Pool Accommodation project at Bombay is to be redesigned by the Department of Urban Development. One of the major projects included in this that of Delhi Metro. The status of the project is highlighted below:-

Delhi metro rapid transit system (Delhi metro rail corporation)

The Delhi Metro Project has several sections in a sequence based on traffic density. The Phase I of the project consist of the following sections

i) ISBT - Central Secretariat - Metro Corridor.

ii) Shahdra - Nangloi Rail Corridor

iii) Sabji Mandi - Naya Azadpur - Rail Corridor.

The phase 1 now consists of only 553 kms. The present estimated cost of the metro rail project is Rs. 5211.0 crores and is scheduled for completion by March 2005. The main consultant has been appointed which will look into the preparation of detailed estimates and action plan for implementation of the project. The deposit work on Shahdra - Nangloi has already started. The work on the preparation of civil construction tenders and procurement of rolling stock etc. Is now in progress.

9

Nineth Plan:Objective, Strategy and Approach

The Eighth Plan had identified "human development" as its main focus. The objectives of the Ninth Plan arising from the Common Minimum Programme of the United front government, the Chief Ministers' Conference on basic minimum services and the suggestions that have been put forward by Chief Ministers of various states during extensive consultations are as follows:

Alleviation of rural poverty has been one of the primary objectives of planned development in India. Ever since the inception of planning, the policies and the programmes have been designed and redesigned with this aim. As such, in the Ninth Plan emphasis has been laid on agriculture and rural development with a view to generating adequate productive employment and eradicating poverty.

Secondly, the draft approach paper of the Ninth Plan aims at a higher growth rate of seven per cent per annum as against the average 5.9 per cent (at market prices) of Gross Domestic Product in the Eighth Plan with its main focus being "growth with equity and distributive justice".

Thirdly, the Ninth Plan also seeks empowerment of women and socially disadvantaged groups such as SCs, STs and OBCs and minorities as agents of socio-economic change and development. It also aims at promoting and developing people's participatory institutions like Panchayati Raj, co-operatives and a large number of self-help groups which have been doing yeoman service in developing the potential of the people.

Fourthly, the Ninth Plan aims at ensuring environmental sustainability of the development process through social mobilization and participation of people at all levels.

Fifthly, the Ninth Plan envisages an employment-oriented growth strategy and an appropriate mix of capital and labour and technology which would lead to efficiency of efficiency of these of resources and ensure higher growth for the economy.

Sixthly, the Ninth Plan gives highest priority to provide the seven basic minimum services of safe drinking water, primary health care facilities, universal primary education, shelter, midday meals, connectivity of villages and revitalizing the public distribution system in a time-bound manner.

Finally, it aims at ensuring food and nutritional security for all, particularly the vulnerable sections of society.

The above stated objectives need to be seen in the context of four important dimensions of state policy, viz (a) quality of life of the citizens; (b) generation of productive employment; (c) regional balance; and (d) self-reliance.

Quality of life is multi-dimensional. It encompasses not only the economic opportunities available to the people, but also their ability to take advantage of these opportunities, and the existence of living conditions which permit a healthy and productive life. Eradication of poverty and provision of basic minimum services are integral elements of any strategy to improve the quality of life. No developmental process can be sustainable unless it leads to visible and wide spread improvement in these areas. The problem of shelter for the poor both in urban and rural areas is particularly acute. Thus, a programme of providing assistance for construction of houses needs to be implemented. The above objectives cannot be achieved merely through increased investment, but a significant change in social attitudes and behavioural responses of the people is required. In this process, the role of women is critical. The process of empowerment of women at the political level has already begun, but it needs to be carried forward into the social and economic spheres as well.

To solve the problem of people's access to basic nutritional requirements, the Ninth Plan will lay emphasis on developing strategies by which the problem can be overcome by integrating the food production and distribution systems with the employment and poverty alleviation programmes. In particular, the public distribution system will be restructured in order to provide food grains at substantially lower prices to the poor in a focused manner and to ensure availability of such commodities in the remote and deficit areas of the country.

One of the objectives of the Ninth plan will be to generate greater productive employment in the growth process itself. During the last decade, there has been relatively rapid growth which generated adequate employment opportunities. However, the quality of employment in terms of the incomes received and the work environment leave much to be desired. Thus, it becomes necessary to shift the focus of employment strategies towards creating conditions whereby employment opportunities lead to significantly better living and working conditions of the people and upholding the dignity of labour. Free and compulsory education of children supported by an adequate midday meal programme in schools is the first step towards this end.

The issue of regional balance operates at both the inter-State and the intra-State levels. There is, therefore, the need to address it in a framework that is more flexible than the political and administrative boundaries of each individual State. The focus regarding the issue of regional balance has traditionally been of industrialization. However, reduction in regional disparities, may be better achieved through greater focus on agriculture and other rural activities. As such, it becomes necessary not only to increase the productivity of agriculture in backward areas, but also to increase the degree of integration between the rural areas and the rest of the country through improved connectivity in terms of transport and communications.

The first, and perhaps most important, component of self-reliance is to ensure balance of payments sustainability and avoidance of excessive external debt. This requires a commitment to sound and prudent macro-economic policies, particularly in fiscal and monetary management matters. The Ninth Plan will be based on a framework of prudent macro-management and greater reliance on non—dept creating external flows for financing balance of payments needs. It will link the inflow of external resources to the level of domestic savings and the long-run ability to service external liabilities.

Relevance and Objectives

"Human Development" had been identified as the main focus in the Eighth Plan. This continues to be the main concern of the Ninth Plan also. The objectives of the Plan are deduced from the Common Minimum Programme (CMP) of the United Front government and the Chief ministers' Conference on basic minimum services as well as extensive consultation with the Chief Ministers of various States. Of the nine objectives identified, in keeping with the figure of Ninth Plan, the first objective lays stress rightly on rural development. The objectives are as follows:

— Priority to agriculture and rural development with a view to generating adequate productive employment and eradication of poverty;

— Accelerating growth rate of the economy with stable prices;

— Ensuring food and nutritional security for all sections of society;

— Providing the basic minimum services of safe drinking water, primary heath care facilities, universal primary education, shelter and connectivity to all in a time-bound manner;

— Containing the growth rate of population;

— Ensuring environmental sustainability of the development process through social mobilization and participation of people at all levels.

— Empowerment of women and socially disadvantaged groups such as Scheduled Castes, Scheduled Tribes and other backward classes and minorities as agents of socio-economic change and development.

— Promoting and developing people's participatory institutions like Panchayati Raj bodies, co-operatives and self-help groups;

— Strengthening efforts to build self-reliances.

The emphasis of the above objectives is to seek to achieve "growth with equity and social justice". These have to be seen in the context of four important dimensions of the state policy which are: (a) Quality of life the Citizens; (b) Generation of productive employment; (C) Regional balance; and (d) Self-reliance.

The fear has been expressed by several experts that the New Economic Policy (NEP) of liberalization and globalization is contrary to the basic philosphy of the Indian Five Year Plans which were based to achieve a socialistic pattern of society with active people's participation. People's participation does figure in the Ninth Plan as the key element to achieve the goals of the Plan.

Prof B.M. Bhatia, an economist of considerable standing is of the opinion that the Planning Commission has lost its utility and function in a free-market-economy. The whole exercise of the approach paper according to him was palpably so arithmetical, albeit circular in reasoning, that one wonders whether it could not be left to a schoolboy to do the job instead of the Yojana Bhavan. He further says that the approach paper has failed to spell out concrete policy for social engineering, that is claimed to be the principal objective of the plan. He further asserts that the planners have been very casual in their task as is evident from the fact that the growth rate for the agricultural sector was put at 3.5 per cent which was revised at the instance of the Prime Minister. This would substantially change the whole structure of the Plan as well as the development strategies underlying it. In view of this change, the entire approach paper should have been drasticaly revised and recast. But the planners had neither patience nor the time to do that. They just took 48 hours to raise the agriculture sector growth rate target from the originally envisaged

3.5 per cent to 4.5 per cent. Could there be a better example of a cavalier approach than the one shown by the present Planning Commission in preparing a five year plan for the country.

The approach paper refutes the idea of non-plan and advocates that the role of planning continues to be highly relevant, although the nature of the instruments available to implement the plan has changed. The planning process today also needs to focus on planning for policy so that the signals that are sent to the economic system induce the various economic agents to behave in a manner which is consistent with the national objectives. In particular, investment patterns would be determined by sectoral policies.

The Ninth Five Year Plan (1997-2002) has the strategy to achieve a seven per cent growth rate for the economy. The approach paper for the Plan was recently endorsed by the National Development Council (NDC) with its final approach paper'would now be put up for public debate before the final document is ready and implemented from 1 April, 1997.

The seven per cent growth in gross domestic product (GDP) would be through a 9.3 per cent annual growth in industrial production, 4.5 per cent growth in agriculture, while the fiscal deficit is to be brought down to four per cent of GDP. The approach document has sought an increase in gross domestic savings rate from the Eighth Plan average of 23.7 per cent to 26.2 per cent in the Ninth Plan. The gap between investment needs and domestic savings can be bridged through increased inflow of foreign capital.

"Growth with equity" has been adopted as the theme of the Plan. The followint are the main objectives to be fulfilled during the Plan period:

— Generation of adequate productive employment and eradication of poverty.

— Acceleration in the growth rate of the economy with stable price.

— Provision for basic minimum services of safe drinking water, primary health care facilities, universal primary education, shelter and connectivity to all villages in a time-bound manner.

— Ensuring food and nutritional security for all, particularly the vulnerable sections of society.

— Containing the growth rate of population.

— Ensuring environmental sustainability of the development process through socila mobilization and participation of people at all levels.

— Empowerment of women and socially disadvantaged groups as agents of socio-economic change and development.

— Promoting and developing people's participatory institutions like Panchayati Raj bodies, co-operatives and self-help groups.

— Strengthening efforts to build self-reliance.

Ninth plan strategy

1. The aim is to make the agriclutural sector grow at the rate of 4.5 per cent per annum.

2. A regionally differntiated strategy is to be adopted, based on agronomic, climatic and environmentally—friendly conditions, on the following lines;

   (i) *North—western high productivity region*: The focus will be on (a) promoting diversification of crops with the emphasis on high–value crops, (b) strengthening linkages with the agro–processing industry and exports, and (c) creation of basic infrastructure.

(ii) *Eastern region with abundant water*: Productivity in this region is very low despite availability of abundant water. In order to increase productivity, emphasis will be on flood control, drainage management, improvement of irrigation facilities and input delivery systems, along with adequate agricultural credit and extension services.

(iii) *Water—scarce region—Peninsular India including Rajasthan*: Low productivity in this region is attributed to water scarcity. The focus will be on development of efficient water harvesting and conservation methods, suitable irrigation packages based on watershed approach and promotion of an appropriate farming system.

(iv) *Ecologically fragile regions including the Himalayasand desert areas*: The emphasis is to be on development of ecofriendly agriculture in these areas.

3. With respect to basic inputs, regional programmes are to be formulated in such a manner as to ensure timely and adequate availability of inputs to the farmer, particularly in the remote, hilly, backward and tribal areas. The approach as regards inputs is as follows:

(i) *Irrigation*: Priority is to be given to completion of ongoing major and medium irrigation projects.

(ii) *Fertilizers*: Consumption of fertilizers in low—use areas and crops is to be increased; imbalances in the use of plant nutrients are to be reduced; an integrated pest management system is to be adopted; emphasis is to be given on use of biotic agents. In order to accomplish these tasks, a programme of soil–testing across the various agro—climatic regions is to be initiated. It is recognized that fertilizer imports need to be curtailed, and hence, output and productivity of fertilizer production units should be increased through better capacity utilization, improvement in energy efficiency in order to reduce production costs, and other measures towards the goal of modernizing the fertilizer industry. (iii) Seeds: The focus will be on promoting a higher seed replacement rate. Then, in the post—GATT period, new plant variety protection rights make it necessary to increase facilities for registration of varieties; steps are to be taken in this direction. (iv) Credit: Efforts are to be made to ensure timely and adequate availability of credit, particularly to small and marginal farmers and tribal farmers at reasonable rates, so that they have the wherewithal for making investment, which would step up production levels.

(v) *Other issues*: Implementation of the National Watershed Development Programme will be intensified for development of rainfed farming areas; the crop insurance scheme. will be focused on to provide security to marginal and small farmers in rainfed areas; in every district, the RIDF is to be used to cover projects which encourage groups of small farmers, artisans and landless labourers, in order to facilitate skill upgradation , processing, better transportation and quqality improvement. These projects can be centred around large agro—based projects or identified sources of regional, national and export demand.

Then, research efforts are to be enhanced in the spheres of biotechnology, microbiology, genetic improvement of crops, genetic upgradation of animal resources, etc. Teaching facilities in the area of agricultural education are to be upgraded, and the existing infrastructure for transfer of technology is to be made more effective and responsive to meet the needs of farmers.

Plan priorities

According to Prof. Madhu Dandavate, Deputy Chairman of the Planning Commission, the Ninth Plan accords "the highest priority to generating adequate productive employment, eradication of poverty, focus on agriculture and rural development with emphasis on radical land reforms".

Pointing out that the power sector constitutes the most crucial infrastructure both for agriculture and industry, he said that the problems of power must be carefully handled in a co-ordinated fashion with due attention for the proper choice of fuels, the adequacy of their availability, the need to rationalize tariff structure, and to prevent transmission and distribution losses.

In fact, the problem of power may reach crisis proportions in the next few years unless urgent action is taken by every state. The financial, managerial and administrative structue of State Electricity Boards (SEBs) and their policies must be changed dramatically and urgently so that the Electricity Boards can raise tariffs to realistic levels, improve the quality of supply, contain power theft and become financially viable. The Finance Minister, Mr. P. Chidambaram, is of the view that the Central and State laws need to be changed to allow SEBs and private electricity companies to function autonomously subject to independent regulatory authorities.

In respect of sectoral strategies, the document emphasizes that agriculture has a vital place in the economic development of the country as it contributes 29.4 per cent of GDP and employs about 64 per cent of the workforce. There has been a significant improvement in agricultural productivity which has helped in reducing rural poverty. It is noted that capital formation (at 1980-81 prices) in agriculture grew at tha rate of 6.05 per cent during 1989-90 to 1994-95. In the accelerated growth scenario for the Ninth Plan, efforts will need to be made to achieve an agricultural growth rate of 4.5 per cent per annum in contrast with 3.5 per cent growth rate during the Eighth Plan period on an average.

The role of basic inputs in agriculture cannot be underestimated. Timely and adequate availabilty of inputs for agriculture and agriculture-related infrastructure will need to receive special attention. Therefore, regional programmes have to be formulated in such a manner as to ensure provision of inputs to the farmer, particularly in the remote, hilly, backward and tribal areas. Likewise, augmentation of irrigation facilities is necessary to increase the gross cropped areas even under rainfed vonditions and invreasing cropping intensity in agriculture areas and assinging priority ot the completion of ongoing projects—both major and minor irrigation.

Another vital input is rural credit. Greater credit flow will be ensured to meet the investment requirements of the farming community for stepping up the growth of production. The approach paper of the Plan stresses that efforts would be made to ensure timely and adequate availability of credit, particularly to small and marginal farmers and tribal farmers at reasonable rates so as to enable them to make investments necessary for higher production. More importantly, the crop insurance scheme is going to receive a big thrust for providing security to marginal and small farmers in rainfed areas during the Ninth Plan period.

Referring to the controversy over poverty estimates exercise, Prof. Dandavate points out that a group in the Plan panes has smoothed out some 'kinks' in the poverty estimate arising out of the appliation of the Lakadwala Committee methodology. He said that the group has suggested that in assessing rural poverty, the agricultural labourers' consumer price index should be used and for estimating urban poverty, the industrial workers' consumer price index should be untilized for updating the poverty line. It is hoped that the Planning Commission would finally decide on this issue during the final draft of the Plan.

The Strategy of development adopted in the Ninth Five Year Plan aims at reaching out to those regions and sections of the society which have been bypassed by the process of development. At the same time, it also has to aim at efficiency of resource use in areas and sectors which have already been developed. Supply—side efficiency and technological transformation have to be interwoven with the economic process of increasing the production potential. In order to sustain a growing and well—diversified economy in the Nith Plan, it would be necessary to evolve judicious public policies towards investment and technology, which can mobilize resources that are lying unutilized in the economy and can unleash wider processes of agricultural growth and decentralized developments linked to national and world markets.

Thrust needs to be given to develop modern communication and information system in the villages. Those could be managed and operated by community initiative or growers' association. This would enable the farming community to know about the latest trend of the prices both in the domestic and international market and also quality of food products of other countries, taste and preference of the consumers. Based on the input structure, the output pattern for major crops during the Ninth Plan has been tentatively worked out. In the output projections, adequate emphasis has been laid on relative self—sufficiency in food production, keeping in view the imperative of maintaining food security in the country. In fact, it culd be stated that the Indian economy attained high rates of growth and better economic stability and resilience during the eighties, among other factors, due to the factor of relative food self—sufficiency. It is important to constantly keep this factor in view while chalking out the broad contours of the Ninth Plan.

The State Agricultural Board should construct Haats with necessary infrastructure facilities at important areas/mandis for small and marginal farmers so as to enable them to get rid of dalall agent and sell their agricultural commodities direct to the buyers/consumers. Tis would also generate a number of employment oportunities in the process of marketing activities, besides better price to the farmers. Necessary infrastructure would need to be created in the major growing areas for encouraging the entrepreneurs to set up food processing industries. It would be more appropriate if encouragement is given to joint ventures with growers' participation as members. An agri–business corporation should be set up for marketing the agricultural produce both in the domestic as well as in international markets. The corporation would establish both forward and backward linkages with the growers and help them to improve quality and productivity. For increasing India's share in the world trade of food and food products, modernizaton of agricultural marketing system would need to be encouraged with more emphasis on quality control, sophisticated and eco—friendly packaging and consumer packs.

Dryland farming and biological software library: There is need for flow of investment in dryland agriculture, which is insufficient at present. It can be suggested that if a part of the huge funds allotted in the Ninth Plan for famine relief in the event of drought could be spent for proper nutrition of poor dry land soils and crops, the recurring problem of famines could be solved to a great extent. Given the level of food stocks of the order of 36.4 million tonnes, food avvailibility has ceased to be a constraint on economic development. Also, while due emphasis would continue to be laid on the diversified crop structure in the Ninth Plan, attention would also have to be paid to the development of dairy, poultry, fisheries, friits and vegetables, tea, coffee, rubber plantation, etc. Development of non—crop oriented agricultural activities would involve, inter alia, strengthening of the existing processing facilities for value—addition operations as also installation of new capacities in these fields. During the Ninth Plan, each village information centre will have one Biological Software Library (BSL) to take care of soil health, earthworm farming and biofertilisers production/supply. Thus, this library will provide all types of organic/biotic inputs at the doorsteps of farmers.

The special needs of water management and its integration with agricultural operations call for a selective and systematic approach to conjunctive use of water at micro and macro levels. This would help eliminate deterious effects on soil and environment and also help optimize the use of water in crop productivity. There is an urgent need to recognize water as a national asset and its proper utilization whould be a top priority area brooking no delay to increase use–efficiency. Low efficiency of irrigation use ranges from 30 to 70 per cent and there is inequality in distribution of water. Increasing problems of soil salinity, water–logging and soil degradation associated with irrigation are also to be looked into. In working out of the production potential of agriculture during the Ninth Plan, the approach to water development strategies at the subregional level is to be vigorously pursued. This approach sets specific targets for projects like tank irrigation, watershed development, modernization and completion of canal system and diversification of cropping sequences in different agro–climatic regions of India. It is also necessary to strengthen the appropriate input structure of irrigation, fertilizer consumption, crop intensity and crop diversification, etc. for building up the production potential of agriculture during the Ninth Plan.

Emphasis should continue to be laid on the Integrated Watershed Development Projects. Various soil and water conservation technologies need to be energetically pursued to raise productivity in the marginal and rainfed land holdings. As per preliminary estimates, the share of irrigated area in gross sown area is likely to be 48.4 per cent in the terminal year of the Ninth Plan diversified agriculture and crop intensification should be propagated with the crop intensity reaching the level of 1.40 by 2001—2002.

It is necessary that institutional finances as advanced by the co—operative credit system and commercial banks and regional rural banks to the agricultural sector should consistently increase during the Ninth Plan. The priority sector lending target set by government for commercial banks should be fulfilled by all the public sector banks during each year of the Ninth Plan. Such a commitment on the part of institutional financing agencies will considerably help in financing development needs in the agriculture and rural development sectors.

The sectoral allocation of the total investment has to be so designed that investment in agriculture and rural development should get a big push in the Ninth Plan. In the Ninth Plan, out of the total investment, the share of agriculture and rural development needs to be increased to about 30 per cent. This is very important, as in recent years, capital formation in the agricultural sector has tended to decline.

The agricultural sector is likely to have a bright future due to the overall expansion of the economy through liberalization, globalization and privatization. The agricultural production, productivity, export and employment is likely to pick up in the future due to its forward linkages with the economy. At the same time, the liberalized economic environment is expected to show some side—effects on crokpping pattern, income distribution and employment. In the overall context, the Ninth Plan hopes to integrate the planning process for the globalization of agriculture.

This, threrfore, establishes the need for evolving a two–prolonged strategy to raise the level of the productivity per unit area when there is no scope for bringing more area under these crops but to release the part of the existing area to meet other economic needs. The two pronged strategy refers to:

— Adoption of available proven technology by all the farmers in a period of five years.

— Strengthening the basefor research, extension and education so that the integrated approach can create an impact in the future.

Proven technology already demonstrated to farmers revolves around use of high—yielding verietal (HYV) seeds or hybrid seeds, organic manure accompanied by chemicalfertilizers, irrigation or adoption of soil and moisture conservation practices, prevention or control of pests and diseases, farm—machineries, agronomic practices and post—harvrest technology. For all food crops, agricultural universities set up in each of the States as also research institutes of the Indian Council of Agricultural Research (ICAR) have already evolved and standardized a package of practicesfor specific regions or areas which are also demonstrated b them or by the Krishi Vigyan Kendras.

In order to achieve the yield potential, the farmers should be enabled to use HYV or hybrid seeds which under a given dose of fertilizer and moisture can express their full yield potential. In respect of rice, the hybrids released for Andhra Pradesh, Tamil Nadu, Karnataka and West Bengal capable of yielding an additional one to 1.5 tonner per hectarethan the besyt variety, have earned for India the distinction of being the second country after China to makethe hybrid technology in rice, a field reality. These hybrids, viz APHR259—1, APHR—2, MGR—1, KRH—1, CNHR—3, DRRH—1 and KRH—4 need to be produced and supplied afresh every year to all the farmers in the area of Telengana and Rayalseema, Tamil Nadu, Karnataka and West Bengal, as only afraction of thearea is presently covered in these States under these hybrids. Likewise, a balanced use of fertilizer nutrients inadequate quantities is necessary to increase yield and sustain soil health and productivity levels. Abrupt increase in fertilizer prices and reduction or removal of subsidy on phosphatic and potassic fertilizers have resulted into unbalanced use of nutrients adversely affecting the productivity of the food crops. Also, application of major and minor nutrients should be made after testing the soil which would help increase productivity and resuce the cost. Basal dose of farm yard manure or biogas slurry is a must for maintaining and enhancing inherent soil fertility. All these aspects are at present ignored by farmers which must be ensured through education and monitoring.

The present status of irrigating the crops either throgh canal or well also needs to be improved consederably. Time method and quantum of water according to the varieties of crops, soil and climate have been evolved which should be judiciously followed. Water is a scarce and very costly commodity, which, if judiciously and scientifically used, will also increase productivity of crops and will not have any adverse effect on soils which we have now been experiencing. Not only is there a most urgent need to conserve water through the use of drip and sprinkler irrgation system but the unused potential of about 13.9 million hectares must also be put to judicious use.

Technological breakthrough would only create the expected impact if agricultural operatons right from land preparation to post—harvest opertions are conducted speedily, effectively and on time for which specific types of farm equipment devised by the research, testing and training centres, power and farm machinery divsion of the agricultural universities as also the Central Institute of Agricultural Engineering are popularized, produced and supplied to farmers. Plant protection, though significantly important, has yet not received the needed attention bythe farmers. For this purpose, a campaign on war footing should be mounted so that all farmers adopt the integrated pest management practices in a time—bound programme. Along with this, losses during harvest and post—harvest operations till the food grains reach the consumers have to be prevented or drastically minimized through adoption of methods already developed for this purpose.

Components of development strategy

In the Ninth Plan, the strategy of development has to be mobelizational in the sense of reaching out to those regions or sections of people who have been bypassed in the process of development and has also to aim at the efficiency of resource use on areas and sectors which have already been developed. Supply side efficiency and technological transformations have to be interwoven withe the economic process of production potential and in this process meet the demands of those who are currentoy left out of the process of development. In working out the production potential in the agricultural sector, the approach of agroclimatic planning, which emphasizes both land and water development strategies at the subregional level, is to be vigorously pursued. This approach sets specific targets for projects like tank irrigation, watershed development, modernization and completion of canal system and diversification of cropping sequences in different agro-climatic regions of India.

For attainment of output targets in various sectors/ subsectors in the Ninth Plan, investment levels have to be increased in critical sectors like agriculture, rural development, industry, power, telecommunications, transport, etc. With increased public investment in infrastructural facilities, private and community investment is also likely to crowd in.

The trend in real investment in the agricultural sector is disturbing and has to be reversed. Fixed capital formation was 8.63 per cent of agricultural GDP in 1984-85, but is only 8.55 per cent in 1994-95 at 80/81 prices. Even if the agricultural incremental capital output ratio (ICOR) is around three, a 12 per cent rate of fixed capital formation is necessary. Increasing levels of investments in the agricultural sector have to be brought about through increased public investment in irrigation, rural government to set up a Rural Infrastructural Development Fund (RIDF) as announced in the Central Budget for 1995-96 will help in financing the ongoing rural projects in backward areas.

The co-operative sector has to participate in increased investment activities in the various sector of the economy. Certain NABARD studies show the self-help co-operatives for decentralized development can generate self-sustaining employment and income but such efforts would require initial refinancing support from outside. Training, infrastructure, including roads, quality control and processing or export home demand areas in each district. The RIDF must meet this challinge, so that benefits of liberalization reach our small farmers.

Integrated watershed development projects oould neet to be closely monitored. Various soil and water conservation technologies eill need to be energetically pursued to raise productivity in the marginal and rainfed land holdings. Improved water management stragegies in irrigated and assured rainfall areas will have to be pursued. As per preliminary estimates, the share of gross irrigated area in gross cropped area is likely to be 46.4 per cent by the terminal of the Ninth Plan. Emphasis will continue to be laid on diversified agriculture and crop intensification will be propagated with crop intensity reasching the level of 1.40 by 2001-2002.

The output structure in the Ninth Plan needs to be conducive to the generation of 8-9 million employment opportunities per year. Emphasis will be laid on high employment elasticity activities like (i) animal husbandry, fisheries, horticulture, etc. (ii) sugar, fish canning and preservation; tobacco pruducts and cotton ginning. For those who are left out on the agricultural and rural growth process, the government is committed to an Employment Assurance Scheme.

In order to achieve the various output levels and to sustain the growing and well-diversified economy in the Ninth Plan, it is necessary to evolve judicious public policies towards investment and technology which can mobilise latent resources which are lying unutilised in the economy and can unleash wider processes of agricultural growth and decentralized developments linked to ;national and world markets.

The perspective plan in the Ninth Plan may, therefore, amongst other strategies have to:

— institutionalize the Accelerated Irrigation Benefit Programme for completing large and medium irrigation programme;

— operationalize the strategy of perspective planning for the water sector being worked out by the special Commission set up for this sector;

— raise fixed investment in the agricultural sector to at least 12 per cent of agricultural CDP; work out the private invesment inducing aspects of public investment in the water, land development, agricultural technology and research and agricultural markets sector;

— carry-forward the agro-climatic planning strategy;

— complete the process of agricultural economic reform, including tariff reform, removal of trade bottlenecks, rural credit reform and liberalization of the co-operative sector; and

— work out the institutional support-base for small farmers and employment for landless labourers

Alternative scenarios

There are two alternative scenarios pertaining to growth parameters envisaged in the Ninth Plan. One focuses on a 6.2 per cent annual rate of growth of the GDP with domestic savings rate rising from 23.7 to 25.2 per cent, the current account deficit rising from 1.3 to 1.7 per cent, investment rate rising from 25 to 26.9 per cent, of the GDP at market price in between the Eighth and Ninth Five Year Plans. The postulated export growth rates in this scenario are 11.4 per cent per annum and 12 per cent per annum for the Eighth and Ninth Plans respectively; the import growth rates for the two plans are put at 13.6 per cent and 11.4 per cent respectively. The incremental capital output ratios (ICOR) underlining the projections are to increase by a mere 10 per cent in between the two plans from 4.24 in the Eighth Plan to 4.34 in the Ninth Plan. The Second scenario envisages a seven per cent annual growth rate of the GDP with the domestic savings rate risings from 23.7 per cent to 26.2 per cent, the current account deficit from 1.3 per cent to 2.4 per cent, investment rate from 24 per cent to 28.6 per cent of the GDP at market price, in between the Eighth and Ninth Plans. The export rate is expected to rise to 14.5 per cent per annum to 15.3 per cent in between the plans. The ICOR is postulated to decline from 4.24 to 4.08 per cent.

It is understandable that the Commission keeps both the two growth rate scenarios in view because of the various possibilities, such as the saving and investment ratios not going very much higher or foreign capital inflows turning out to be lower than anticipated.

Without the opportunity and time to examine in depth the values and the inter-relationships postulated, amongst the parameters, their intenal consistency in any scenario has to be just assumed to be valid. There can be many a slip between the cup and thelip, as the say. In any case, even in the past when the uncertainies resulting from the globalization were much less, the growth rate achievements turned out to be lower than targeted; with the fevour for glovalization expanding, though in the midst of highly contradictory political signals, the growth rate becomes even more amenable to influences beyond the pale of a convincing prediction of that rate for any five year scenario. We can only hope that the average annual growth rate during the Ninth Plan would at least be 6 per cent annum..

It may be pointed out that the momentum which the world economy gained during the sixties has yet to return. Neither the rate of world economic growth nor that of the growth of world trade has come out of what is turning out to be the rather longest recession market economies have had since the end of that era. The East Asian economies which have been the most positive influence on whatever world growth there has been in the meanwhile are themselves upset by the recent deceleration of their exports and growth rates.

In such circumstances and with our own exports and imports fluctuating sharply every now and then, uncertainities in the way of the fulfilment of our growth targets are also an important parameter to reckon with. Since the advocay of globalization is likely to remain vociferous at least during the Ninth Plan period, the chances of the experience of shortfalls of the Eighth Plan type not being repeated are hardly bright.

Apart from strengthening infrastructure, the Ninth Plan aims at:

— maximizing the growth of productive employment and reducing poverty through higher priority to agriculture and rural development;

— rapid economic growth without inflation;

— providing for food and nutritional security for all but most of all for the vulnerable sections of the society;

— supplying to all, basic minimum services like safe drinking water, primary health care facilities, universal primary education, shelter and connectivity, in a time-bound manner;

— checking population growth;

— ensuring environmental-friendly sustainable development through wider peoples' participation than hitherto;

— increasing political and economic empowerment of women and other socially handicapped people including OBCs and minorities so that they become effective agents of socio-economic change;

— encouraging and fostering decentrialisation through Panchayati Raj and co-operative institutions; and

— building up self-reliance.

Private sector

It is difficult to be assured that these objectives will be backed by economic policies different from those of the previous plan. If the intention is that by a greater substitution of private capital for the govermental one, we will be nearer the goal of a more co-ordinated growth-equity nexus, we are frankly off the mark. The prospects of the private sector being an effective remedy for resource deeficiency depend largely on the national pool of savings being larger. Provided the private investors are always thrifty and the government always wasteful, privatisation could raise savings somewhat. But if the public sector's waste is always viewed as misplanced welfare or populist and the private sector's thrift as always being efficiency-oriented, and certainly not related to welfare, this method of raising savings, even if there are no other problems, could be questioned. Currently, the welfare motives of even the NGOs are being viewed with scepticism because they are every now and then using government as a source of their own funding. But the more serious difficulty is that the private sector today regards encouraging consumerism as such a cardinal principle of today's market that it cannot as expected to add to national savings in the same measure as expected. Both its self-seeking postures and also its initiative performance in respect of encouragement to often excessively competitive consumption dissuade us from believing that increasing substitution of the private sector in place of govenment can help in achieving many of the above enumerated objectives of the Ninth Plan except very marginally.

Indirectly it could do that if the growth rate was accelerated and with that the rate of growth of employment too was pushed up with no dip in the real wage rates of the employed.

From that angle, the emphasis on giving priority to agricultural production is welcome. But here too as elsewhere, constraint in respect of resources (say for an infrastructure like irrigation) is a bottleneck and shuold not be handled in terms of privatisation and by such superficial attempts as Infrastructure Development Fund etc.

However, while the State has to be at the commanding heights if the growth-equity nexus has to be co-ordinated well enough to enable the Ninth Plan to achieve its various objectives, the improvement in the work ethos of the public sector and fixing up of criminal liability on those wasting public funds must be urgently attended to. All those who oppose judicial activism or other serious attempts to fight corruption are merely tending to protect the vested interest of the few against the larger interests of the many. Corruption is rightly cited amongst the most negative of factors against the

State assuming commanding heights; and since in India's circumstances today, the market would be incapable of bringing about growth equity co-ordination, continuance of corruption can only help detractors of public intervention rather than the vast masses of people for whome the entire exercise of planned development has always been really intended.

Action plans

Targets envisaged under the Ninth Plan document are not difficult to be achieved at all. However, in order to achieve the target of 230 million tonnes of food production by the end of the Plan period, formulation of a perspective plan for five years indicating targets cropwise, seasonwise, yearwise and areawise taking into consideration the production potential at current technological level on one hand and annual action plan focusing the strategic planning for achieving the targets on the other, is absolutely essential.

The annual action plan should include detailed estimates of required inputs, viz high yielding varietal seeds or hybrid seeds, okrganic manure and chemical fertilizers, farm machinery and equipment, irrigation, pesticides and post—harvest facilities areawise. Besides, sources of their availability from various agencies, viz private, co-–operative and government sectors should be indicated so as to make them available on time. Transfer of technology through field level trained extension staff as well as mass media will have to be ensured. In fact, past experience has very well confirmed and established that our extension services at field level has been inefficient which should be made most responsive to the present needs. A modified system from thelesson learnt on "Training and Visit System" to suit different agro—ecological regions and social system may be necessary.

The State level corporations and boards, viz Electricity Boards, Seed Corporation, Ground Water Development Corporation, Agro—Industries Corporations, Soil Testing Laboratories, Krishi Vigyan Kendras, Marketing Boards/Federations, Co–operative organizations and the like primarily responsible to play the vital and catalytic role in the promotion and growth of food grain production in particular and other farm commodities in general should also be made to respond and commit themselves for showing the expected results rather than detailing excuses. Input delivery and marketing system which involve the above agencies needs to be revamped without any delay.

In order to reduce the cost of production per unit quantity and increase productivity, production and profitability of the food grain production, there is an urgent need to ensure the folowing:

— The seed industry both n public and private sectors should not only produce quality seeds of food crops but also guide farmers in respect of time, method of sowing and amount of seeds to be used along with agronomic practices to be adopted for optimum productions.

— The fertilizer industry should arrange for soil testing and advising farmers on the time and method of application and amount of chemical fertilizers along with manure to be used for specific food crops.

— The pesticide industry should educate farmers on integrated pest management in respect of food crops concerned.

— The authorities concerned with the supply of canal or ground water should counsel farmers on a continuing basis about the time and method of application of water as also quantum of water to be applied so as to optimize the use of water for specific food crops.

— The suppliers of farm implements and machineries must advise users for specified types of farm operations to be conducted as per schedule which can minimize the cost of okperations. It is high time that these agencies are not only directed to supply quality inputs on time at reasonable rates but also provide full extension support to growers. They should be held responsible for poor quality, late deleivery, high rates and inefficient extension services which have adversely affected soil helath, crop health and production.

Development aspects

Post—harvest facilities have been found grossly inadequate in almost all the States. They should be properly installed particularly in respect of preservation, transport, processing and storage at consumer level.

Research in all aspects should be a continuing process which calls for alloccaton of substantial financial resources, equipment, laboratories and trained manpower. Endeavour should be made to allocate at least one per cent of the Gross Domestic Product (GDP) as against hardly 0.3 per cent today. Besides, the private sector as also the financial institutions should be encouraged to contribute funds to this area in one or the other form. Duplication of research work should be avoided and targets for research results should be considered necessary. At the university level, effective integration among research, extention and educational wings should be established in order to create the desired impact at field level.

Biogas plants already installed and lying out of order throughout the country should immediately be activated through Panchayati Raj or private sector effort inorder to make available enriched organic manure to the fields which have been showing soil–sickness. Similarly, an intensive drive for popularizing compost–making at the farm level and adoption of green manuring and biofertilizers by the farmers should be launched. This will alone help restore soil productivity and mend the damage done by chemical fertilizers.

All the districts, if not the blocks besides the Krishi Vigyan Kendras should have facilities of soil and water testing. However,l all blocks should have well–organized and efficient input delivery system.

Though continuous and heavy dose of subsidy is not desirable, production, procurement and distribution of food grains may have to be subsidised inview of:

— these being items of daily requirement by one and all;

— their productivity and profitability per unit area and time cannot be ckmpared with cash crops; and

— a slight increase in their cost of production would trigger off chain reactions on Indian economy. Thus, all–out steps including a strong political will may be necessary to reduce their cost of production and ensure that farmers do not lose interest incultivating them. Besides, a viable framework for subsidizing food grain production, procurement and distribution may have to be evolved.

As cost of production varies considerably among different agro–ecological zones as well as food grains raised by canal water and through use of diesel engines and wlectric pumpsets, the procurement price should be based taking into consideration these variances.

The approach and attitude of the bank personnel towards financing food grain prodction should be in tune with the changing socio–economic necessity. Not only procedures of lending need to be simplified but adequate autonomy also should be given to banks in respect of deciding the scale of financ, margin, security, rate of interest, model of financing, etc rather than imposing everything on them. The National Bank for Agriculture and Rural Development (NABARD) has done yeoman service in preparing the potential linked plan for the districts indicating yearwise targets for the Ninth Plan period which should be achieved in close co—ordination with village and block Panchayati raj institutions.

Planning and implementation of the annual action plan should be developed over to village and block PRIs and its achievements be reviewed and monitored by the District PRI. Needed infrastructural support along with extension services should be properly identified and appropriately planned in advance to be provided by the State government on time.

Unlike the Eight Five Year Plan of which the structural framework claimed more than a three-year time under the exercise of repeatedly reconstituted Planning Commission by as many as three Prime Ministers appearing in the see-saw political scene since 1989 to get itself approved in May 1992, the approach paper to the Ninth Five Year Plan has happily received approval of the National Development Council on 16 January, 1997 which still leaves two-and-half-month period to complete the tenure of the current Plan. The approach paper to the Ninth Plan, now available, will reap the benefit of being commented upon widely in various media. This is a definite advantage and, if everything goes well, the Ninth Plan comprising the period from 1 April, 1997 to 31 March, 2002 will take off in time without suffering a delay like the pre-Eighth Plan two-year plan holiday.

The approach to the Ninth Plan is undoubtedly bold and highly ambitious. The Plan envisages an annual economic growth rate of seven per cent per annum with an increase of savings and investment rates of 26.2 per cent and 28 per cent respectively, within the limit of ceiling on current account deficit at 2.4 per cent of GDP. The Prime Minister, Mr H.D. Deve Gowda had called for collective efforts to raise the huge resource quantum of Rs. 8,75,000 crore for implementing the Plan.

The approach paper to the Ninth Plan does initiate a departure from traditional lines of the past in more than one way.

First, the States are being given a wider latitude in the affairs of rural development under a basket of programmes complex with, however, an added responsibility of mobilizing additional funds.

Secondly, the role of government has been deeply examined against the backdrop of a fast-changing economic scenario and emerging dynamism in the international politico-economic horizon that is increasingly necessitating a larger role of the private sector.

Thirdly, the role of involvement of people in the process of nation building through of nation building through decentralized planning has received deeper attention than in the VIII Plan.

Fourthly, the question of growth with social justice and equity has received greater focus with stock taking of achievements in the areas of basic minimum services and a renewed emphasis on quick realization of the remaining tasks.

Fifthly, the need for an effective family welfare and population policy has been spelt out as an indispensable factor in the planning process and the employment generation target is aimed at eight million jobs per year with the emphasis on high employment-elastic activities in the agro-allied areas of animal husbandry, fishery, horticulture, dairy farming, fish preservation and the like.

The important thrust areas as highlighted in the approach paper are agriculture, infrastructure and the social sector areas which have by and large remained neglected during the VIII Plan. The Ninth Plan expects to achieve an agricultural growth rate of 4.5 per cent annually which is looked upon as a chief engine of poverty removal and rural development. Though the output of agricultural sector during the VIII Plan grew by 3.5 per cent per annum, the approach paper expects that a higher rate of public investment in irrigation, soil conservation, flood and drought preventive measures, marketing infrastructure and in sectoral diversification to high value crops will achieve the Ninth Plan target of 4.5 per cent of annual output growth.

The loss of community reality and participation jeopardize many values of the democratic tradition. Those generous impulses that grow out of an awareness of a local common good are weakened. One is merely lost in the amorphous anonymity of a huge population.

As a consequence, the ordinary citizen becomes less and less articulate and makes fewer contributions to the decisions that shape his own destiny or the collective destiny. The democratic experience, whereby the voice of the ordinary citizens at the local grass roots has been heard in higher-level decisions, is lost. So a method of work that promises to increase the responsibility of the citizens, is pertinent to the treatment of the malaise of our time.

Much of the literature on community development is more expressive of the writer's enthusiasm to do good than of any discipline of description and evaluation. Both the enthusiasm and discipline are necessary if this field of work with people is even to approach the fulfillment of its promise,

As to values, let it be stated immediately that development is always normative. That is, it takes place in the midst of actions that serve chosen goals. No scientist (social or any other kind), when he takes part in development, can be content with description only. He must approve actions and evaluate results in the light of some scheme of values towards the attainment of which the development is directed. The paradox for the scientist is that he will never describe man as he is. He will need also to describe man in the process of becoming and this latter task requires planned development that seeks chosen goals.

In regard to community development and people's participation, the emerging consensus clusters round a concept of the improvement of people, the underprivileged, the overprivileged, and all in between. Improvement is evaluated in terms of democratic skills, responsibility to serve growing awareness of a common good, ethical sensitivity, and willingness to co-operate. All other improvements are judged good or bad by reference to what is happening to the people involved.

In the preceding paragraphs we have emphasized upon some value loaded normative ideas which may appear like Utopia but they are the sine qua non of all the development strategy. If we look into the successive Five Year Plan documents from the I Plan to the VIII Plan, it is evident that by and large they have been laudable and reflected the pious dreams of the founding fathers of the nation. However, on the performance side, we have always drawn, if not blank, at least little achievements. The Ninth Plan document emphasizes more on rural infrastructure, the social sector and equity, which are based on the Common Minimum Programme of the United Front government. No doubt, the approach is very laudable but again it is a million dollar question as to what we will achieve at the end of the Ninth Five Year Plan. Instead of lamenting over this question, in the succeeding pages the approach to Ninth Five Year Plan is being discussed in brief and finally our observations on various aspects of the approach paper are given.

The main thrust of the Ninth Plan has been to evolve a shared vision of and a shared commitment to the national objectives and the development strategy not only in the government at all levels but also among all other economic agents. No development strategy can be successful unless each component of the economy works towards a common goal and purpose with the full realisation of the role that has to be played within an overall structure of responsibilities. Some of the tasks needed in respect of rural development are given below:

— The principal task during the Ninth Plan, therefore, is to build on the Eighth Plan, while tackling the problems that have emerged, particularly in areas such as capital formation in agriculture, social sector, regional disparity, and fiscal deficits. Indian economy is still vulnerable and the operation of a more open economic system has to be tempered by judicious public interventions to ensure that these vulnerabilities are gradually overcome.

— Since the planning is done for the entire nation, the strategies for resource augmentation need to cover not only the government at all levels but also those which would be available to other sections of the people.

— Since not all parts of the country are equally endowed to take advantage of growth opportunities, planned intervention is needed to ensure that large imbalances do not occur .

— The Indian economy still has a large number of its citizens who live in acute poverty both in rural and urban areas. Special employment programmes targeted to these people will continue in the Ninth Plan. Special attention will need to be paid to unorganized labour, particularly the agricultural landless labourer.

— There exist large disparities across the various social groups. The disadvantaged groups include members belonging to Scheduled Castes and Scheduled Tribes, other backward classes and minorities. In addition, women and children and the physically handicapped and disabled are also vulnerable. For these sections of society State intervention is required in order to provide them with adequate opportunities for education and employment in an attempt to involve them productively in the development process.

— It is heartening to note that the Plan has identified people's initiative and participation as a "key element" in the process of development, particularly in improving the effectiveness of development outlays which has been declining over the years. It has also recognized that the role of the government should be to facilitate the process of people's involvement by creating the right type of institutional infrastructure, particularly in rural areas. The progress on this front so far has not been entirely satisfactory primarily due to the fact that the other tiers of the government were not fully integrated into the development strategy. The Plan also asserts that the process of social mobilization and development of people's initiatives cannot be achieved without the active support and involvement of the political system at all levels. In the Plan, the Panchayati Raj bodies in rural areas will be directly involved in the development process. People's involvement via their elected representatives will be realized through "democratic—decentralization".

— Co-operatives will be rejuvenated to enlist people's active participation in these societies. They will be liberated from tight bureaucratic control. Self-help groups, associations of workers or small producers, etc. are other forms of institutions which will be encouraged to actively involve people in planning process and implementation. Government will seek active "partnership" with the voluntary sector in organizing and promoting these institutions.

— Domestic entrepreneurship, which is the backbone of the development process, will be fully encouraged through measures to enhance their competitive strength and to facilitate their growth and efficiency. In particular, the small-scale and village and home industries will be provided the proper environment for growth and diversification.

— While new initiatives are being taken for additional investment, optimum utilization of the existing infrastructure should not be neglected. This needs to be done by technology upgradation, systems improvement and ensuring public utilities function on commercial lines. Most importantly, care should be taken to ensure that in the provision of these services, the rural areas are provided their due share both in terms of magnitude as well as technology suited to their needs.

— In regard to subsidies, emphasis is laid to move to a system of transparent subsidies directed towards specific target-groups in a selective manner.

— The Indian Planning process had always laid emphasis on measures to ensure sustainability of the development process not only in economic terms, but also in terms of social and environmental factors. The Ninth Plan will carry this tradition further and consolidate on the creation of conditions for sustainable development.

It is some satisfication that six years after the so-called "revolution" of liberalization and globalization, we are still talking of planning the growth of the Indian economy. At one stage, the chorus in favour of the miracles of the market was so loud, that one thought that one could just sit back and hope that growth, employment generation, poverty removal, internal and external price stability and social justice, all would just automatically come along one after another in easy succession or even simultaneously, and the Planning Commission would become and anachronism and wither away!

Planning did not, of course, produce any miracle. But it did emphasize the fact that investment in the areas of national priority such as capital goods and infrastructure needed to be substantially raised if the economy was to maximize its rate of growth of national income. In fact, about 80 per cent of public sector investment were directed at achieving that objective. There was bureaucratic red tape, there was a poor work ethos, there was corruption but there was no fault in the objective and none, therefore, in the rationale for having a planned mixed economy in the country.

The Ninth Plan seems to be veering round to that view after we lost six precious years in the wake of the "revolution". But it is still not doing that with the conviction which had gone with the earlier plans barring the last one. The Eighth Plan fumbled with indicative versus target planning with a greater focus on indicative posture particularly in respect of the corporate industrial sector on which much globalization has remained focused.

The consequence of that fumbling has been the mounting arrears of investment in infrastructure even after the controversial sop of counter-guarantees was offered to some foreign investors. Whether the Ninth Plan has been forewarned about the total inadequacy of foreign private investment in Indian infrastructure at least on the basis of the Eighth Plan experience, is unclear. But if seeks to go on repeating emphasis in that investment, thus trying to be a mere 'facilitator' rather than 'doer' in the infrastructure sector, it may end up with a much lower rate of growth than seven per cent; what is worse, it may produce a more undesirable content of economic growth than hitherto.

The earlier rate of growth of durable consumer goods was 12 per cent plus and the new one could be 17 per cent plus. Will that be regarded as enriching the growth content in a poor country particularly when the infrastructure growth is hardly exceeding three per cent per annum!

Thus while we welcome the Ninth Plan's commitment to seven per cent rate of growth of output, we are unclear now with an obsession for the great prowess of the foreign investor, and a gradual abandonment of the role of the State as a doer in place of that of the facilitator., even in the infrastructure sector, the commitment will be carried through.

Indicative planning

Since there is in this a danger that the invisible preference for indicative planning which was in evidence in some parts of the Eighth Plan is brought forward to the Ninth Plan as well, a word about the relevance of this type of planning might be in order here.

Indicative planning is an attempt by the Planning Authority to project relative demands and supplies of goods with some given time horizon in mind. Its aim is to plan in a manner that market players and also the State, if it too is amongst them, are enabled to prevent falling into an excess or deficient demand situation. It is expected to assist a balanced allocation of resources in the economy.

Assuming that the purpose of planning is to augment supplies of infrastructure, capital goods, technology, wage goods, national security and a pollution-free growth, (these priorities have remained crucial throughout the planning period and should remain so in the Ninth Plan as well), how will mere indication of supply deficiencies meet our purpose? The hope that once the deficiencies are identifies, the local or foreign private investors could be induced to remove them is sheer bravado. The growth of infrastructure in terms of market rules raises a host of issues beginning with the rate of return and ending with the entire question of external economy if private investors insisting on adequate risk coverage and a smaller time horizon for recovery of their fixed capotal investments, charge exhorbitant prices for that infrastructure. Further, the resulting higher prices of infrastructure services may turn out to be antipeople. The tendency of the market to raise prices in areas of scarcity (and infrastructure is such an area) is unavoidable. As for governmental control and regulation of monopolist price fixing, brought in against privately run infrastructure, there could be the same type of problems which have been generally used to decry governmental role in economic activities.

India's development goals—growth with social justice and self-reliance, with particular emphasis on eradication of poverty and human development—have remained more or less unchanged throughout the plan period since 1951. Early strategies for achieving these goals entailed large investments in the public sector for infrastructure development and creation of industrual base, regulation and licensing of the privae sector to channelize investments into priority areas, import restrictions to protect the domestic industries and limitations to foreign investments.

Social justice was expected to result from economic growth as well as through direct including health, education, etc. While these strategies had helped in creating an industrial base and self-sufficiency in food production, they did not lead to a pattern of develoment and growth rates sufficient enough to eradicat poverty and achieve social justice.

Shift in strategy

The need for a shift in strategy to a competitive industrial environment and open trade regime was recognized for quite some time. The attempts made in the eighties were, however, too feeble to make a significant impace. A shift in economic strategy towards a more openand more competitibve economy began in 1991 in the aftermath of severe macro-economic imbalances particularly in the balance of payments situation and in the fical position of the government.

There was also a growing recognition that much more attention was needed to addres human development in all its many facets to achieve broad-based economic growth along with equity and social justice. The experience of fast growin East Asian countries where human development precede ecnomic growth underscored the importance of investment in human development. The experience of these countries, further, highlights the fact that the gains from economic growth gets widely distributed via employment and this can be facilitated by universal primary of widespread skills.

The economic reforms initiated in 1991 included stablilization measures and structural adjustment policies. Besides, fiscal and exchange rate correction, the measures included deregulation of industry, partial disinvestment of public sector enterprises, encoragement of foreign investment—both direct and portfolio, liberalization of foreign trade and an array of measures to achieve structural reform of institutions in the financial sector and capitctor and captial markets. The reforms strategy also included measures to promote employment opportunities in agriculture, industry and social sectors. A number of target-oriented programmess aimed at poverty alleviation and provision of vasic minimum social services to the poor also got strengthened.

The VIII Plan (1992-97) formulated in the wake of introduction of the reforms strategy attempted to imbibe the ethos of the reforms. But in its detailed structural characterixtics it was broadly as continuation of the earlier plans. Theis has resulted in several constraints in the implementation of the VIII Plan and also. perhaps, decelerated the progress of economic reforms.

In the approach to the Ninth Five Year Plan (1997-2002), it is realized that the growth pattern of the VII Plan (1992-97) did not benefit the poor and the underprivileged. The Ninth Plan, therefore, contemplates to usher in a new era of people, oriented planning in which the government and the people, particularly the poor, can fully participate. Though this participatory planning process, it is expected to ensure equity and accelerate the rate of growth of the economy and thus raise the agricultural and rural incomes and to target these with programmes which aim at small, medium, and marginal farmers and landless labourers. Provision of irrigation water and inputs on a widespread basis in different agro-climatic regions of the country, backed by suitable policy measures for creating infrastructure, would be the most important the creation of adequate employment opportunities through a broad-based programme of development and economic growth.

These need to be accompanied by measures which (BMSs) such as sage drinking water, availability of primary health service facilities, universalisation of primary education, provision of public housing assistance to all shelterless poor families, nutritional support to children, connectivity of all villages and habitations by roads, and public distribution system targeted to the poor. While the objectives of this programme have been decided through mutual consultation, the States have been give full opportunity to decide on the phasing of the target for each specific sector. The achievement of these targets would be jointly monitored by the State and the Central governments. This approach is an ideal blends of national commitments with local initiatives. In addition, the process of development that is being contemplated would empower all the disadvantaged sections of the population, especially the Scheduled Castes (SCs), and minorities to integrate them in the mainstream. Besides, women and children and the physically handicapped and disabled are also vulnerable. Fore these sections of society, planned State intervention would be required in order to provide them with adequate opportunities for education and employment in an attempt to involve them productively in the development process. Above all the role of the government would be to facilitate the process of people's involvement by creating right types of institutional infrastructure, particularly in rural areas. Panchayati Raj bodies in rural areas are to be directly involved in the development process and people's involvement through their elected representatives would be realized. Cooperatives would be strengthened and self-help groups, association of workers/producers, etc. encouraged. The government would seek active partnership with the voluntary sector in organizing and promoting these institutions. In the light of the foregoing discussion and in the context of four important dimensions of State policy, viz quality of life, generation productive employment, regional imbalance, and self-reliance, the approach paper spells out the following objective:

— Priority to agriculture and rural development with a view to generating adequate productive employment and eradication;

— Accelerating the growth rate of the economy with stable prices;

— Ensuring food and nutritional security for all, particularly the vulnerable sections of society;

— Providing the basic minimum services of sage drinking water, primary health care facilities, universal primary education, shelter, and road connectivity to all habitations in a time-bound manner;

— Containing the growth rate of population;

— Ensuring environmental sustainability of the development process through social mobilization and participation of people at all levels;

— Empowerment of women and socially disadvantaged groups such as SCs, STs, OBCs, and minorities as agents of socio-economic change and development;

— Promoting and developing people's participatory institutions like Panchayati Raj bodies, co-operatives, and self-help groups; and

— Strengthening efforts to build self-reliance.

The approach paper adopted by the National Development Council on 16 January, 1997 envisages a seven per cent annual growth rate in Gross Domestic Product (GDP) as against the 5.9 per cent GDP llikely to be achieved during the VIII Plan. It is assumed by the Planning Commission that domestic savings can be pushed up from the current level of 23.7 per cent GDP to 26.2 per cent. This is based on the optimistic belief that government expenditure reduction can be effected bringing down the budgetary deficit and mobilizing resources by public sector enterprises.

The Finance Ministry has been cautious and favoured a 6.2 per cent GDP growth rate with a public sector outlay of Rs. 20,04,000 crore. Even budgetary support for the plan cannot be more than Rs. 3,00,000 crore. But he figure has been fixed at Rs. 3,70,000 crore with a higher level of taxation of corporate profit etc.

A difficult task: There are three related aspects which make the tasks of Ninth Plan formulation and implementation difficult.

First, a higher percentage of population below the poverty line, ie 37.27 per cent of population in 1993—94 has to be taken care of in anti–poverty programmes in the place of 16.82 per cent assumed by the earlier government. This will call for more resources. It is curious to note that between 1987–88 and 1993–94, rural poverty has gone down only to a small extent even though agricultural growth has been high. But in the later period, when agriculture growth was not high, rural poverty has gone down to a much greater extent. This is an evidence of the fact that agricultural development alone is not–sufficient for rural development and poverty removal.

Secondly, the growth rate of agriculture is envisaged to be 4.5 per cent it is doubtful whether this can be achieved unless there is adequate thrust on both fiscal and human resource inputs. That is why the local resource mobilization strategy has to give a prominent place to human resource development investment like education, health, nutrition, etc.

Thirdly, the saving as a percentage of GDP over 26 per cent may be on the high side and, therefore, labour will have to be used as a substitute for the limited capital.

When there is local planning and local resource mobilization, the objective of rural development can be achieved with accelerated growth of agriculture and its productivity. In fact, in the case of rural societies like what we have in India, rural development will imply also social change and rural transformation as well as development. All these are complementary to each other in several ways for accelerating the pace of rrural development.

It has been found that there can be growth in literacy, which is a prerequisite for rural development, when educational facilities, communication facilities, communicable roads and access to electricity are improved.

The issues we now have to consider are: (a) Why there are such unutilized resources in the rural areas; (b) how real are the opportunities for such local resource mobilization; (c) In the process of such mobilization how rural development can take place; and (d) What is the role of human resources development in this process. It is the contention of this paper that when there is a shortage of resources at the macro—level for implementing the plan, additional resources are best mobilized at the local level. In the very process of mobilizaton of non—financial resources, new oportunities for meeting localy perceived needs will be found and exploited.

The first novelty of the Ninth Plan is that the Planning Commission has decided to give more freedom to the State governments in formulating their plans. The Planning Commission has decided that in consultation with the Union Ministry of Finance, it will indicate the probable amount of Central assistance available to each State and the State governments would be left free to determine the size of their plans. It may be recalled in this context that the earlier practice followed was that the State governments would propose specific size of the States' annual plans. The Planning Commission would scrutinize them in detail and then extract a promise of additional resource mobilization from the States before approving the plan size. This gave unnecessary credibility to the size of the States' plans. Every state would push the plan size to unrealistically high level hoping that the Planning Commission would provide additional plan assistance. This never happened. As a result, many States used to reduce their plans by December each year and wide gaps used to emerge between the original plan size and the final actual plan. What is more, the plan size came to be politicized at the State level. Nobody would accept the size of the plan lesser than the previous years' and it had to be necessarily higher at least by 10 per cent. This kind of politicisation has been removed during the Ninth Five Year Plan period. The Planning Commission indicates the gross and net plan assistance available to each State and leaves the final size of the plan to be determined by the State government depending upon its capacity to raise additional revenue. This is the first change in the process of planning introduced by the Planning Commission during the Ninth Five Year Plan period.

The second change is that while determining the Central assistance to the State plans, the financial resources which used to flow from the financial institutions like LIC/NABARD/IDB/GIC plus statutory liquidity ratio (SLR) market borrowings were treated as Central government transfers. Though the Central government has control over the borrowing powers of the State governments, particularly when they are indebted to the Central government, these sources of funds are the prerogative of the State governments. The State governments are free to raise funds through banks and other financial institutions depending upon the financial viability of the projects and their capacity to service the debt. However the Planning Commission and the Union Ministry of Finance have evolved a unified borrowing policy to protect the interests of poorer States and minimise the adverse impact of public borrowing on the economy. Therefore, these financial institutions were asked to co-ordinate their direct lending to the State governments. In this ways, the Planning Commission used to treat SLR and other such borrowings from the developmental financial institutions as part of Central assistance. This practice was disliked by States like West Bengal an, therefore, the Planning Commission has now changed the accounting format in such a way as to show institutional finance and SLR borrowing as States' own resources available for plan purpose. This does not change the resource position of the States in any way. But it goes a long way in giving them and they need not be at the mercy of the Central government to raise funds from lending institutions.

Thirdly, for the first time the approach paper recognized the federal nature of the Indian planning system and has devoted a separate chapter explaining how the Planning Commission is going to decentralize not merely plan formaulation but also the entire planning process including monitoring of implementation. The document recognizes the implications of the far-reaching political change that has taken place in India. From the inception of the planning regime, the Central government used to be formed by a national party which used to dictate terms to the state governments But in the 1996 elections, no national party secured a majority and a number of regional parties have joined hands to form the United Front government at the Centre. This is an unprecedented change in the political scenario. Consequently, the Planning Commision's thinking had to reflect this changed situation and give more voice to the State governments in the planning process. At the same time, the State governments are made to realize that they have to mobilize adequate additional resources and harmonize their budgets with a view to reducing fiscal imbalance in the economy.

Furthermore, the Planning Commission has been persuading the Central ministries to transfer a large number of Centrally-sponsored schemes (CSS) along with the corresponding funds to the State governments so that the Central domination in the development process and priorities of the States is reduced. For instance, about 1823 Centrally-sponsored schemes with an outlay of Rs. 16,038. 19 crore were being implemented during the Eighth Plan period. The Chief Minister's conference held in July, 1996 expressed the view that the number of CSS should be reduced and transferred to the States. But the Central ministers are reluctant to transfer many schemes. They agreed to transfer the schemes worth Rs. 1,300 crore only. Therefore, the Planning Commission has taken the initiative and is persuading the Central ministries to transfer more schemes along with the funds to the State governments as per the decision of the NDC which has laid down that CSS outlay sould not exceed one-sixth of total Central assistance. In 1979-80, 71 CSS were transferred to the states with an outlay of Rs. 2,000 crore. While this is not a new phenomenon as it was done earlier also, it still augurs well for the States autonomy. The only occasion when it was done on a large scale was during the Janata Party rule which again gave prominence to true federal structure in the planning process.

The reconstituted Planning Commission believes that the principal task of planning in the post-reform era in our federal framework is to evolve a shared vision of and a shared commitment to the national objectives and the development strategy not only in the government at all levesl but also among all economic agents. The principal objective of the Ninth Plan is to build on the succsses of the VIII Plan, whike tackling the problems that have emerged, particularly in agriculture, living standard of the poor, infrastructure, social sector, regional disparity and fiscal deficits. The IX Plan will facilitate broadening and deepening the economic reforms process to ensure that the fruits of development reach the backward regions of the country and benefit the poorer sections of the society in a time-bound manner.

The conference of State Chief Ministers held in july 1996 made a commitment to provide seven basic minimum services universally by AD 2000. They are (i) safe drinking water, (ii) access to primary health care, (iii) universal primary education, (iv) public housing assistance for the homeless, (v) extension of the midday meal scheme, (vi) road connectivity to all villages, and (vii) food security through the public distribution system for all families below the poverty line. The IX Plan will attempt to operationalize this commitment.

The approach to the IX Plan outlines a long-term fiscal policy stance indicating methods by which resources of the governments at all levels can be augmented in order to reduce and eventually eliminate the revenue deficit at all levels.

Along with aggregate economic growth, balanced regional development has been an essential component of our development strategy from the inception of planning. since not all regions of the country are well-endowed or equipped to take advantage of the growth objectives provided by the market, planned intervention continues to be essential to ensure reduction in regional imbalances.

Our society continues to have a sizeable number of members who still suffer from abject poverty and deprivation. A vast majority of them do not get an opportunity to participate in the market economy. They are neither able to contribute nor receive anytying from the market process. Special employment programmes to ensure adequate incomes for these sections of the society will continue to be an integral part of the IX Plan. Fruther, appropriate public policies including skill-endowment to the market economy will be part of the Plan.

Increasing the welfare of the socially and ecnonmically disadvantaged groups, including the Scheduled Castes, Scheduled Tribes and backward classes as well as minorities, handicapped and disabled and women and children is another objective of the Ninth

Plan. Planned State intervention is essentisal in order to provide these groups with adequate opportunities for education and employment to enable them to participate productively in the development process.

The Ninth Plan has introduced a number of correctives to reverse many of the unsustainable trends in the programmes and projects of previous plans. It has also laid stress on (1) maintenance and better utilization of existing assets/capacities in the one hand and early completion of incomplete projects on the other, so that productivity of the existing assets improves and benefits realized early, (2) approval of limited number of projectrs which are operationally viable and can be completed within a short period and for which adequate funds are available. And further, the aproval and monitoring process would become more scientific and rigorous, and (3) a genuine push towards decentralization and people's participation in the planning process through institutional reforms and strengthening the Panchayati Raj and the different models of people's instirutions. The Centre and the States will work jointlly to overcome most of the deficiencies in prograamme formulaion and implementation.

All these strategies have certainly greater relevance in improving the efficiency of economic organization and ensuring social justice.

But there are two important constraints.

First, whether the public sector can provide adequate funds for planned development. Public investment as a whole, as mentioned earlier, is targeted to be no more than 33 per cent of the total investment as against 36.5 per cent realized during the VIII Plan. Fiscal and revenue deficits are still quite high and there is no possibility that they can be contained during the period of the Ninth Plan. The Planning Commission proposes to increase presumptive income tax on the basis of reliable reference list of facilities such as telephones, cars, gas and electricity connections. In addition, it also suggests to augment non-tax revenues through revision of irrigation charges and royalties on mines. It is doubtful, whether the government can tale such hard decisions. Populism is the source of fiscal crisis both in the Centre and the states and this continues unabated even when there is financial bankruptcy at many levels.

Secondly, where is the political will to realize th objectives laid down in the Ninth Plan? Most of the politicians have lost their credibility. The bureaucratic system has become ineffective to respond to the changes that have become inherent in the new environment. Even the Panchayati system is controlled by a number of petty and corrupt politicians. They are not likely to inspire confidence among the people. The NGOs who are sometimes called 'sacred cows' have lost their sacredness. Many of them are mere mercenariess. All the agents of change are more gor less ineffective to brin about any radical change either in the economy or in the social structure. The old desperation may frustrate new hopes. The onmly positive note that we can enshrine is that "if hopes were dupes, the fears might be liars.

The approach paper of the Ninth Plan was approved by the National Development Council (NDC) on 16 January. In conformity with the objectives specified in the Common Minimum Programme (CMP), the Ninth Plan aims at increasing the annual growth rate to seven per cent of GDP during the plan period. To achieve such a high rate of growth, the approach paper suggests to increase the savings rate to the extent of 26.2 per cent and investment rate to the extent of 28.6 per cent while putting a ceiling on the current account deficit at 2.4 per cent of GDP. While a high rate of economic growth is desirable for increasing the overall size of the economy, it is doubtful whether we can be able to achieve the target envisaged in the Plan.

There seems to be a number of constraints which may hinder the process of increased capital formation. First, we may not increase domestic savings to the extent of 26.2 per cent. Public sector savings in the VIII Plan were only 1.6 per cent. To increase this rate to the extent of 2.8 per cent seems hardly feasible. there has been no improvement in the operational efficiency of public sector enterprises during the last five or six years. and the government sctor may have to increase its expenditure on the basis of the recommendations of the fifth Pay Commission and on account of subsidies which may continue for a long time, because of political uncertainty. It is estimated that open subsidies absorb nearly 20 per cent of the tax revenues of the government, both the Centre and the States taken together. Besides, there are a number of hidden subsidies whose magnitude and quantum are probably much moe than open subsidies. According to some estimates, 16 per cent of GDP goes into subsidies both explicit and implicit. No attempt is made to reduce these subsidies. On the other hand, competitive politics and populism (as we see in Punjab and Andhra Pradesh) may dreve many state governments towards bankruptcy. A target of seven per cent annual growth requires hard decisions. But there is little political will to take such decisions.

There is no guarantee that the government can increase tax revenue to meet such additional expenditure. The Deputy Chairman of the Planning Commission feels that public savings can increase through improvement in the taxes net of subsidies. He believes that tax compliance can be improved and the tax GDP ratio increased. He says, as against 85 per cent of the population in Denmark and Sweden which pay income tax, in India only 0.8 per cent pays income tax. He therefore, proposes to tax the visible expenditure of the creamy layer and include more people in the tax net. He also hopes to rope in some of the black money through apropriate schemes. But the uncertainty that has been created with the Minimum Alternative Tax (MAT) and the reverses that have taken place in the case of Presumptive Tax do not give encouraging results.

The private corporate sector and the household sector and the household sector may not also increase their savings due to inflation which may increase to the extent of nine to 10 per cent. The government will have to increase th administered prices of petroleum products since the oil pooln deficit is expected to increase to Rs. 18,000 crore by the end of March 1996. If the administered prices of petroleum products are not inreased, the current account deficit may be much more than 2.4 per cent of GDP which may increase fiscal deficit to a large extent. To improve the household savings, the Deputy Chairman has plans to introduce a set of incentives for small savers. But experience, however, shows that more incentives for small savers do not bring about a higher savings rate; on the other hand, they may only channilize more savings rate; on the other hand, they may only channelize more savings into financial assets, leaving the totality unchanged.

Secondly, the accelerated rate of growth of seven per cent per annum is again based upon 4.5 per cent growth in agriculture and 9.3 per cent in industry. In spite of favourable monsoons for a period of consecutive se ven to eight years, the rate of growth of agriculture in the VII Plan was 3.35 per cent and may be 3.5 per cent in the VIII Plan. There is no guarantee that monsoon would be as favourable in the coming years. If the fiscal deficit increases in the plan period, the government may not have adequate resources to increase investment in agriculture. And the poor infrastructure may retard the growth of industries.

It admitted by the planners that sustained growth of the economy depends on adequate availability of basic infrastructural facilities, such as power, transport and communications and irrigation of adequate quality. The VIII Plan has fallen significantly short not only of the targets, but also of the VII Plan in these areas, as indecated in primarily due to the slower pace of investment than had been contemplated.

It has been mentioned in the approach paper that efforts at containing the fiscal deficit of the government have fallen diproportionately on public investment, particularly in those sectors which are more dependent on budgetary support. The share of capitall expenditure in the total expenditure of the government has declined sharply from around 30 per cent at the beginning of the VIII plan to 24 per cent The IX plan may also face the same difficulty. Further, it is noticed that public investment as a whole is targeted to be no more than 33 per cent of the total investment against the 36.5 per cent realized during the VIII Plan (The VIII Plan targeft was 43 per cent). This is justified on the ground of reducing the fiscal deficit to the extent of four per cent of GDP. But the state of the economy as it prevails now does not proviede any optimism either in regard to growth or reduced rate of fiscal deficit.

Another area which again seems doubtful is lower incremental capital-output ratio [(ICOR) 4.08% as against 4.24% during the VIII plan]. If investment from external sources comes to 2.4 per cent as envisaged in the approach paper in the shape of Foreign Direct

Investmint, they are bound to be capital-intensive projects. But the approach paper indicates three areas which may reduce ICOR. One area is to encourage small-scale labour-intensive industrial development with short gestation periods. According to statistics, 40 per cent of total manufacturing is labour-intensive. If this balance can be maintained, it is possible to realize lower ICOR, particularly with shorter gestation periods.

Further, it is assumed that reforms will phase out obsolete technologies and usher in higher material and energy efficiency. Thirdly, improvement in the efficiency and productivity of the five infrastructural sectors, viz irrigation, mining, power, railways, and communications. No definite proposal has been given to implement these assumptions. In many cases, the actual implementation of some of these proposals is in the hands of State governments, most of whom openly divert their plan funds for non-plan expenditure. All this implies that the rate of growth envisaged in the approach paper leaves too many loose ends which may frustrate the hopes and aspirations of the planners.

Despair and hope of the ninth plan

Gandhi had said: "India's soul lives in villages". India will perish if we don't take care of them. He advocated the model of development from bottom—upwards—to top. But the model we have followed is from top-down-to bottom. This model believes in trickle down and percolation theory of development. People were actively involved neither in the planning process nor in the implementation of various programmes, activities and schemes.

There is an interesting dialogue between the Mughal emperor, Akbar and and Birbal about the result of policies and programmes imposed on people from above.

Akbar was a benevolent and popular ruler. He felt that nobody would violate his or his state's order. Birbal was of the opinion that nobody could execute the order unless people were consulted and involved. Akbar wanted to test the validity of Birbal's argument. An order was issued that the people should pour one jug of milk each during the night in the four reservoirs dug for this purpose in the city. Next morning both of them found that the reservoirs were full with water instead of milk. The people, on enquiry, informed that they poured water into the reservoirs as they did not have milk to spare. They also wanted to send the message across to the king and his administrators that such orders should not be issued without consulting and involving them. People must be taken into confidence and should be explained in detail about the aims and objects of plans and schemes to get their participation.

With the advent of freedom, India faced many problems. As the task of immediate relief and rehabilitation of refugees was on the way to completion, the government began to think in terms of rebuilding the country and reawakening the people.

This made the government adopt planning as a way and method to deal with the complicated problems to change and transform the socio-economic life of the people. Thus, came the Five Year Plan—a model of human patience, skill and endeavour; a documented account of the resources both human and material, and suggestions for their optimum utilisation. A constructive revolution had begun in the form of a series of development schemes, national as well as State.

In a sense, the First Five year Plan might be described as the mother of all subsequent plans. Planning had become fashionable everywhere in the world at the end of the Second World War. In India, various government departments in Delhi, Bombay and other State capitals, had prepared plans for the development of the economy. The Indian government after taking over from the British did not discard these plans. It sifted out the mere feasible schemes and incorporated them into what came to be known as India's First Five Year Plan. However, it was merely, a priority list for government expenditure than a real plan. The objective of the First Five Year Plan was to prevent the government from squandering money and to set out in general terms the ideals of social and economic equality.

Had the Plan failed, planning might well have been set aside, but the Gods favoured and two excellent monsoons made the Plan a success. Let us see what two of the Gandhian stalwarts had to say about the Plan.

R. K. Patil, the then Member of the Planning Commission took the draft of the First Five Year Plan For discussion with Vinoba. Vinoba found that the Plan as far as he was concerned was of no use to him as there was no mention of employment and food self-sufficiency. He felt that the only useful thing it contained was the "pin" and the rest could be consigned to the waste-paper basket.

A telegraphic message was sent by Nehru, the then Prime Minister to Vinoba to come to Delhi and apprise the members of the Planning Commission with his views. Vinoba replied promptly to Nehru that as per his wish he had started for Delhi, but on foot. Of course, he would have nothing to say to the members as they were highly knowledgeable and experts in their respective fields. However, in his pad-yatra from Wardha to Delhi, he would ascertain from people their opinions about their needs and priorities. On reaching Delhi he asked the learned members about the methods and ways by which they would like to achieve self-sufficiency and self-reliance in food. The reply of the global market and import our items in the global market and import grains at competitive rates from the would market. This did not satisfy Vinoba Bhave. He was of the opinion that every country had to be self-sufficient, the country would not be able to maintain its independence. He felt disenchanted with the ways of the government and felt that is was necessary to prepare the people who would bring pressure on policies and programmes of government.

J.C. Kumarappa served as a representative of the Sarva Seva Sangh in the Planning Commission Advisory Board. Form New Delhi Railway Station, he engaged a tonga to reach the venue of the Board meeting in the South wing of Rashtrapati Bhavan. At the outer gate, a young officer commanded the driver to get off the road. When Kumarappa intervened that he had every right to use a public road, the office replied that he was clearing the road for Panditji (Nehru), the then Prime Minister. On Kumarappa's assertion that he was also attending the same meeting, he was allowed to proceed. But he had to encounter the same trouble at the subsequent gates too, though succeeding ultimately in his attempts. He strongly protested against this treatment to the military secretary warning him that he would ride on a bullock-cart to the meeting place if the meeting continued for the following day. In the meeting, when the question of road came up, Kumarappa pointed out that bullock -cart drive was as good a citizen as Prime Minister in a democracy and that he was insulted by denying him the use of a public road. Agreeing to the quality of all citizens in a democracy, Jawaharlal Nehru explained that the restriction "bullock carts not allowed" was to save them from would be accidents due to the frequency of military lorries on the road. To this Kumarappa quipped that a simple man like him would put up a board there "motor cars and lorries are not allowed," thereby restraining the source of danger rather than the possible victim". A peal of laughter rent the air in response to his ready wit and simple plan speaking.

He said: "Instead of burying Gandhi into our heart we are burying him deep into the earth." We wish our leaders and representatives would ponder over his words. He had the courage to tell Vinoba that he was 'number one thief" in India. Vinoba who was taken aback by this unexpected charge from his bosom friend asked for clarification. Kumarappa calmly told him that he was merely referring to his hoarding the lands, obtained through Bhoodan without proper arrangements for their distribution. Binoba immediately understood the truth behind his statement and thereafter expedited the distribution of lands to the needy.

It is necessary to recall in this context that the planning Commission was pushed to the background in the background in the wake of liberalization and structural reform programme. Though the Eighth Five Year Plan was approved by the National Development Council and the States' Eighth Five Year Plans were discussed and approved, the intellectual importance of the Planning Commission was reduced during the period 1991-95. This was partly because the Planning Commission did not change its thinking in keeping with the international wave and partly because the Planning Commission was critical about specific policy package of liberalization and structural reforms. There was also some difference in the perceptions of the Union Ministry of Finance and the Planning Commission on specific policy issues like the quality of intellectual input which the planning Commission used to provide to the policy-makers in the government had declined. Therefore, during the last two years of the Eighth Plan the Planning Commission was simply ignored.

The United Front government has decided to restore the intellectual status of the Planning Commission. It has reconstituted the Planning Commission with an eminent person who was Union Finance Minister as the Deputy Chairman. He took the task seriously and revived the image of the planning Commission. The Planning Commission completed the Annual Plan discussions for 1996-97 in a record time and prepared the approach paper as indicated by the Planning Commission. It may look a trivial matter to mention here that the Prime Minister Mr H.D. Deve Gowda, who is the Chairman of the Planning Commission, convened the first meeting of the full Commission on 16 August, 1996 and he saw to it that the meeting was held in Yojana Bhavan to boost the morale of its personnel. After Jawaharlal Nehru, no Prime Minister had visited Yojana Bhavan to preside over the full meeting of the Planning Commission Mr H.D. Deve Gowda not only presided over the full meeting but also provided broad guidelines for the Ninth Five Year Plan. Further, the Prime Minister had convened a meeting of the Chief Ministers in July 1996 to take them into confidence in formulating a crash programme for ensuring basic minimum services to the rural people. This meeting gave an opportunity for the Planning Commission to gauge the feelings of the State governments. The Planning Commission had requested the Chief Ministers to indicate their views on the Ninth Five Year Plan in the course of the 1996-97 Annual Plan discussions. After receiving the written views of the state governments and after several internal meetings of the Planning Commission, the approach paper was finalized.

The official planners have been very brave, indeed foolhardy, to scale up from 3.5 per cent to 4.5 per cent, reportedly under political pressure, the agricultural growth rate target for the Ninth Plan. This may please the powerful lobby of rich farmers and pander to their high growth ambitions. But it casts grave doubts on the veracity and credibility of the planning exercise, especially so when the sharp set-back to agricultural production in 1995-96, a good monsoon year, should have made the planners doubly cautious in their approach to the ticklish problems and uncertain prospects of Indian agriculture.